Practitioner's Guide to Trusts, Estates and Trust Returns

Larry H. Frostiak, CA, CFP, TEP
John E.S. Poyser, BA, LLB, TEP

© **2004 Thomson Canada Limited**

All rights reserved. No part of this publication may be reproduced, stored in a retrieval system, or transmitted, in any form or by any means, electronic, mechanical, photocopying, recording, or otherwise, without the prior written permission of the publisher (Carswell).

Carswell and all persons involved in the preparation and sale of this publication disclaim any warranty as to accuracy or currency of the publication. This publication is provided on the understanding and basis that none of Carswell, the author/s or other persons involved in the creation of this publication shall be responsible for the accuracy or currency of the contents, or for the results of any action taken on the basis of the information contained in this publication, or for any errors or omissions contained herein. No one involved in this publication is attempting herein to render legal, accounting, or other professional advice.

Library and Archives Canada Cataloguing in Publication

Frostiak, Larry H.

Practitioner's guide to trusts, estates and trust returns / Larry H. Frostiak, John E.S. Poyser

Includes index.
ISBN 0-459-28115-1

1. Trusts and trustees — Taxation — Canada. I. Poyser, John (John E. S.)
II. Title.

KE5864.T7F76 2004   343.7105'264
C2004-905576-3
KF6499.ZA2F76 2004

Composition: Computer Composition of Canada Inc.

One Corporate Plaza	**Customer Relations:**
2075 Kennedy Road	Toronto 416-609-3800
Toronto, Ontario	Elsewhere in Canada/U.S. 1-800-387-5164
M1T 3V4	Fax 1-416-298-5094
Internet: http://www.carswell.com	
e-mail: carswell.orders@thomson.com	

We dedicate this publication to lawyers, accountants, trust administrators and trust officers who practice in the trust and estate profession. We sincerely hope our work will assist you in interpreting the complex array of issues you encounter and create valuable insights for the advice and planning you provide to your clients.

Foreword

As trust, estate and tax issues become more onerous and exceedingly more complex in Canada, the United States and other countries around the world, the need to focus one's attention on the opportunities and advantages of tax and estate planning, both domestic and international, has never been greater. In fact, it is becoming increasingly more difficult to effectively assist the high net-worth individual without significant input into the implementation of an effective estate or tax plan. Many of the tried and true strategies that were historically employed by trust, estate and tax practitioners in assisting clients in their generation to preserve and transfer assets from one generation to the next are no longer available. Additionally, the mobility of high net-worth clients is much greater today and the likelihood of a client having assets domiciled in multiple jurisdictions is much more prevalent. As a result, practitioners, today more than ever, expend enormous time and effort deciphering the complicated provisions of the Act and the associated regulations, bulletins and circulars, not to mention the voluminous case law, in an attempt to assist their clients in the preservation, creation and succession of wealth. It is relevant to point out that this recent evolution towards tax, trust and estate planning is not limited merely to the practice of law. Today, investment advisors, insurance professionals, trust officers, accountants and many other professionals are being pushed by their clients to provide such advice. It is not surprising that for such professional advisors, one of the most useful tools in estate and tax planning is the "trust". Although "trusts" are often heralded by practitioners as a remarkable tool for the discreet and tax-effective management of all types of property (domestic and international), the utilization and effectiveness of trusts are generally not well understood. Although complexity should never be a valid reason for not exploring all possible alternatives, not all practitioners have the ability and/or experience to provide assistance when the planning involves the use of a "trust." The bottom line is that "trusts" and their effective implementation and utilization is generally not well understood.

It is clear in my mind that the *Practitioner's Guide to Trusts, Estates and Trust Returns* is an important piece of work and fills a definite void. Nowhere are the principles required to implement domestic trust and estate planning better laid out than in Frostiak and Poyser's *Practi-*

FOREWORD

tioner's Guide to Trusts, Estates and Trust Returns. Upon first reading the manuscript, I was immediately impressed with the book's comprehensive and substantive material, not to mention the authors' clear and concise writing style. This text is sure to become the standard text for trust and estate planning, and brilliantly demonstrates that an extremely difficult area can be broken down into manageable sections – from the planning phase to the reporting phase. The book clearly lives up to its title – it truly is a guide – designed to walk you through the entire planning and reporting phase. For everyone aspiring to build a practice in this area, whether a lawyer, accountant, insurance planner, financial planner, rookie or seasoned veteran, this is the book to have on your shelf.

Paul R. LeBreux, LLB, LLM, TEP
October 2004

Paul R. LeBreux is recognized as one of Canada's leading international tax lawyers. Paul is also Chair of STEP (Society of Trust and Estate Practitioners) Canada, the leading professional body for the trust and estate profession worldwide. In Canada, there are currently about 2,000 STEP members from the legal, accountancy, corporate, trust, banking, insurance and related professions, involved at a senior level in the planning, creation, management of and accounting for trust and estates and related matters, and includes some of the most experienced and senior practitioners in their fields.

Acknowledgements

The editorial committee to this text consists of the following individuals:

John R. Delaney, BA, LLB
Inkster Christie Hughes, Winnipeg.

Douglas G. Gorman, BA, LLB, TEP
The Estate House by Gorman & Koski, LLP, Barristers and Solicitors, Edmonton.

Timothy C. Matthews BSC, LLB, BCL, Q.C., TEP
Stewart McKelvey Stirling Scales, Halifax.

Kim G.C. Moody CA, TEP
Moody Shikaze Boulet LLP, Calgary.

Philip J. Renaud, BA, LLB, Q.C., TEP
Duncan & Craig LLP, Edmonton.

The expertise and input of the editorial committee is gratefully acknowledged, as is the assistance of Larry's wife Jayne, and also Angie Bachalo and Jane Wilson in reviewing and administering the manuscript and in assisting with the research of this text during its creation.

TABLE OF CONTENTS

Introduction xxi

Part I – Basic Estate and Trust Planning

Chapter 1 – An Overview of Trust Law

1. The Nature of a Trust 3
   1.1 Trusts as Relationships 4
   1.2 Parties to a Trust 5
       (a) The Beneficiary 5
       (b) The Settlor 7
       (c) The Trustee 7
   1.3 Division of Ownership 8
   1.4 The Three Certainties 9
       (a) Certainty of Intention 10
       (b) Certainty of Subject Matter 11
       (c) Certainty of Objects 11
2. Creation of a Trust 12
   2.1 By Law 12
   2.2 By Express Words or Conduct 13
3. Distinguishing Trusts from Other Relationships 14
4. Provincial Considerations 16
   4.1 The Rule in *Saunders v. Vautier* 17
   4.2 Perpetuities and Accumulations 19
5. The Relationship Between Tax Law and Trust Law 21

Chapter 2 – Types of Trusts and Basic Planning

1. Testamentary Trusts 23
   1.1 Summary 23
   1.2 General Comments Relating to Testamentary Trusts 23
       (a) Definition of Testamentary Trust 23
       (b) Qualifying and Non-Qualifying Testamentary Trusts 25
           (i) Trusts Created by Will 25
           (ii) Successive Testamentary Trusts 26

ix

TABLE OF CONTENTS

		(iii)	Blended Trusts	26
		(iv)	Insurance Trusts	26
		(v)	RRSP Trusts	28
		(vi)	Trusts Arising by Operation of Dependants' Relief Legislation	29
		(vii)	An Estate	30
		(viii)	Trusts Settled with Property from an *Inter Vivos* Trust	32
	1.3	Special Features		33
		(a)	Taxation at Graduated Rates	33
		(b)	Flexible Year End	33
		(c)	No Installment Taxes	34
	1.4	Things You Need to Know		34
		(a)	Loss of Status as a Testamentary Trust	34
		(b)	Opportunity to Seek Reassessments	36
		(c)	Attributing Losses to Deceased's Terminal Return	37
		(d)	Testamentary Trust Enjoying Income from Business, Farming, Fishing and Rentals	37
		(e)	Rollovers into Testamentary Spousal Trusts	37
		(f)	Separate Taxpayer Status for Multiple Testamentary Trusts	38
		(g)	Minimum Tax	40
		(h)	Designated Income	40
2.	*Inter Vivos* Trusts			41
	2.1	Summary		41
		(a)	Gifting	42
		(b)	Sale or Gift to an *Inter Vivos* Trust	43
	2.2	General Comments Relating to *Inter Vivos* Trusts		46
		(a)	Definition of *Inter Vivos* Trust	46
	2.3	Special Features		47
		(a)	Tax Consequences to the Contributor or Settlor	47
		(b)	Tax Consequences of an "Interest" in the Trust to the Beneficiary	49
		(c)	Attribution	50

TABLE OF CONTENTS

		(d)	Taxation of Income, Losses, Capital Gains and Capital Losses	52
	2.4	Things You Need to Know		52
		(a)	Minimum Tax	52
3.	Spousal Trusts			53
	3.1	Summary		53
	3.2	General Comments Relating to Spousal Trusts ...		54
		(a)	Definition of Spousal Trust	54
		(b)	Qualifying Spousal Trust	57
		(c)	Tainted Spousal Trust	58
4.	Trusts for Minor Beneficiaries			60
	4.1	Summary		60
	4.2	General Comments Relating to Trusts for Minor Beneficiaries		61
		(a)	Attribution to Non-Arm's Length Transferor Under 74.1(2)	61
			(i) The Minor	62
			(ii) The Transferor	62
			(iii) The Type of Income	63
			(iv) The Transfer Transaction and Type of Property	63
			(v) Miscellaneous Points Relating to 74.1(2) Attribution	64
		(b)	Pent Up Income Attributed to Minors Under 104(18)	65
		(c)	Kiddie Tax under Section 120.4	70
	4.3	Things You Need to Know		72
		(a)	Whether "In-Trust Accounts" Qualify as Trusts	72
		(b)	Payments Made Outside Trustees' Discretion	74
5.	Alter Ego and Joint Spousal or Common-Law Partner Trusts			74
	5.1	Summary		74
	5.2	General Comments Relating to Alter Ego and Joint Spousal or Common-Law Partner Trusts ...		75
		(a)	Requirements for a Qualifying Alter Ego Trust	75

TABLE OF CONTENTS

        (b)   Requirements for a Qualifying Joint Spousal or Common-Law Partner Trust ... 76
        (c)   Planning Opportunities 77
              (i)   Probate Avoidance 77
              (ii)   Confidentiality 79
              (iii)   Control of Capital 79
              (iv)   Incapacity Planning 80
              (v)   Creditor-Proofing 80
              (vi)   Avoiding Dependants' Relief Legislation 80
              (vii) Jurisdiction Shopping 81
    5.3   Special Features 81
        (a)   No Disposition at Insertion 81
        (b)   Opting Out Available for Alter Ego Trusts 83
        (c)   No Deemed Disposition at Twenty-One Years 83
    5.4   Things You Need to Know 84
        (a)   Cannot Fund Testamentary Trust 84
        (b)   Attribution of Income to Settlor 85
        (c)   Principal Residence Exemption 85

Part II – Taxation of Trusts and Beneficiaries

Chapter 3 – Taxation of Trusts

1.   Tax Residency of a Trust 91
2.   Minimum Tax 94
3.   Treatment of Income Generally 95
    3.1   The General Rules Relating to Inclusion and Deduction of Income 95
    3.2   Exceptions to the General Rules 96
    3.3   Special Kinds of Trusts Governed by Special Rules 97

Chapter 4 – Taxation of Beneficiaries

1.   Determining Whether Income is Payable 99
    1.1   Discretionary Income Distributions 99

TABLE OF CONTENTS

	1.2	Non-Discretionary Income Distributions	99
2.	Income in the Form of Benefits Conferred by the Trust		103
3.	Income in the Form of Outlays for the Upkeep of Trust Property		106
4.	Income Designations under 104(13.1) and 104(13.2)		108
5.	The Preferred Beneficiary Election		112
	5.1	Summary	112
	5.2	Determining if the Preferred Beneficiary Election is Available	116
		(a) Considerations Relating to Characteristics of Trusts	116
		(b) Considerations Relating to Beneficiary	116
	5.3	Calculations Under the Preferred Beneficiary Election	118
		(a) Calculating the Deduction	118
		(b) Calculating Beneficiary Income Under the Preferred Beneficiary Election	120
	5.4	The Mechanics of Making the Preferred Beneficiary Election	121
	5.5	Miscellaneous Considerations in Employing the Preferred Beneficiary Election	123
6.	Non-Resident Beneficiaries		123

Chapter 5 – Attributions to Contributor Under Subsection 75(2)

1.	General Considerations	125
2.	Potential Reversion under Subsection 75(2)	126
3.	Control Over Destination	127
4.	Gate Keeping	128
5.	Considerations Relating to Contributor	129
6.	Factors Relating to Property	130
7.	Considerations Relating to Type of Income	131
8.	Miscellaneous Points Relating to Subsection 75(2) Attribution	132

TABLE OF CONTENTS

Chapter 6 – Dispositions of Trust Property

1. Capital Distributions to Beneficiaries 135
    1.1 Spousal or Common-Law Partner Trusts 135
    1.2 Personal Trusts Other than a Spousal or Common-Law Partner Trust 137
2. Deemed Realizations 139
    2.1 Deemed Realizations at Twenty-One Years 140
    2.2 Deemed Realization on Emigration 144
    2.3 Deemed Realization on Certain Amendments 145
    2.4 Trust Transfers or Mergers 146

Part III – Filing Requirements and Administration by CRA

Chapter 7 – General

1. Who Should File? 149
2. Where to File 151
3. How to File 151
    3.1 Paper Return, Summary and Slips 152
    3.2 Filing on Magnetic Media 152
4. Filing Requirements and Deadlines 153
5. Interest and Penalties 153
6. Liability of Trustees and Personal Representatives 155
7. Clearance Certificates 156

Chapter 8 – Administration

1. Filing Information 159
2. Assessments and Reassessments 160
3. Notice of Objection 161

Part IV – Preparing the T3 Trust Information and Income Tax Return

Chapter 9 – Completing the Information Return

1. Name of Trust 165
2. Name of the Trustee, Executor, Liquidator or Administrator 166

TABLE OF CONTENTS

3.	Mailing Address	166
4.	Trust Account Number	166
5.	Telephone Numbers	167
6.	Residence of Trust	167
7.	Type of Trust	168
	7.1 Testamentary Trust	168
	7.2 *Inter Vivos* Trust	169
8.	Taxation Year	170
9.	Amended Return	171
10.	Final Return	171
11.	Official Language	171
12.	Deemed Resident	171
13.	Other Information Required	173
	13.1 Multiple Trusts	173
	13.2 Change in Ownership	174
	13.3 Terms of the Trust Amended or Varied	175
	13.4 Continuously Resident in Canada	176
	13.5 Additional Capital Contributed	176
	13.6 Incurred a Non-Arm's Length Debt	177
	13.7 Election to Defer the Deemed Realization Day	178
	13.8 Income Payable to Beneficiaries	179
	13.9 Transfer from Non-Grandfathered *Inter Vivos* Trust	180
	13.10 Distribution to Beneficiary	181
	13.11 Additional Contribution of Property	183

Chapter 10 – Calculating Total Income

1.	Line 01 – Taxable Capital Gains	191
	1.1 General Rules	191
	1.2 Reserve for Proceeds Not Due	193
	1.3 Utilizing Capital Losses	195
2.	Line 02 – Pension Income	198
3.	Line 03 – Actual Amount of Dividends from Taxable Canadian Corporations	198
4.	Line 04 – Foreign Investment Income	199
5.	Line 05 – Other Investment Income	200
6.	Line 06 – Business Income	202
7.	Line 07 – Farming Income	203

TABLE OF CONTENTS

8.	Line 08 – Fishing Income	203
9.	Line 09 – Rental Income	203
10.	Line 10 – NISA Fund 2	206
11.	Line 11 – Deemed Realizations	206
12.	Line 19 – Other Income	208
	12.1 Death Benefit – Other than CPP or QPP	209
	12.2 Registered Retirement Savings Plan (RRSP)	210

Chapter 11 – Calculating Net Income

1.	Line 21 – Carrying Charges and Interest Expenses	211
	1.1 Interest Expenses	211
	1.2 Re-Loaned Funds	212
	1.3 Other Carrying Charges and Expenses	213
2.	Line 24 – Trustee Fees Deductible from Income	213
3.	Line 25 – Allowable Business Investment Losses	214
4.	Line 40 – Other Deductions from Total Income	216
5.	Line 43 – Upkeep, Maintenance and Taxes of a Property Used or Occupied by a Beneficiary	217
6.	Line 44 – Value of Other Benefits to a Beneficiary	217
7.	Line 47 – Total Income Allocations and Designations to Beneficiaries	218
8.	Line 49 – Gross-Up Amount of Dividends Retained or Not Designated by the Trust	219

Chapter 12 – Calculating Taxable Income

1.	Line 51 – Non-Capital Losses of Other Years	221
2.	Line 52 – Net Capital Losses of Other Years	222
3.	Form T3A – Request for Loss Carryback by a Trust	224
4.	Line 53 – Capital Gains Deduction for Resident Spousal or Common-Law Partner Trust Only	225
5.	Line 54 – Other Deductions to Arrive at Taxable Income	226

Chapter 13 – Summary of Tax And Credits

1.	Line 81 – Total Federal Tax Payable	227
2.	Line 82 – Provincial or Territorial Tax Payable	228

TABLE OF CONTENTS

3.	Line 83 – Part XII.2 Tax Payable		228
	3.1	Designated Income	229
	3.2	Designated Beneficiary	230
4.	Line 85 – Tax Paid by Installments		231
5.	Line 86 – Total Tax Deducted		231
6.	Line 88 – Refundable Investment Tax Credit		232
7.	Line 90 – Part XII.2 Tax Credit		232
8.	Line 91 – Other Credits		232
	8.1	Newfoundland and Labrador Research and Development Tax Credit	232
	8.2	Yukon Mineral Exploration Tax Credit	233
	8.3	Yukon Research and Development Tax Credit	233
	8.4	British Columbia Mining Exploration Tax Credit	234
9.	Line 94 – Refund or Balance Owing		234
10.	Line 95 – Amount Enclosed		235
11.	Line 100 – Refund Code		236
12.	Name and Address of Person or Company (Other than Trustee, Executor, Liquidator or Administrator)		236
13.	Certification		236

Chapter 14 – Trust Schedules and Forms

1.	Schedule 1 – Dispositions of Capital Property		239
	1.1	Meaning of "Disposition"	243
	1.2	Qualified Small Business Corporation Shares ("QSBCS")	245
	1.3	Qualified Farm Property	247
	1.4	Mutual Fund Units and Other Shares	249
	1.5	Bonds, Debentures, Promissory Notes, and Other Similar Properties	250
	1.6	Real Estate and Depreciable Property	251
		(a) General Comments	251
		(b) Non-Arm's Length Transfers	252
		(c) Valuation Day (V-Day) Considerations	253
		(d) Land	254
		(e) Principal Residence	255
	1.7	Personal-Use Property	256
	1.8	Listed Personal Property (LPP)	256

TABLE OF CONTENTS

	1.9	Information Slips	257
	1.10	Capital Gains (or Losses) from Reserves	257
	1.11	Capital Gains from Gifts of Other Capital Properties	258
	1.12	Total Losses Transferred under 164(6)	259
2.		Schedule 2 – Reserve on Disposition of Capital Property	259
3.		Schedule 3 – Eligible Taxable Capital Gains	261
4.		Schedule 4 – Cumulative Net Investment Loss	262
5.		Schedule 5 – Beneficiary Spouse or Common-Law Partner Information and Spousal or Common-Law Partner Trust's Capital Gains Deduction	267
6.		Schedule 6 – Trusts' Agreement to Allocate the Basic Exemption from Minimum Tax	269
7.		Schedule 7 – Pension Income Allocations and Designations	269
8.		Schedule 8 – Investment Income, Carrying Charges, and Gross-Up Amount of Dividends Retained by the Trust	272
	8.1	Line 1 – Actual Amount of Dividends from Taxable Canadian Corporations	272
	8.2	Lines 2 to 4 – Foreign Investment Income	272
	8.3	Lines 5 to 10 – Other Investment Income	274
	8.4	Lines 11 to 15 – Carrying Charges and Interest Expenses	274
	8.5	Lines 16 to 21 – Calculating the Gross-Up Amount of Dividends Retained or Not Designated by the Trust	275
9.		Schedule 9 – Income Allocations and Designations to Beneficiaries	276
10.		Schedule 10 – Part XII.2 Tax and Part XIII Non-Resident Withholding Tax	280
11.		Schedule 11 – Federal Income Tax	284
12.		Schedule 12 – Minimum Tax	289

TABLE OF CONTENTS

Part V – Completing the T3 Summary and T3 Slips

Chapter 15 – Filing Requirements

1.	General	299
2.	Completing the T3 Summary	300
3.	Completing the T3 Slips	302
	3.1 Dividends	305
	3.2 Capital Gains	306
	3.3 Other Income Allocations and Designations	306
	3.4 Tax and Other Credits	310
4.	Filing the T3 Summary and T3 Slips	311
	4.1 Filing	311
	(a) Paper Filing	311
	(b) Magnetic Media	311
	4.2 Distributing the T3 Slip	312
	(a) Paper Filing	312
	(b) Magnetic Media	312
5.	Amending, Cancelling or Issuing Duplicate T3 Slips	312
	5.1 Amended Slips	312
	5.2 Cancelled Slips	313
	5.3 Duplicate Slips	313
6.	Amending the T3 Summary	313

Part VI – Appendices

Appendix A: Interpretation Bulletins and Information Circulars	319
Appendix B: Technical Interpretations	323
Appendix C: Marginal Tax Rates	327
Index	331

Introduction

This publication is written with the view to providing lawyers, accountants, trust administrators and trust officers with a resource handbook addressing the income tax issues presented by personal trusts as well as detailed assistance in the completion of the T3 Trust Information and Income Tax Return. The text also reviews and provides in-depth commentary on trust and estate planning concepts and an explanation and discussion of the use of various types of trusts.

This text does not purport to cover the taxation of trusts in its entirety. It deals only with personal trusts. Certain types of other trusts receive special treatment under the *Income Tax Act* (referred to as the "Act").[1] Many of these other trusts, to the extent that they are unique, fall outside the scope of this publication. Practitioners dealing with these types of trusts should consult outside material.

For instance, this publication does not deal with the types of trusts listed below.

- Amateur athlete trusts

- Employee trusts

- Master trusts[2]

- Related segregated fund trusts[3]

- Retirement compensation arrangement trusts[4]

- Trusts whose direct beneficiaries are one of the above-mentioned trusts

- Trusts governed by an eligible funeral arrangement

---

1 R.S.C. 1985, c.1 (5th Supplement).
2 Paragraph 149(1)(o.4).
3 Section 138.1.
4 Subsection 207.5(1).

INTRODUCTION

- Cemetery care trusts

- Unit trusts

- Commercial trusts (certain trusts in which all interests have been vested indefeasibly and in which no interest can become effective in the future, generally known as "commercial trusts")

- Employee benefit plans

- Employee profit sharing plans

- Deemed *inter vivos* trusts for religious congregations[5]

- Mutual fund trusts

- Pension fund trusts

- Health and welfare trusts

- Non-resident trusts[6]

- Foreign retirement arrangements

- Vacation pay trusts

- Trusts with charitable purposes

This text outlines positions taken by Canada Revenue Agency (referred to as "CRA"), that are corroborated with the applicable Interpretation Bulletin, Information Circular or Technical Interpretation references cited in the footnotes. No opinion is given whether such CRA positions are correct and whether they would stand up to a court challenge.

These positions are discussed on the basis that a practitioner filing returns would want to do so based on what CRA will accept, and not on

---

5 Subsection 143(1).
6 Trusts resident in countries other than Canada are not, generally, taxed under our Act.

INTRODUCTION

what CRA ought to accept or what might be forced on CRA if the matter ultimately were to proceed through the courts. The text does point out, however, where divergent views or contradictory rulings have been issued, or when challenges are currently ongoing. CRA's resource materials, including the Interpretation Bulletins, Information Circulars and Technical Interpretations referred to in the text, have not been reproduced within the body of this work, as they are readily available to the practitioner by accessing either the Carswell or the CRA Web sites. Extensive referencing and cross-referencing of relevant CRA materials and commentary within the text provides the practitioner with the necessary link to undertake further review on a particular matter or tax issue.

CRA also publishes a T3 Guide each year that provides the practitioner with assistance in preparing the T3 Return, T3 Summary and related supplementaries for an estate or trust, on a line-by-line basis. This text is intended to be a stand-alone resource that can be consulted in lieu of the CRA Guide. Portions of this text, dealing with the T3 Return on a line-by-line basis, will therefore paraphrase some of the material found in the CRA Guide.

Trusts or equivalent arrangements in Quebec are not covered in this text. Some provisions of the Act are specific to Quebec,[7] and the provincial laws of Quebec are based on the civil code, not the English common law, and depart fundamentally from the laws in other provinces and territories.

---

7 See, for example, paragraph 248(3)(b).

Part I
Basic Estate and Trust Planning

Chapter 1
An Overview of Trust Law

1. The Nature of a Trust

A trust is a relationship under which a person, called the settlor,[1] transfers property to another person, called the trustee, who holds that property for the benefit of another person, called the beneficiary.

The definitions used in purely legal treatises tend to be more detailed and arcane. For example:

> All that can be said of a trust, therefore, is that it is the relationship which arises whenever a person called the trustee is compelled in equity to hold property, whether real or personal, and whether by legal or equitable title, for the benefit of some persons (of whom he may be one, and who are termed beneficiaries) or for some object permitted by law, in such a way that the real benefit of the property accrues, not to the trustees, but to the beneficiaries or other objects of the trust.[2]

This expanded definition recognizes the ability to establish a purpose trust.[3]

---

[1] In the case of a trust established under a will, the settlor is often referred to as the "testator." See 1.2(b) of this chapter entitled, "The Settlor."

[2] W.W. Keeton and L.A. Sheridan, *The Law of Trusts*, 10th ed. (1974), at p. 5. This definition is cited with approval in Canada's leading text on the law of trusts, D.W.M. Waters, *Law of Trusts in Canada*, 2nd ed. (Toronto: Carswell, 1984), at p. 5.

[3] See 1.2(a) of Chapter 1 entitled, "The Beneficiary" for a discussion on this point.

PART I — BASIC ESTATE AND TRUST PLANNING

1.1 Trusts as Relationships

The law does not recognize a trust as a legal entity. A trust is the relationship between persons relative to property held under that relationship. Thus, unlike a corporation or flesh and blood person, a trust cannot be named as a defendant in a legal suit or sue in its own name as plaintiff. A trust cannot own property in the name of the trust and a trust cannot enter into a contract as a party. Instead, in each of those instances, it is the trustees who have to personally stand in the place of the trust. It is the trustees who are named as plaintiffs in a suit on behalf of the trust or as defendants if the trust is sued. It is the trustees whose names appear as legal owner on title to the trust property, and any contract entered involving the trust is entered by trustees in their own names as the contracting party, not by the trust itself. As an exception, a trust is deemed to be an individual for income tax purposes[4] and, while the trustees are liable for the tax, the trust itself can be treated and discussed as a taxable entity in its own right aside from its trustees.

The specific terms of the relationship are normally detailed in the document creating the trust. Where that document does not contain that detail or no documentation exists creating the trust, the terms of the relationship are determined by the spoken words and conduct of the parties or by reference to the general laws that have developed to deal with trusts. Those laws are found in a body of judge-made case law, originating in medieval England, later adopted and developed here in Canada and supplemented by statutes enacted by provincial and territorial governments.[5]

---

4 Subsection 104(2). The actual wording is that "A trust shall ... be deemed to be in respect of the trust property, an individual," making it clear, *inter alia*, that for purposes of enforcement, CRA will look to the trustees and not to the trust.
5 Each province or territory has, for example, enacted a statute dealing with trusts, generally entitled, The Trustee Act. For additional detail on this point see heading 4 of this chapter entitled, "Provincial Considerations."

CHAPTER 1 — AN OVERVIEW OF TRUST LAW

1.2 Parties to a Trust

Generally speaking, there are three parties to a trust – the settlor, the trustee and the beneficiary. Trusts frequently have more than one trustee or more than one beneficiary, and occasionally have more than one settlor.

While a trust will generally have the three parties referred to above, a person can simultaneously fill one, two or three of those roles. Thus, a single person can be the settlor, trustee, and beneficiary of his own trust.[6] This general rule is subject to some exceptions. If one person is to fill all three roles, there should be at least one other beneficiary of the trust, either now or in future, with some vested or contingent right to receive income or capital, or to enjoy the use of the property. If that condition is not met the trust may not be a trust, as the whole of the legal and equitable ownership of the trust property is entirely enjoyed and controlled by the same person, and that person will be properly characterized as the outright owner the property.[7]

(a) *The Beneficiary*

The beneficiary is normally the person who is entitled to the use, enjoyment and advantage derived from the property. If the trust property is in the form of investments, that entitlement might be in the form of access to income. If the trust property is a summer home, that entitlement might be in the form of a right to use the summer home for recreational purposes. A beneficiary is said to have a "beneficial interest" under the trust or in the trust property. A beneficiary can be a human being or a corporation and, subject to the exception posed by "purpose trusts" as discussed below, a beneficiary must be a legal person.

The beneficiary will normally be a person or a group of persons who are specifically named or who are part of an identifiable class.[8] An

---

6 Waters, *supra*, note 2 at p. 5.
7 See 1.3 of this chapter entitled, "Division of Ownership" for more detail and explanation on this topic.
8 As an example, "my children."

PART I — BASIC ESTATE AND TRUST PLANNING

exception to this is found in "purpose trusts." Under a purpose trust there is no beneficiary in the normal sense. The trust property is held not for the benefit of a person or group of persons, but to further a purpose. The laws of Canada only recognize purpose trusts under limited circumstances. Our laws will allow a purpose trust to exist for charitable purposes[9] or if the trust qualifies as one of a closed set of special purpose trusts finding their origin in the English courts in the mid-1800s, such as trusts for the care of graves or funeral monuments or trusts for the care of specific pets. Otherwise, if a trust is established for a purpose rather than for the benefit of a beneficiary, the courts can strike down the trust.[10]

A trust qualifies as charitable if it serves a purpose that can be characterized as falling into any one of the following four categories laid out in England in 1891:[11]

1. the relief of poverty,
2. the advancement of education,
3. the advancement of religion, or
4. other activities beneficial to the community.

Beneficiaries are often divided into different types or according to different characteristics. Income beneficiaries are often distinguished from capital beneficiaries. An income beneficiary is one who is entitled to receive and enjoy distributions of income from the trust. A capital beneficiary is one who is entitled to receive capital from the trust in the form of capital distributions taking the form of cash distributions or the transfer of assets from the legal ownership of the trustees into the legal

---

9 Originating in England with *Morice v. Bishop of Durham* (1805), 10 Ves. Jun. 522, 32 E.R. 947 (Ch. Div.).

10 This rule of law has given rise to colourful examples. See *Re Shaw*, [1957], 1 W.L.R. 729, [1957] 1 All E.R. 1067, affirmed [1958] 1 All E.R. 245n (C.A.) (dealing with the last will and testament of George Bernard Shaw and his failed attempt to establish a trust to fund the development and popularization of a new English alphabet); *Re Gwyon*, [1930] 1 Ch. 255 (Ch. Div.) (dealing with the last will and testament of a clergyman and his failed, and bizarre, attempt to establish a trust to provide for the annual purchase of new knickers for young boys in England).

11 *Pemsel v. Special Commissioners of Income Tax*, [1891] A.C. 531 (U.K. H.L.). For more detail on each category see Waters, *supra*, note 2 at pp. 551-601.

ownership of the capital beneficiary. Contingent beneficiaries are often distinguished from beneficiaries with a vested interest. A beneficiary with a vested interest has a beneficial interest in the trust property that is already perfected, and that beneficial interest does not depend on the occurrence of some future condition or contingency to come into effect. A contingent beneficiary has no vested interest and will not enjoy a beneficial interest in the trust unless some future contingency occurs.

(b) The Settlor

The settlor is the person who contributes or settles property to the trust. For the purposes of this text, this generally involves a voluntary contribution of property into the trust, but can also include a contribution into a trust that is mandated by the terms of a contract or is otherwise made in return for financial consideration. A trust can have one or more settlors under trust law. Where a trust is established through the terms of a last will and testament, the settlor is the maker of the will, since it is that individual who causes property to be inserted into the trust after his death. Where established through a trust agreement, or trust deed or trust indenture, the settlor is generally the person who contributes the initial property into the trust.

The settlor of the trust must be the owner of the property that is to be settled into the trust. The settlor must also have the necessary mental capacity to establish the trust. The level of capacity varies in some measure with the type of trust, and the standard is higher for establishing a trust to take effect upon the death of a settlor under a will than it would be in establishing a trust taking effect during the settlor's lifetime, under a trust agreement or trust deed.[12]

(c) The Trustee

The trustee is the person who holds the property and is under an obligation to administer it under the terms of trust for the benefit of the beneficiary or beneficiaries. The trustee is said to owe a fiduciary duty to the beneficiaries, meaning a duty to place the interests of the benefi-

---

12 Waters, *supra*, note 2, at p. 94.

ciary or beneficiaries ahead of his own interests, at all times, and to act with honesty and care in the discharge of his duties. This duty is described as being a duty of the utmost good faith.

The trustee is given authority to administer and deal with the trust property, either expressly in the document creating the trust or by the operation of provincial and territorial laws that govern trusts and their use in the various jurisdictions across Canada. A trustee's authority will often include the discretion to perform acts or make decisions. A discretion is the ability of the trustee to use his own judgment, and such discretion is generally immune from challenge provided that a trustee's discretion is exercised in good faith and without regard to irrelevant considerations.

1.3 Division of Ownership

A key component to understanding the existence and operation of a trust is understanding the division of ownership that is possible under the English common law. Ownership of property can be divided into two types of ownership – beneficial and legal. The owner of property normally enjoys both types concurrently. Legal ownership involves the right to have the title registered in the owner's name, and the incidents that flow from title, including the power to sue for the recovery of the property or the power to dispose of the property. Equitable ownership of property involves the right to enjoy the property, including the right to use the property or enjoy income generated from the property, whether immediate or deferred. A trust, by its essence, involves the division of ownership between the trustee, who holds the legal ownership, and the beneficiary, who gains or enjoys the equitable ownership.

The division of ownership finds its origins in two separate court systems that operated in tandem in England before the development of modern trust law. The common law courts recognized legal ownership in property, but did not admit the existence of equitable ownership. The Court of Chancery, on the other hand, sprang up to recognize situations where the legal owner of land ought not, in good conscience, be allowed unfettered enjoyment to property owned by him, but instead, ought to be subject to an overriding claim of some other person who had a claim

CHAPTER 1 — AN OVERVIEW OF TRUST LAW

in conscience to the use and enjoyment of the property. This might occur where, for example, person A contributed all of the purchase money for a parcel of land, but for reasons of secrecy, or some other reason, asks person B to stand on title for him as legal owner. If B then proposed to unilaterally sell the land and keep all of the sale proceeds, the common-law courts would not interfere. The Court of Chancery would interfere, however, and order that the sale proceeds ought to be paid by B to A. Referred to as a court of equity, Chancery could not order that the legal ownership of the property change, but it could make orders against the person who holds that legal ownership. Thus, a Court of Chancery could order that the legal owner was personally obliged to deal with the property or sale proceeds in a way that benefited the equitable owner. The two types of courts were later merged, but the distinction in law between legal and equitable ownership lives on as a primary tenet of trust law.

1.4 The Three Certainties

This text assumes that a practitioner is in fact dealing with a trust. This assumption, in practice, may not always be correct.[13] There will be occasions where a written document exists purporting to create a trust, yet no trust exists. There will be other occasions where no written document is in place, but a trust nonetheless is in existence.

In deciding whether a trust is present or not, a court will generally go through an analysis of the "three certainties." These can be viewed as conditions precedent to the existence of a trust.[14] If any one of them is not present, then no trust exists and, except in the case of an estate,[15] the relationship and the parties to it will generally be taxed as if no trust exists.

The three certainties are:

---

13 See for example the discussion on in-trust accounts appearing under the topic "Trusts for Minor Beneficiaries," at 4.3(a) of Chapter 2 entitled, "Whether 'In-Trust Accounts' Qualify as Trusts."
14 See generally Waters, *supra*, note 2 at pp. 107-128.
15 An estate does not qualify as a trust in law, but is treated as a trust for the purposes of income tax pursuant to subsection 104(1).

PART I — BASIC ESTATE AND TRUST PLANNING

1. certainty of intention,
2. certainty of subject matter, and
3. certainty of objects.

(a) Certainty of Intention

The person creating the trust must intend to create the trust, and that intention must be clear to outside observers. The most obvious evidence of intention will be an express reference in any written document establishing the trust, such as the last will and testament or a trust deed or indenture. If the settlor expressly declares the intent to create a trust, or to have property held by one person for the benefit or use of another, this element will generally be met.

The intention to create a trust will be less clear in cases where the trust springs up by words or conduct, or where the documentation dealing with the relationship is ambiguous or too brief to be of significant use in determining the intent of the settlor. Where that is the case, the courts give careful scrutiny to the conduct of the settlor in setting up the relationship and to the conduct of the parties to the relationship over the time the property in question is being held and administered.

If a trust is created by operation of law, as is the case where a trust is established by the courts as a constructive trust or a resulting trust, the courts, in essence, find or construct that intention from the conduct of the parties and are willing to do so over the vociferous objection of the notional settlor who generally takes the position, in defending the claim, that he had absolutely no intention of creating a trust and intended, in fact, to keep the property in question as his own and for his continuing benefit.

A trust often fails for lack of intention to create a trust when the transfer of property is found to be a gift from donor to donee rather than a contribution from settlor to trustee. A gift is often made, in a will or by a living person, with concurrent words that express the hope held by the donor for the future use of the property (for example, "it would be nice if you passed that on to your children"). In that case, such words do no more than state or imply a hope, or at best a moral obligation on

CHAPTER 1 — AN OVERVIEW OF TRUST LAW

the recipient, and will not ground a trust and oblige the recipient to deal with the property as forming the contents of a trust after receiving it. If it is clear from other wording or from the circumstances that property is intended to be given to the recipient outright, for his ownership and to do as he will, then even stronger language may fail to establish the necessary intent to create a trust. The words "in trust" or similar formulations do not end the question if other conduct or words suggest a contrary conclusion.[16]

Where a trust is established in a bid to minimize income taxes, the courts may give special scrutiny to this requirement, demanding a clearer statement of intent than would otherwise be necessary on the part of the settlor to create a trust.[17]

(b) Certainty of Subject Matter

The property that is to be held in the trust has to be known with sufficient certainty at the time the trust is to be created or the trust cannot be said to exist. It must be possible to point to the property that is to be governed by the trust. This requirement means that the property must either be described in the trust instrument or there must be a formula or method given to identify the trust property at the relevant time.[18] This situation can occur through conduct, as where particular property is given or transferred from settlor to trustee and is then earmarked and held separately by the trustee as distinct from the trustee's other property.

(c) Certainty of Objects

For a trust to exist, the person or purpose to be served or benefited must be known with sufficient certainty. If the objects of the trust are persons, then they must be named or must be part of an identifiable class. "My

---

16 *Canada Trust Co. v. Davis* (1912), 25 O.L.R. 633, 2 D.L.R. 644 (C.A.), affirmed (1912), 46 S.C.R. 649, 23 O.W.R. 308, 8 D.L.R.756, 1912 CarswellOnt 754 (S.C.C.).
17 *Minister of National Revenue v. Ablan Leon (1964) Ltd.*, [1976] C.T.C. 506, 10 N.R. 113, 76 D.T.C. 6280, 1976 CarswellNat 228 (Fed. C.A.).
18 Waters, *supra*, note 2 at p. 119.

brothers" is an ascertainable class, but "my friends" is not.[19] That class need not be a closed one, and could be "my grandchildren" for example, provided that the class is described with sufficient certainty that it can be ascertained at any relevant future moment.

As indicated earlier, a trust can also be established to serve or further a purpose rather than to benefit a collection of ascertainable beneficiaries, in which case the purpose has to be stated with sufficient certainty to ground the trust.[20]

2. Creation of a Trust

2.1 By Law

A trust can be established by operation of law. This situation can occur where a statute enacted by Parliament or a legislature expressly provides that a trust is imposed by operation of the statute,[21] or where a statute confers discretion on a court to impose a trust.[22]

Trusts can also arise in the context of judicial intervention in cases where a court has found that a person, by his conduct, has given rise to a trust for the benefit of another, as is the case with resulting trusts and constructive trusts.[23]

---

19 Waters, *supra*, note 2 at pp. 123-124 (including a larger discussion of qualifying and non-qualifying phrases with references to relevant case authority).
20 See 1.2(a) of this chapter entitled, "The Beneficiary."
21 As might be the case, for example, under various provisions found in federal and provincial pension legislation that imposes a trust on employer's property for un-remitted pension contributions. A more comprehensive listing of statutory trusts can be found in Waters, *supra*, note 2 at pp. 25-26.
22 As might be the case, for example, under dependant's relief legislation in various provinces that confer the power on the court to impose a trust to hold property that is to be paid to a dependant pursuant to a court order granting a payment or distribution to the disabled person from the property of the deceased. As another example, trustee legislation allows a court to impose terms of trust over an inheritance or other amount to be received outright by a minor or a person who is incapacitated and otherwise unable to handle his affairs.
23 See Waters, *supra*, note 2 at pp. 17-20.

CHAPTER 1 — AN OVERVIEW OF TRUST LAW

Where trusts arise by operation of law, the intent of the settlor to create a trust is either deemed to be present or is simply disregarded. Thus the "certainty of intention" normally required for the existence of a trust[24] is not a requirement in these circumstances.

2.2 By Express Words or Conduct

The most common way in which a trust will be established is by express words set out in a trust agreement, trust declaration or last will and testament.

It is also possible to establish a trust by words expressed orally, not in writing, provided that the three certainties are present and the necessary evidence can be marshalled to prove the existence of the trust. As an exception, in some provinces and territories it is not possible to verbally create a trust to hold real estate.[25] A verbally established trust is also not possible where a trust is to be established on the death of the settlor, as provincial and territorial wills legislation generally require that a trust must be in writing if it is to be established by testamentary instrument.

Finally, it is possible for a settlor to establish a trust, and the terms of that trust, if the presence of the three certainties is implied by his conduct. The terms of that trust cannot be easily ascertained, but can be ascertained at least in some measure by reference to provincial and territorial legislation dealing with trustees or by application to the courts.

---

24 See discussion earlier at 1.4(a) of this chapter entitled, "Certainty of Intention."
25 This rule has its origins in England under the *Statute of Frauds*, 1677, (29 Cha. 2), c. 3, which provided that trusts holding land had to be established in writing. The rule continues in operation in Alberta, Saskatchewan, Manitoba, Newfoundland, and the territories and has been varied but continues to have effect to varying degrees in Ontario, Nova Scotia, New Brunswick, British Columbia and Prince Edward Island. For a full discussion, see Waters, *supra*, note 2 at pp. 188-189.

PART I — BASIC ESTATE AND TRUST PLANNING

3. Distinguishing Trusts from Other Relationships

A trust relationship can be distinguished from other similar relationships.

A trust is not the same as an estate.[26] The personal representative of an estate takes title to the property of the deceased and is obliged to handle that property with many of the same duties of good faith that attach to a trustee, but the division of ownership which is one of the hallmarks of a trust relationship is absent. The beneficiary of a trust holds the equitable title to the property of the trust while the trustee holds the legal title. The beneficiary of an estate however does not, as a rule, enjoy a beneficial interest in the assets while they are under administration and form part of the estate. The role of the trustee and the personal representative of an estate are very similar but not identical.[27] The beneficiary of an estate does not have a claim over the assets during the executor's year, as an example. While an estate is not the same thing as a trust, there are many situations where the terms of a last will and testament will stipulate that a trust is to be established holding some or all of the assets of the estate after the administration of the estate proper is complete. In wills where this intent is not clearly expressed, it can be difficult to determine the date on which the estate ends and the trust begins, particularly if the personal representatives of the estate and the trustees of the trust are one and the same person or group of persons.[28]

A trust can also be distinguished from other relationships,[29] including the following:

- *Bailment* – Under a bailment one person holds possession of personal property that belongs to another. It can arise in a number of

---

26 See generally, Waters, *supra*, note 2 at pp. 34-42.
27 Provincial legislation governing trustees often includes personal representatives of estates under the rubric "trustee" but does not treat them coextensively. See, for example, the *Trustee Act*, R.S.O 1990, c. T.23 (Ontario), and *The Trustee Act*, C.C.S.M. c. T160 (Manitoba).
28 For more detail on this point see 1.2(b)(vii) of Chapter 2 entitled, "An Estate."
29 For a comprehensive discussion on this topic see D.W.M. Waters, *Law of Trusts in Canada*, 2nd ed. (Toronto: Carswell, 1984), at pp. 31-87.

CHAPTER 1 — AN OVERVIEW OF TRUST LAW

situations, such as where one person agrees to store the property of the other or borrows an item of property from the other. The legal and beneficial ownership of the property never passes to the person who gains possession of the property. The tax position of the parties does not change in any way in the typical course of a bailment.

- *Agent and Principal* – Agency is a relationship that arises typically but not necessarily, under a contract, in which one person gives another the power to enter into contracts on his behalf or to otherwise alter his legal rights in some way. To the extent that the agent may deal with property belonging to the principal, the legal and beneficial ownership in that property never passes to the agent, but remains with the principal. The tax positions of the parties do not change by virtue of the relationship.[30]

- *Powers of Appointment* – A power of appointment arises where a person, called a donor, gives a power to another person to dispose of property owned by the donor, and the power includes the discretion to exercise that power as he sees fit, or not at all. A trust does not arise. A trustee is obliged to deal with property to further the terms of the trust, while a person receiving property under a power of appointment is enabled to deal with the property, but is not obliged to. A trustee is obliged to apply the property for the enjoyment of the beneficiary or beneficiaries of the trust, but the holder of a power has no such obligation. The holder of a power can give the property to himself, while a trustee cannot do so unless he is concurrently a beneficiary of the trust.

- *Powers of Attorney* – A power of attorney over property appoints a person, referred to as the "attorney," to handle property owned by the person who grants the power of attorney. The attorney gains the power to deal with the assets, but never becomes the legal or beneficial owner of the property. No trust is in place, and the tax position of the person appointing the attorney does not change. In similar

---

[30] A bare trust is said to be a relationship of agency. From Waters, *ibid.* at pp. 27-29. "The usually accepted meaning of the term 'bare,' 'naked' or simple trust is a trust where the trustee or trustees hold property without any further duty to perform except to convey it to the beneficiary or beneficiaries upon demand."

PART I — BASIC ESTATE AND TRUST PLANNING

fashion to a trustee, an attorney cannot apply the property in question for the advantage or enjoyment of the attorney.

- *Committeeship (or Guardianship)* – A committeeship or guardianship over property is a court ordered arrangement conferring power under provincial or territorial statute on a person, called a committee or guardian, to administer property on behalf of a person who is unable to manage his affairs and who owns the property. Like an attorney under a power of attorney, the committee or guardian does not gain legal or beneficial ownership of the property, which remains with the owner, and no trust is created. In similar fashion to a trustee, a committee or guardian cannot apply the property in question for the advantage or enjoyment of the committee or guardian.

- *Gifts* – A gift of property is frequently confused with a trust. Under a gift, the whole of the legal and equitable ownership in property is given by a person, called the donor, to a recipient, called the donee. The donee receives the whole of the ownership interest formerly enjoyed by the donor. No division of ownership occurs. The confusion arises where a person makes such a gift but couples it with a statement of their hope relating to the ultimate use (*e.g.*, "with the hope he will let his son use the property as well") or relating to the ultimate destination of the property (*e.g.*, "with the expectation that he will ultimately leave the cottage to his daughter when he passes away").[31]

4. Provincial Considerations

Income tax law is a matter of federal jurisdiction and will remain constant from province to province and territory to territory across Canada.[32] The laws that apply to trusts and govern property, however, are a matter of provincial and territorial jurisdiction, not federal jurisdiction. As a result, those laws will vary in some degree across the provinces and territories

---

31 See also the discussion on this topic that appears at 1.4(a) of this chapter entitled, "Certainty of Intention."
32 Some provisions of the Act are specific to Quebec but, as noted in the introduction to this book, the scope of this text does not extend to Quebec.

CHAPTER 1 — AN OVERVIEW OF TRUST LAW

of Canada. A detailed comparison of the laws from jurisdiction to jurisdiction is beyond the scope of this text.

All of the provinces and territories, other than Quebec, began with the same starting point. Canadian provinces and territories adopted the laws of England as their own law as they became independent entities and established their own civil courts.[33] Much of the provincial and territorial law that applies to trusts will be the same across the territories and provinces. The laws have diverged, however, primarily by virtue of legislative changes. Among the most significant areas of difference are the laws that apply to variation of trusts and to the rules that apply to perpetuities and accumulations.

4.1 The Rule in *Saunders v. Vautier*

The law that applied to the variation of trusts in England is referred to as the rule from *Saunders v. Vautier*.[34] The rule provides, in essence, that a trust can be terminated or varied with the concurrence of its beneficiaries and without requiring the concurrence of the courts or, for that matter, the trustees. This assumes that the beneficiaries are able to give that concurrence, and thus the rule does not extend to situations in which the beneficiaries have yet to attain the age of majority or are incapacitated and unable to consent on their own behalf to a change. In those latter instances, the courts retained a supervisory jurisdiction to protect the interests of the vulnerable beneficiaries and court approval was required for any windup or amendment of the trust. This rule has

---

33 As each province was created and established civil courts, its judge-made case law (referred to as the "common law") began to evolve on its own. The highest court of appeal remained the English Privy Council, and not the Supreme Court of Canada, until the mid-1900s. As a result, the judge-made law of England continued to mould the judge-made common law of Canadian provinces and territories for as much as eighty or ninety years after provinces established their own systems of law until the right of appeal to the Privy Council was extinguished. Current English law remains influential on Canadian courts today but is not binding in any way.
34 (1841), 4 Beav. 115, 49 E.R. 282 (Rolls Ct.), affirmed (1841), 1 Cr. & Ph. 240, 41 E.R. 482 (Ch. Div.).

PART I — BASIC ESTATE AND TRUST PLANNING

not been uniformly adopted across Canada,[35] and at least some jurisdictions, including Manitoba and Alberta,[36] require court approval for the amendment or windup of a trust even where adult, capacitated beneficiaries unanimously consent to the change. In such cases, any amendment of the trust conducted without court approval will be ineffective, and court approval should be obtained where an amendment to the trust is required for tax purposes. It may be possible to circumvent court approval if the trust contains an express mechanism granting the ability to amend the trust without court approval, but an opinion should be secured from legal counsel in the jurisdiction applicable to the trust before proceeding on the basis that an amendment has been validly effected.

In those provinces and territories in which the rule in *Saunders v. Vautier* does apply, some trusts will be more susceptible than others to variation. The rule will not apply where the draftsperson of the trust has included a generation of contingent beneficiaries that include minors or additional generations of contingent beneficiaries including minors. When trusts are drafted for income tax purposes, they generally do not contain provisions to preclude or dissuade such applications.[37]

---

35 For more detailed reviews of the law on this point see Keith B. Farquhar, "Recent Themes in the Variation of Trusts" (2001) 20 E.T.P.J. 181 and A.J. McClean, "Variation of Trusts in England and Canada" (1965), 43 Can. Bar. Rev. 181.

36 From Waters, *supra*, note 29 at pages 979-980. The Wills and Estates section of the Canadian Bar Association is attempting to pull together a table that compares provincial and territorial laws as they relate to succession, but that table is still in the preparation stage.

37 Waters, *supra*, note 29 at p. 966:
Tax considerations have encouraged the drafting of single beneficiary trusts, and trusts with simple successive interests, such as a gift over from the first to a second and final beneficiary. In these circumstances the will draftsman can more easily create a situation where the testator's scheme of proprietary arrangements can be brought to nothing by premature termination, and as a result it becomes particularly important for the draftsman to be able to recognize almost instinctively a future and likely *Saunders v. Vautier* situation.

CHAPTER 1 — AN OVERVIEW OF TRUST LAW

4.2 Perpetuities and Accumulations

Canada also inherited laws from England that restricted trusts under rules that applied to perpetuities and accumulations. Accumulations rules generally prohibit the accumulation of income in a trust beyond a specified period of time, generally twenty-one years. At the end of that period of time, the income must be paid out each year to a beneficiary. As each province and territory was established and became responsible for its own provincial law, it adopted and implemented the laws of England as they stood at the time. Accumulations laws were evolving in England while various provinces came on line and, thus, different provinces received the law in different forms. Many provinces then legislated changes to the laws they had adopted relating to accumulations. Thus, the laws on this point differ greatly from jurisdiction to jurisdiction.[38] The rule against accumulations no longer exists in Manitoba[39] and has effectively been removed from operation in Alberta[40] and British Columbia,[41] where the permitted accumulation period has effectively been extended to the effective life of the trust under perpetuities legislation.

The rule against perpetuities is related to the rule against accumulations and arose in England in the 1600s.[42] The rationale behind the rule is subject to debate, and in its original form made interests in a trust void if they did not vest within a given length of time, normally expressed as being within a life or lives in being and twenty-one years. The property in the trust did not have to be distributed in that time frame, but the terms of trust had to be such that a court could look at the pool of beneficiaries, current and contingent, at the time the trust was established and be satisfied that the trust property would have vested in known

---

[38] An effort to canvass the difficult laws in this area is found in Waters, *supra*, note 29 at pp. 284-287. An opinion specific to the province or territory in question should be solicited from a lawyer where the applicability of accumulations law is important to a given situation.
[39] *Perpetuities and Accumulations Act*, R.S.M. 1987, c. P33 (abolishing the rule).
[40] *Perpetuities Act*, R.S.A. 2000, c. P-5.
[41] *Perpetuity Act*, R.S.B.C. 1996, c. 358.
[42] *The Duke of Norfolk's Case* (1682), 3 Ch. Cas. 1, 22 E.R. 931 (Ch.).

PART I — BASIC ESTATE AND TRUST PLANNING

persons by the time the current beneficiaries had passed away plus an additional period of twenty-one years.

After the rule against perpetuities became the law in various provinces and territories in Canada, they set about amending it. In some jurisdictions it has been amended to allow the courts to take a wait and see approach, not declaring trust provisions void at the outset but allowing the trust to operate until the question of vesting is answered with the passage of time. Manitoba, alone among the provinces and territories in Canada, has abolished the rule in its entirety.[43] In doing so, it joined a small handful of North American jurisdictions, including Alaska, that allow for trusts to be established over longer terms and for successive generations, free from the fetter on perpetuities imposed by the English common law.

The rule reflects a judicial expression of social policy from a bygone era. Some commentators question its current relevance. James Watt was working on his improvements to the steam engine when the rule was developed. From the perspectives of tax planning and legacy planning, the ability to establish trusts of longer duration is often considered to be an advantage. The laws on this point, like those applying to accumulations, differ greatly from jurisdiction to jurisdiction.[44]

The rule against perpetuities is often confused with the deemed disposition of trust property that occurs every twenty-one years under subsection 104(4) of the Act. The rule against perpetuities is a principle from the law of trusts and deals with the validity of trusts and the length of time property can be held in a trust before it vests. The perpetuity period will generally be far longer than twenty-one years, as it extends over the life of the initial collection of beneficiaries plus twenty-one years. It can be viewed as mandatory in the sense that a trust has to comply in a jurisdiction where the rule against perpetuities is in operation or the trust risks invalidity. The twenty-one year deemed disposition is a tax rule, having nothing to do with the validity of the trust. Nothing in

---

43 *Supra*, note 39, s. 4.
44 An effort to canvass the difficult laws in this area is found in Waters, *supra*, note 29 at pp. 284-287. An opinion specific to the province or territory in question should be solicited from a lawyer where the applicability of perpetuities law is important to a given situation.

CHAPTER 1 — AN OVERVIEW OF TRUST LAW

the tax rule will require the windup of the trust, and the terms of trusts need not include any provision requiring the wind up of the trust as a mandatory step to avoid the disposition.

5. The Relationship Between Tax Law and Trust Law

Trust law and tax law do not always parallel each other. The differences often have to be borne in mind, as case law and commentary in one area may not be applicable or relevant in the other. The income of a trust for tax purposes is calculated under the Act and is not the same as the income of the trust under trust law, and there will be occasions where the income figures have to be distinguished one from the other. Whether a trust is "testamentary" or not under the *Income Tax Act* is key to determining its tax treatment, but a separate body of law has developed that deals with whether a trust can be characterized as testamentary or not for the purposes of the various provincial wills acts.[45] The case law and principles in one area will not be applicable or relevant in the other, and will be misleading if considered in the wrong context.

Under trust law, an estate is not a trust,[46] but is treated as such under the Act for income tax purposes.[47] There may be occasions where a trust has a settlor under trust law, but does not have a settlor for tax purposes,[48] or occasions where a trust exists under trust law that is not considered to be a trust for certain provisions of the Act.[49]

---

45 Waters, *supra*, note 29 at pp. 157-161.
46 See heading 3 of this chapter entitled, "Distinguishing Trusts from Other Relationships."
47 Subsection 104(1).
48 Subsection 108(1), definition of "settlor," subparagraph (b) (certain *inter vivos* trusts do not, by definition, have a settlor where contributions have been made by more than one person). For additional commentary on this topic, see also 13.5 of Chapter 9 entitled, "Additional Capital Contributed."
49 Subsection 108(1), definition of "trust."

Chapter 2
Types of Trusts and Basic Planning

1. Testamentary Trusts

1.1 Summary

A testamentary trust is one that arises on and as a consequence of an individual's death. Common forms of testamentary trusts for tax purposes include estates, trusts established under the terms of a person's last will and testament, trusts established by judges under dependants' relief legislation, and insurance trusts. A qualifying testamentary trust enjoys advantageous tax treatment under the Act, including taxation at graduated rates (rather than the top rate payable by *inter vivos* trusts), a flexible year-end, and freedom from installment taxes. A trust can fail to qualify as a testamentary trust or lose its status and become disqualified in a variety of ways, including situations where a living person contributes property to the trust or pays capital expenses on behalf of the trust.

1.2 General Comments Relating to Testamentary Trusts

(a) *Definition of Testamentary Trust*

A "testamentary trust" is defined as a trust that arises "on and as a

PART I — BASIC ESTATE AND TRUST PLANNING

consequence of the death of an individual."[1] The definition goes on to specifically *include* the following:

- an estate; or

- a trust established under the terms of the taxpayer's will;[2] or

- a trust established by an order of a court in relation to the taxpayer's estate made under any law of a province that provides for the relief or support of dependants.[3]

Specifically *excluded* from the definition, however, even if it otherwise meets the terms of the definition, will be the following:

- a trust or estate that is created or settled by a person other than the individual whose death has caused it to come into existence;[4] or

- a trust that has received a contribution of property otherwise than by an individual on or after the individual's death and as a consequence thereof[5] (this exclusion does not apply to testamentary trusts created before November 13, 1981, and trusts created before that date are subject to special rules).[6]

An additional exception has been proposed under Draft Technical Legislation of February 27, 2004, that would exclude any trust from characterization as testamentary if the trust incurs a debt or other obligation to a beneficiary.[7] This will not extend to a debt owed to the

---

1. Subsection 108(1), definition of "testamentary trust."
2. Paragraph 248(9.1)(a), this provision of the Act is brought into the main definition by a specific inclusion in subsection 108(1).
3. Paragraph 248(9.1)(b).
4. Subsection 108(1), definition of "testamentary trust," paragraph (a).
5. Subsection 108(1), definition of "testamentary trust," paragraph (b).
6. Subsection 108(1), definition of "testamentary trust," paragraph (c).
7. M.N.R., Special Release IT 04-01, "Draft Technical Amendments and Explanatory Notes To Amend the Income Tax Act" (February 27, 2004) at clause 45 (for a commentary on an earlier version of the same amendments, see Barry S. Corbin, "Tightening the Noose on Testamentary Trusts" (2003) 22 E.T.P.J. 175). See also Department of Finance comfort letter dated April 28, 2004, relating to proposed paragraph (d) of subsection 108(1) of the Act, defining "testamentary

CHAPTER 2 — TYPES OF TRUSTS AND BASIC PLANNING

beneficiary on account of income or capital that the beneficiary is entitled to under the terms of the trust, or to a debt owed to a personal representative or trustee on account of fees for services to the estate or trust, or to amounts expended by a personal representative or trustee on behalf of the estate or trust, as might be the case if a personal representative pays funeral expenses on behalf of a deceased and then seeks reimbursement, provided that reimbursement is made within twelve months of the expenditure by the personal representative or trustee.[8]

(b) Qualifying and Non-Qualifying Testamentary Trusts

Because *inter vivos* and testamentary trusts are subject to different rules and because of the tax advantages inherent in qualifying as a testamentary trust, characterization is an important issue. Before filing, carefully ensure that the trust is in fact a testamentary trust within the meaning of the Act.[9] Very little case law has been generated on the point and much of the material available on the point is in the form of non-binding technical interpretations published by CRA.

(i) Trusts Created by Will

Trusts created under the terms of a person's last will and testament will qualify as testamentary by virtue of clear wording in the Act. The definition of a testamentary trust[10] includes a trust referred to in subsection 248(9.1), and that subsection expressly includes trusts created under a taxpayer's will.

---

trust." Proposed paragraph (d) of the definition "testamentary trust" is an anti-avoidance rule that is intended to prevent the use of a testamentary trust for income-splitting purposes. The Department of Finance comfort letter suggests that modifications will be made to proposed subparagraph (d)(iii) of the definition so that a testamentary trust will not lose its status by virtue of failing to pay interest to its debtors, under certain circumstances.

8 M.N.R., Special Release IT 04-01, *ibid.* at clause 45.
9 Also note that a trust that would clearly qualify as testamentary can lose that characterization if it falls prey to any of the disqualifying events discussed later in this chapter at 1.4(a) under the title "Loss of Status as a Testamentary Trust."
10 Subsection 108(1), definition of "testamentary trust".

PART I — BASIC ESTATE AND TRUST PLANNING

(ii) Successive Testamentary Trusts

A testamentary trust is frequently set up for a surviving spouse on express terms that when the surviving spouse passes away the remaining contents of the trust for the spouse will then be divided into a series of testamentary trusts for the children. Under those circumstances, the trusts for the children appear to qualify as testamentary trusts on a continuing basis.[11] Thus it appears that assets can be flowed through a series of successive testamentary trusts established under the terms of a taxpayer's will without losing qualifying status.

(iii) Blended Trusts

CRA appears to take the position that two or more testamentary trusts might be merged together to form a single trust and that the blended trust would under those circumstances maintain its status as a testamentary trust.

Likewise, when an individual gifts property in her will to an existing testamentary trust (*e.g.*, when the will of a parent directs that some portion of the estate is to be placed in a testamentary trust previously created by the will of a grandparent for the benefit of the children of that parent), the contribution does not disqualify the existing trust as a testamentary trust because the contribution is made by an individual on or after that individual's death and as a consequence thereof.[12]

(iv) Insurance Trusts

The proceeds of an insurance policy can be used to fund a trust separate and apart from the estate of a deceased person, thereby establishing a testamentary trust while maintaining probate avoidance, confidentiality

---

11 M.N.R., Technical Interpretation 9801035, "Successive Trusts and Definition of Trust" (September 22, 1998).
12 M.N.R., Technical Interpretation, 2000-0059755 "Trust Receives Property from an Alter Ego Trust" (March 23, 2001) (the wording of the Act is less than completely clear on this point and the position is not binding on CRA).

CHAPTER 2 — TYPES OF TRUSTS AND BASIC PLANNING

and creditor proofing.[13] The terms of trust can be set out in a trust declaration or trust agreement, distinct from a person's last will and testament, but can also be set out in the will itself provided that the provisions establishing the insurance trust are carefully kept distinct from the provisions that govern the estate. If the trust is to be a qualifying spousal trust, however, the terms of the insurance trust must be set out in the will,[14] and not in a side document.

The following requirements must be met before an insurance trust will qualify as a testamentary trust.[15]

- No property can be settled on the trust by the settlor prior to her death.

- The payment of the insurance proceeds has to result from the death of the person creating the trust.

- The deceased person creating the trust must be the owner of the insurance policy.

- The deceased person must enter into an insurance designation that designates the trustee of the trust as the beneficiary of the proceeds at death.

- The insurance designation must qualify as a testamentary instrument.

---

13 See generally Barry S. Corbin, "Separate Insurance Trusts: Eating One's Cake and Having it Too" (1992) 12 E. & T.J. 105.

14 This being one of the requirements of subsection 70(6); also see M.N.R., Technical Interpretation 9625975, "Testamentary Spousal Trust" (October 7, 1996).

15 Insurance trusts have been the subject matter of extensive commentary in nonbinding technical interpretations: M.N.R., Technical Interpretation 9238555, "Trust" (February 4, 1993); M.N.R., Technical Interpretation 9625975, *ibid.*; M.N.R., Technical Interpretation 9605575, "Testamentary Trust – Insurance Proceeds" (December 17, 1996); M.N.R., Technical Interpretation 2000 – 0059755, *supra*, note 12; M.N.R., Technical Interpretation 2000 – 0005135, "Trust — property from alter ego trust" (March 23, 2001) (both of the latter technical interpretations issued on the same day, with nearly identical titles, and each contain an extensive discussion on point).

PART I — BASIC ESTATE AND TRUST PLANNING

In considering the last of those points, an instrument is said to be "testamentary" if each of the following requirements are met:[16]

1. no consideration passes,
2. the document has no immediate effect,
3. the document is revocable, and
4. the position of the deceased and the donee does not immediately change.

The latter two requirements may mean that the beneficiary designation cannot be revocable if the insurance trust is to qualify as a testamentary trust.

(v) *RRSP Trusts*

CRA has taken the position that a testamentary trust might be funded by RRSP proceeds funneled into a freestanding testamentary trust via a beneficiary designation appointing the trustees of the trust as the beneficiaries of the plan.[17] The issue is not whether death will bring the fair market value of the registered investments into income in the year of death – it will. The question is whether the plan proceeds can be used in an analogous manner as insurance proceeds might be used to fund a freestanding testamentary trust, outside of the estate and without the payment of probate fees. The following statement of requirements was expressed by CRA:

> It follows therefore that in order for a trust, funded from the proceeds of an RRIF or RRSP available on the death of an individual and the terms of which have been established during the individual's lifetime separate from

---

16 *Elliot v. Turner*, [1944] O.W.N. 185, [1944] 2 D.L.R. 313, 1944 CarswellOnt 120 (H.C.). For a more general discussion of when an instrument can be said to be testamentary see *MacInnes v. MacInnes* (1934), [1935] S.C.R. 200, 2 I.L.R. 14, [1935] 1 D.L.R. 401, 1934 CarswellOnt 139 (S.C.C.) (a document is said to be testamentary if "the person executing it intends that it shall not take effect until after his death, and it is dependent upon his death for its vigour and affect...").

17 M.N.R., Technical Interpretation 2002-0143685, "*RRSP/RRIF and Testamentary Trusts*" (January 29, 2003).

CHAPTER 2 — TYPES OF TRUSTS AND BASIC PLANNING

his will, to be viewed as a "testamentary trust" within the meaning of subsection 108(1) of the Act, the following conditions must be met:
(a) The trust was created by the deceased individual or his legal representative;
(b) The deceased individual had designated the trust as the beneficiary of the RRSP or RRIF;
(c) The designation of the trust as beneficiary of the RRSP or RRIF is considered under the applicable provincial legislation to be a testamentary instrument;
(d) No property can be contributed to the trust prior to the receipt of the proceeds of the RRIF or RRSP on the death of the individual; and
(e) No property is contributed to the trust otherwise than by an individual on or after the individual's death and as a consequence thereof.[18]

The requirement to meet provincial legislation may be the only impediment on the list. It appears, generally, that the beneficiary designation will qualify as a testamentary instrument,[19] but some issues may remain on a province-by-province basis relating to the mechanics of the beneficiary designation itself and whether a trustee can be designated as the legal owner of the proceeds to hold the funds in trust for another.[20]

(vi) Trusts Arising by Operation of Dependants' Relief Legislation

A trust established by a court order will be testamentary if the order is pronounced under a provincial law providing for the relief or support of dependants.[21] Different provinces will have different laws in place for the relief or support of dependants, and those statutes may or may not

---

18 M.N.R., Technical Interpretation 2002-0143685, *ibid.*
19 See Anne Werker, "Non-Insurance RRSP Designations – Testamentary Dispositions of Property that Do Not Form Part of the Estate" (2003) 22 E.T.P.J. 103.
20 Barry S. Corbin, "The 'Separate RRSP Trust'" (2003) 22 E.T.P.J. 360.
21 Subsection 108(1), definition of "testamentary trust" (expressly including as testamentary any trust described in subsection 248(9.1), specifically referring to any trust created "by an order of a court in relation to the taxpayer's estate made under any law of a province that provides for the relief or support of dependants" – trusts established under other forms of legislation do not appear to qualify).

provide the authority to the court to establish a trust when fashioning relief for a dependant.[22]

(vii) An Estate

An estate is not a trust,[23] but is afforded the status of a testamentary trust for income tax purposes.[24] If the personal representatives of a deceased are obliged to distribute the assets comprising the estate then that tax treatment will not be available indefinitely, and the trust will lose its qualifying status at such time as they ought to have been able to distribute the assets.[25] Generally speaking, CRA will look at the executor's year as the natural duration of an estate in those circumstances and allow status as a testamentary trust over the course of that year, but may look to the facts of each case to extend that treatment over a longer period or to limit it to a shorter period.

Generally speaking, the administration of an estate would be considered to be complete when the beneficiaries are ascertained, the assets have been gathered in, the debts and specific bequests have been paid, the value of the residue has been ascertained, and the final accounts of the estate have been approved by the residuary beneficiaries or have been passed by a court.[26]

Where the executors are in a position to distribute an estate to beneficiaries and succeed in winding up the estate prior to the end of

---

22 In Manitoba that jurisdiction exists and is found in paragraphs 9(2)(b) and (c) of *The Dependants' Relief Act*, C.C.S.M. c. D-37 (S.M. 1989-90, c. 42).
23 See generally D.W.M. Waters, *Law of Trusts in Canada*, 2nd ed. (Toronto: Carswell, 1984) at p. 34.
24 Subsections 104(1) and 108(1), definition of "testamentary trust".
25 M.N.R., Technical Interpretation 2002-0172475, "Administration of Estates" (May 30, 2003). Also see *Grayson v. Minister of National Revenue* (1989), [1990] 1 C.T.C. 2303, 90 D.T.C. 1108, 1989 CarswellNat 459 (T.C.C.) (failed effort to treat trust as ongoing during years following completed administration), and *Hall v. R.*, 2003 TCC 410, 2003 D.T.C. 779 [2003] 4 C.T.C 2544, 2003 CarswellNat 1823 (T.C.C. [Informal Procedure]) (estate treated as ongoing trust while distribution delayed by fee dispute and assets still to be collected).
26 M.N.R., Technical Interpretation 9526815, "Executor's Year Passing Beneficial Ownership Estate" (May 24, 1996).

CHAPTER 2 — TYPES OF TRUSTS AND BASIC PLANNING

the executor's year but do not do so, CRA will take the position that all of the income and capital of the estate has been paid to the beneficiaries and, accordingly, all of the income is taxable in the hands of the beneficiaries on their T1 returns.[27] This will occur unless the trustees designate income under subsection 104(13.1) or (13.2) to be trust income,[28] or unless any one beneficiary of the trust objects to that treatment with respect to the executor's year, in which case the income of the estate for that year will be taxed as trust income and not beneficiary income, not just for the beneficiary who lodges the objection but for all of the beneficiaries.[29]

Where the executors are unable to wind up the estate and it remains open and holding assets for a longer period, the income will generally continue to be that of the estate and will not be included in the income of the beneficiaries.[30]

Where the executors are charged under the terms of the will with the obligation of passing the estate assets over to trustees to hold under the terms of a long-term trust the estate will be wound up as of that date that occurs, or ought to occur, and the trusts will thereafter be treated as distinct taxable entities.[31]

---

27 M.N.R., Technical Interpretation 9526815, *ibid.*
28 M.N.R., Technical Interpretation 9526815, *supra*, note 26 (making the designation will often be advisable, as where the beneficiaries are high income earners and the income can be taxed more efficiently in the estate). See heading 4 of Chapter 4 entitled, "Income Designations Under 104(13.1) and 104(13.2)."
29 M.N.R., Interpretation Bulletin IT-286R2, "Trusts – Amount Payable" (April 8, 1988), at paragraph 6 (note that the income cannot be taxed in the hands of the trust by virtue of beneficiary objection if it has actually been paid out, but the income in that event should be subject to the opportunity to designate it as trust income under 104(13.1) and (13.2)).
30 M.N.R., Technical Interpretation 9526815, *supra*, note 26; also see *Roy v. Minister of National Revenue* (1977), [1978] C.T.C. 2180, 78 D.T.C. 1123, 1977 CarswellNat 457(T.R.B.).
31 M.N.R., Technical Interpretation 9526815, *supra*, note 26.

PART I — BASIC ESTATE AND TRUST PLANNING

(viii) Trusts Settled with Property from an Inter Vivos Trust

CRA takes the position that a trust created pursuant to the death of a lifetime beneficiary of an *inter vivos* trust will be refused characterization as a testamentary trust. Despite an early technical interpretation that suggested that it may be possible to fund a testamentary trust using the proceeds of an *inter vivos* trust,[32] and notwithstanding continuing debate on the point, a series of later technical interpretations have expressly superseded the earlier interpretation and suggest that such trusts would fail to qualify as testamentary trusts.[33]

In the heart of the analysis, CRA states:

> However, since it is our understanding that a person cannot transfer his or her property on or after his or her death otherwise than by will or other testamentary instrument, the transfer of property from an alter ego trust to a trust created after the death of the settlor of the alter ego trust is not a transfer of property by the settlor of that alter ego trust.[34]

Another reason is cited:

> Furthermore, in the case of property which has been transferred to an alter ego trust prior to the death of the settlor, the property does not belong to the settlor at the time of the settlor's death and thus, the property cannot be considered to be a contribution by the settlor as a consequence of the settlor's death to a trust that is created subsequent to the settlor's death.[35]

---

32 M.N.R., Technical Interpretation 9613875, "Definition of a Testamentary Trust" (September 11, 1996).
33 M.N.R., Technical Interpretation 9818696, "*Inter Vivos* Vs. Testamentary Trusts" (August 7, 1998); M.N.R, Technical Interpretation 9901435, "Status of Successive Trusts" (February 16, 1999); M.N.R., Technical Interpretation 2000-0059755, *supra*, note 12; M.N.R., Technical Interpretation 2000-0005135, *supra*, note 15; M.N.R., Technical Interpretation 2001-0079285 "Status of Successive Trusts" (November 2, 2001).
34 M.N.R., Technical Interpretation 2000-0005135, *supra*, note 15.
35 M.N.R., Technical Interpretation 2000-0005135, *supra*, note 15.

CHAPTER 2 — TYPES OF TRUSTS AND BASIC PLANNING

1.3 Special Features

Testamentary trusts enjoy special features not available to *inter vivos* trusts.

(a) *Taxation at Graduated Rates*

Testamentary trusts are taxed at graduated rates in the same manner as an individual.[36] This basis of taxation permits a degree of income-splitting with the beneficiaries of a testamentary trust, as income payable to the beneficiaries can be retained and taxed within the trust at the same graduated rate structure as is available for a living individual. The ability to access multiple levels of the graduated tax rate system through the use of multiple testamentary trusts can, however, be subject to review and ministerial discretion by CRA.[37] Also, there is a provision in the Act[38] that prevents a personal trust from claiming any personal tax credits, as set out in section 118, in computing federal income taxes payable.

(b) *Flexible Year End*

The trustees of a testamentary trust enjoy the ability to select a fiscal period[39] for tax purposes other than a calendar year, provided that the taxation year does not exceed twelve months from the date of death. Once the taxation year is established, it cannot be changed without the concurrence of the Minister.[40]

The first taxation year of the estate begins on the day after the date of death of the deceased taxpayer. The trustee, administrator or executor

---

[36] Subsection 117(2), this gives rise to a variety of estate planning opportunities. See also Appendix C in Part VI entitled, "Marginal Tax Rates" for a schedule detailing the various combined federal and provincial or territorial tax rates applicable to testamentary trusts.
[37] For additional commentary on this point see 1.4(f) of Chapter 2 entitled, "Separate Taxpayer Status for Multiple Testamentary Trusts."
[38] Subsection 122(1.1).
[39] Paragraph 249.1(1)(b).
[40] Paragraph 104(23)(a).

of the estate can choose a year-end for the first taxation year. Thereafter, each taxation year must be twelve months in duration unless a shorter year is requested and approved by CRA. A request for a change in taxation year[41] must be submitted in writing to the Director of the local district taxation office and should be accompanied by a statement signed by the trustee or personal representative explaining the reasons for the change.[42] Permission is not required if the taxation year is terminating early as the result of the windup of the estate or trust.[43] Where permission is required, the change in taxation year will only be granted if the Minister is satisfied that the change is sought for sound business reasons other than simply obtaining tax benefits.[44]

(c) No Installment Taxes

Installment taxes need not be paid on income generated in a testamentary trust, it being sufficient that any income taxes are paid within ninety days from the end of the taxation year.[45] This provides tax deferral on income taxed in the hands of the trustees.

1.4 Things You Need to Know

(a) Loss of Status as a Testamentary Trust

A trust can be created on terms that clearly make it a qualifying testamentary trust at the outset, but it can lose that status in a number of ways after it has come into existence. The most common reason results from mismanagement by the trustees. A testamentary trust that loses its status will be taxed, as a result, as an *inter vivos* trust. The following are some

---

41 While the term "fiscal period" is proper in other contexts, and is used frequently in the context of trusts and estates, the phrase "taxation year" is actually considered to be the more proper in this context (see M.N.R., Technical Interpretation 9406256, "First and Last Taxation Year of Testamentary Trust" (September 7, 1994)).
42 M.N.R., Interpretation Bulletin IT-179R, "Change of Fiscal Period" (May 28, 1993), at paragraph 4.
43 M.N.R., Interpretation Bulletin IT-179R, *ibid.* at paragraph 5.
44 M.N.R., Interpretation Bulletin IT-179R, *supra*, note 42 at paragraph 2.
45 Paragraph 104(23)(e).

CHAPTER 2 — TYPES OF TRUSTS AND BASIC PLANNING

of the events which can result in the loss of status as a testamentary trust:

- if property is contributed or settled into the trust by a living person,[46] as would be the case if a beneficiary borrows money and voluntarily adds it to the trust;[47]

- if a beneficiary or some other person pays capital expenses on behalf of the trust;[48]

- if a beneficiary of an estate pays income taxes on behalf of the deceased on account of their terminal return that would normally be the obligation of the trustees;[49]

- if the trustees fail or refuse to make a mandatory capital distribution to a beneficiary of the trust;[50] or,

- under proposed amendments to the Act discussed earlier, if the trust incurs an obligation to a beneficiary or a person not at arm's length to a beneficiary.[51]

---

46 Subsection 108(1), definition of "testamentary trust," at subparagraph (b); but see M.N.R., Technical Interpretation 9319185, "Compensation Received by Testamentary Trust" (November 29, 1993) (a contribution of property to a trust generally implies that the trust receives the property without any value being given in return to the contributor, and thus a testamentary trust will not be disqualified by a loan to the trust, or by an asset received into the trust by virtue of a purchase for full face value by the trust, or by a payment into the trust by a trustee in settlement of a claim by the trust against the trustee).
47 *Greenberg Estate v. R.*, [1997] 3 C.T.C. 2859, 97 D.T.C. 1380, 1997 CarswellNat 1007 (T.C.C.).
48 M.N.R., Technical Interpretation 2002-0154435, "Payment of Trust Expenses by Beneficiary" (April 17, 2003).
49 M.N.R., Technical Interpretation 9233787, "Election Under 104(13.1) and (13.2)" (January 1, 1992).
50 M.N.R., Technical Interpretation 2002-0172475, *supra*, note 29; also see remarks to that effect set out in the "T3 Guide" published by CRA.
51 M.N.R., Special Release IT 04-01, "Draft Technical Amendments and Explanatory Notes To Amend the Income Tax Act" (February 27, 2004) at clause 45.

PART I — BASIC ESTATE AND TRUST PLANNING

(b) Opportunity to Seek Reassessments

Under current tax provisions, the trustees of a testamentary trust can file reassessments and seek refunds for taxation years as far back as 1985.[52] This opportunity extends to testamentary trusts and to individuals but not to other forms of trusts, such as *inter vivos* trusts or to corporations.[53] If a return was filed previously for a taxation year, a refund can be sought by submitting a written request or, if returns were not filed, by filing the returns along with documentation or explanations to support the claimed refund.[54] The provision was enacted as part of the 1991 "Fairness Package" and requests are granted subject to ministerial discretion,[55] and that discretion may be exercised in favour of a taxpayer if they were simply unaware that a deduction or credit was available.[56] If unsatisfied with the Minister's decision on a refund request, the taxpayer can ask that the request be reconsidered by the Director of the appropriate district office or Taxation Centre. The review process is subject to judicial review but only in limited circumstances, such as where the minister's decision is made in bad faith, is contrary to law, or is based on irrelevant considerations.[57]

If a request is granted, the refund will bear interest from the date the return is filed or the date the request for adjustment of the past return is received.[58]

52　Subsection 152(4.2). See generally M.N.R., Information Circular 92-3, "Guidelines for Refunds Beyond the Normal Three Year Period" (March 18,1992). Under proposed changes introduced in the 2004 Federal Budget, the opportunity to file reassessments and seek refunds will be limited to a ten year period, as opposed to going back to 1985.
53　See M.N.R., Information Circular 92-3, *ibid.* at paragraph 6.
54　See M.N.R., Information Circular 92-3, *supra*, note 52 at paragraph 8.
55　The wording of the subsection is permissive, not mandatory.
56　See M.N.R., Information Circular 92-3, *supra*, note 52 at paragraph 9.
57　*Barron v. Minister of National Revenue*, [1996] 3 C.T.C. 121, 110 F.T.R. 315, 1996 CarswellNat 1464, 96 D.T.C. 6262, [1996] F.C.J. No. 461 (T.D.), reversed 1997 CarswellNat 7, [1997] 2 C.T.C. 198 (Fed. C.A.), leave to appeal refused (1997), 223 N.R. 78 (note) (S.C.C.).
58　See M.N.R., Information Circular 92-3, *supra*, note 52 at paragraph 22.

CHAPTER 2 — TYPES OF TRUSTS AND BASIC PLANNING

Opportunities may also exist above and beyond those described above to seek reassessments for past taxation years in the application of the designated income sections of the Act.[59]

(c) Attributing Losses to Deceased's Terminal Return

The personal representative of an estate can elect to apply net capital losses realized in the estate against income on the deceased's year of death return.[60]

The personal representative of an estate can also elect to have losses on stock options held by the deceased treated as a loss from employment on the deceased's terminal return for the year of death.[61]

(d) Testamentary Trust Enjoying Income from Business, Farming, Fishing and Rentals

Where a testamentary trust is the sole proprietor of the business, or if the business is owned by a partnership of testamentary trusts, the trust is exempt from special rules that otherwise apply to the calculation of income.

(e) Rollovers into Testamentary Spousal Trusts

A rollover is available allowing for the transfer of capital property from a deceased taxpayer into a qualifying spousal trust.[62]

---

59 See 1.4(h) of this chapter entitled, "Designated Income" for a discussion on this point.
60 Subsection 164(6). For a more extensive discussion, see 1.3 of Chapter 10 entitled, "Utilizing Capital Losses."
61 Subsection 164(6.1).
62 Paragraph 70(6)(b). See heading 3 of Chapter 2 entitled, "Spousal Trusts."

PART I — BASIC ESTATE AND TRUST PLANNING

(f) Separate Taxpayer Status for Multiple Testamentary Trusts

Each distinct and separate trust will generally be treated as a separate taxpayer.[63] This is often an advantage when dealing with testamentary trusts, as each trust will be entitled to access the graduated tax system, providing an opportunity for income splitting. The Minister of Finance enjoys discretion, however, to tax multiple trusts as one, aggregating all of the income and treating it as if it were earned by a single trust.[64] This discretion can be exercised only if both of the following two conditions are met: substantially all of the property in the various trusts has been received from the same settlor,[65] and the various trusts are "conditioned so that the income thereof accrues or will ultimately accrue to the same beneficiary, or group or class of beneficiaries."[66]

It follows that if two trusts have been created by two separate distinct settlors, the ministerial discretion to tax them as one will not be available, as where a husband and a wife each establish their separate last wills and testaments and create a separate trust for the same child. It also follows that if one settlor establishes two trusts, each with a separate income beneficiary, the ministerial discretion to tax them as one will not be available, as where a parent establishes three separate trusts for each of three different children.[67]

The situation is less clear in other circumstances and CRA has declined to take a specific position when asked to issue technical interpretations dealing with the following situations.

---

63 Subsection 104(2).
64 Subsection 104(2).
65 Paragraph 104(2)(a).
66 Paragraph 104(2)(b).
67 *Mitchell v. Minister of National Revenue* (1956), 16 Tax A.B.C. 99, 56 D.T.C. 521, 1956 CarswellNat 172 (T.A.B.) (dealing with a precursor section to the current 104(2)); also see M.N.R., Technical Interpretation 9306245, "Multiple Trusts Created by a Single Person" (May 20, 1993) and M.N.R Technical Interpretation 9304865, "Multiple Trusts Settled by a Single Person" (May 20, 1993).

CHAPTER 2 — TYPES OF TRUSTS AND BASIC PLANNING

- Where separate trusts are created having some common income beneficiaries, as would be the case where a will establishes two testamentary trusts, the first trust having the surviving spouse as the income beneficiary and child number one as residual beneficiary, and the second trust having the surviving spouse as the income beneficiary (in common with the first trust) but having child number two as the residual beneficiary.[68]

- Where a deceased person seeks to establish five separate trusts for his children and grandchildren, one for child A alone, one for child B alone, one for child B and the two grandchildren sired by child B, and one for the combined benefit of child A and child B.[69]

In each of those circumstances, CRA declined to indicate whether the trusts would attract the ministerial discretion to be aggregated and taxed as one, but cited the following factors to be considered on a case-by-case basis in making the decision:

- whether or not there was a clear intent by the testator, as evidenced by the terms of the will, to create separate trusts;

- whether or not the trusts had common beneficiaries;

- whether or not the assets of each trust were segregated and accounted for separately (*e.g.*, separate bank accounts, no undivided interests in property, separate accounting records); and

- the conduct and powers of the trustees.[70]

---

68 M.N.R., Technical Interpretation 9714835, "Aggregation of Testamentary Trusts" (June 30, 1997) (it should be noted that paragraph 104(2)(b) does not consider the ultimate capital beneficiaries of the trust relevant, only the income beneficiary, and therefore CRA could easily have taken the position that ministerial discretion applies in such circumstances).
69 M.N.R., Technical Interpretation 2002-0162865, "Unification of Trusts" (November 19, 2002).
70 M.N.R., Technical Interpretation 9714835, *supra*, note 68; and for additional material see answer to Question 8 of the 1998 APFF Round Table, document 9M19190.

PART I — BASIC ESTATE AND TRUST PLANNING

While separate taxpayer status is normally an issue only when considering testamentary trusts, the ministerial discretion under subsection 104(2) applies equally to *inter vivos* trusts, and the ministerial discretion will be less likely to be exercised against *inter vivos* trusts where the trusts are irrevocable and the settlor has not retained any power to dispose of the trust property or vary the trust terms.[71]

Separate taxpayer status will not be attained simply by virtue of the fact that each trust has different capital beneficiaries.[72] In similar fashion, the fact that two trusts have different trustees, or that they operate consecutively and never exist at the same time, will not be effective in ousting the ministerial discretion to treat them as one for tax purposes.[73]

(g) Minimum Tax

A testamentary trust is entitled to the $40,000 minimum tax exemption.[74] A more general discussion relating to minimum tax is contained in other areas of this publication.[75]

(h) Designated Income

The provisions of the Act that allow income to be payable or, in fact, paid out to a beneficiary but be designated and taxed as trust income are of particular use in dealing with testamentary trusts.[76]

---

71 See M.N.R., Interpretation Bulletin IT-406R2, "Tax Payable by an *Inter Vivos* Trust" (May 11, 1990), at paragraph 4; and see also M.N.R., Technical Interpretation 9304865, *supra*, note 67.
72 See the wording of paragraph 104(2)(b) and the commentary set out earlier in note 68.
73 M.N.R., Technical Interpretation 9238787, "Minister's Discretion — 104(2)" (January 25, 1993).
74 Paragraph 127.53(1)(b).
75 See heading 12 of Chapter 14 entitled, "Schedule 12 – Minimum Tax" and also heading 2 of Chapter 3 entitled, "Minimum Tax."
76 See M.N.R., Interpretation Bulletin IT-342R, "Trusts – Income Payable to Beneficiaries," (March 21, 1990). See also commentary in heading 4 of Chapter 4 entitled, "Income Designations Under 104(13.1) and 104(13.2)."

CHAPTER 2 — TYPES OF TRUSTS AND BASIC PLANNING

2. *Inter Vivos* Trusts

2.1 Summary

There are a number of ways in which property can be transferred to achieve an individual's estate planning objectives.

A common misconception is that a degree of "estate-planning" can be achieved on an *"inter vivos"* basis by simply affecting a gift or a transfer of property or by transferring title of the property to an intended beneficiary,[77] either directly or on an "in-trust" basis. While this may seem to be a direct and simple method, it can trigger many tax problems and other complications. CRA generally considers that a transfer of property, or a transfer of an interest in the property, results in a beneficial change of ownership and a corresponding disposition for tax purposes in the hands of the transferor.

Similarly, the creation of an "in-trust" account intended to benefit a minor child or grandchild does not necessarily except the attribution provisions from applying to the transferor, even in respect of capital gains or losses arising on the property. The absence of formal documentation can cause CRA to argue that no trust, in fact, was created or that the parent or grandparent can exercise so much control over the investment that, in fact, there never was a beneficial transfer of ownership. In this case, all income (including capital gains) would be taxable to the transferor.

Typically, the type of asset considered for a "gift" or transfer would include an appreciating asset, such as:

- real estate (a cottage for instance);
- a stock portfolio;
- shares of a family owned business; or
- farm property.

---

77 Paragraph 69(1)(c).

PART I — BASIC ESTATE AND TRUST PLANNING

(a) *Gifting*

An outright gift of property for no consideration can create a number of problems, not the least of which is the potential for a taxable capital gain on the deemed disposition of the property resulting from the "gift."

Also, future income earned on the transferred property might be attributed back to the transferor (where the beneficiary is a spouse or a minor child), since inadequate consideration was received on the transfer.

A number of other problems can also occur, specifically:

- loss of control over the asset transferred or gifted;

- the loss or availability of elective provisions in the Act, such as sections 51, 85, or 86;

- the absence of any liquidity of the transferred asset;

- potential valuation issues and a potential concern over subsection 69(1) of the Act; and

- possible application of the superficial loss rules under paragraph 40(2)(g) of the Act.[78]

The "simple act" of transferring title to another person or registering the property in "joint ownership" with another person can trigger these disastrous consequences.

For these reasons, the estate practitioner should consider other methods of achieving an *inter vivos* estate freeze, including:

- a sale of the property at fair market value, for fair market value consideration;

- utilization of a subsection 85(1) holding company "freeze" of the assets in favour of the intended beneficiaries;

---

78 Section 54, definition of "superficial loss."

CHAPTER 2 — TYPES OF TRUSTS AND BASIC PLANNING

- utilization of a subsection 86(1) freeze of an existing corporation in favour of the intended beneficiaries; or

- an exchange of convertible property subject to the tax deferral provisions of subsection 51(1).

(b) Sale or Gift to an Inter Vivos Trust

The control issue to the "freezor" can be addressed by effecting a transfer or sale of the asset to an *inter vivos* trust.[79] The contributor or settlor can then exercise control over how the property is used, either by the selection of trustees or by restrictions specified in the trust document.

Care must be taken to ensure that the trust is appropriately structured so that the income attribution rules of the Act are not triggered, where minor children or a spouse are beneficiaries of the trust.

An *inter vivos* trust is, in common terms, a trust that is created by a living person. Under the Act, an *inter vivos* trust is defined as a personal trust that does not qualify as a testamentary trust.[80] This means that a trust that is established by virtue of an individual's will could conceivably be taxed as an *inter vivos* trust if it failed to qualify as a testamentary trust.

For tax purposes, when a settlor transfers property into an *inter vivos* trust, the transfer of these assets will result in a disposition for tax purposes, which could create a tax liability. Generally, there is no "tax-free" rollover into an "*inter vivos* trust," excepting certain *inter vivos* trusts, which are specifically defined as an "alter ego trust"[81] or a "joint spousal or common-law partner trust."[82]

---

79 See also M.N.R., Interpretation Bulletin IT-209R, "*Inter Vivos* Gifts of Capital Property to Individuals Directly or Through Trusts" (May 18, 1983) for additional commentary.
80 Subsection 108(1).
81 Alter ego trust, subsection 248(1); see also paragraph 104(4)(a).
82 Subsection 248(1); see also paragraph 104(4)(a).

PART I — BASIC ESTATE AND TRUST PLANNING

Consequently, the use of an *inter vivos* trust for estate planning purposes is generally only used where the transferred property will not create an immediate tax liability to the settlor.

A second sobering tax implication for the settlor is that income of the trust will be attributed back to that individual, should the settlor retain a reversionary interest or right to the capital of the trust.[83]

Income attribution to the settlor can occur if:

- the property of the trust can revert back to the settlor; or

- the settlor reserves the right to determine later who receives property from the trust; or

- the settled property of the trust can only be disposed of with the consent of the settlor.

In effect, the use of an *inter vivos* trust for effective estate and tax planning requires the settlor to give up control of the asset settled into the trust.

However, an *inter vivos* trust does have its place in an effectively engineered estate plan. For example, an *inter vivos* trust is an excellent vehicle to introduce as a new equity shareholder, in connection with a subsection 86(1) reorganization of capital, a subsection 85(1) holding company freeze, or an exchange of convertible property under subsection 51(1) of the Act.

A trust can also be used as a "stand-alone" vehicle to establish a freeze for family assets such as a cottage property. Many cottages purchased thirty or forty years ago now have market values in excess of $500,000. The accrued gain on the family cottage can result in a capital gains tax on the "last-to-die" scenario. At that time, the ability to access the principal residence exemption may not be available or could be diminished significantly, depending on other real estate properties owned by the deceased person. The use of an *inter vivos* trust to deal with this type of property can create a "certainty" to the estate plan.

---

83 Subsection 75(2).

CHAPTER 2 — TYPES OF TRUSTS AND BASIC PLANNING

For these reasons, it is not uncommon to consider gifting or "selling" the cottage property to an *inter vivos* trust, thereby shifting the future appreciation to children or grandchildren.

In many cases, the immediate capital gain realized on a gift or sale can be managed. Very often, the significant increase in the cottage value has occurred because of capital repairs, renovations or additions to the property. These costs should be tracked and added to the "adjusted cost base" for tax purposes to determine the true capital gain reportable on a disposition.

Alternatively, the settlor (generally the parent or grandparent) may have access to her principal residence exemption and may be able to gift or sell the cottage property to an *inter vivos* trust without triggering any capital gains tax.

The *inter vivos* trust would acquire the transferred property with an adjusted cost base equal to the fair market value of the cottage property at the time the trust is settled. In effect, the gift or transfer to the trust creates a "step-up" in the adjusted cost base (ACB) of the property for tax purposes.

The trust can continue to hold this property for the benefit, use and enjoyment of all beneficiaries. However, all and any future capital gains earned on the property from the date the trust is created or "settled" to its twenty-first anniversary will, on the twenty-first anniversary date of the trust, be subject to capital gains tax. Because of this factor, ownership of the trust property (the cottage) would generally be transferred on a tax-deferred "roll-out" basis to the beneficiaries immediately prior to such date.[84]

This strategy effectively defers the capital gains tax on the cottage until the eventual owners (or their spouses) pass away. It is therefore an effective tool to achieve a significant degree of tax deferral.

---

84 Subsection 107(2). See also additional commentary contained in 2.1 of Chapter 6 entitled, "Deemed Realizations at Twenty-One Years."

2.2 General Comments Relating to *Inter Vivos* Trusts

(a) Definition of **Inter Vivos** *Trust*

As mentioned earlier, an *inter vivos* trust is defined to include any personal trust, other than a testamentary trust.[85] The term "*inter vivos*" is derived from the Latin root, meaning "among the living." Accordingly, an *inter vivos* trust is a personal trust created during the lifetime of the settlor.[86]

A personal trust can be either "testamentary" or "*inter vivos*." A personal *inter vivos* trust must be a trust however, in which no beneficial interest was acquired for consideration payable either to the trust or to a person who contributed property to the trust. The person or related persons creating an *inter vivos* trust may acquire all interests in the trust without affecting its status as a personal trust.

A spousal or common-law partner trust can be either testamentary or *inter vivos*, whereas an alter ego or joint spousal or common-law partner trust can only be established during the lifetime of the contributors, as an *inter vivos* trust.

Note also that an *inter vivos* trust does not become a testamentary trust on the death of the contributor or settlor. For this reason, an *inter vivos* trust is often referred to as a "living trust."

However, it may not always be clear from the onset whether a trust is *inter vivos* or testamentary in nature. While it is clear that a valid *inter vivos* trust can be created either verbally or by written document, if the trust is to operate upon the death of the settlor it must comply with the will-making requirements for that jurisdiction. For instance, a trust may appear to be created on an *inter vivos* basis, but if the transfer of the trust

---

85 Subsection 108(1).
86 It also includes a testamentary trust that has, for any reason, lost that status. See also 1.4(a) of Chapter 2 entitled, "Loss of Status as a Testamentary Trust."

property is to take effect on the death of the contributor or settlor, the trust may in fact be considered to be a testamentary trust.[87]

Conversely, where a trust document takes immediate effect, though certain actions are to be performed after the death of the contributor or settlor, the trust is not contingent upon the death of the contributor or settlor and would, therefore, be *inter vivos*.[88]

2.3 Special Features

There are four principal aspects relating to the taxation of property transferred or settled upon an *inter vivos* trust. These are:

1. the taxation consequences to the contributor or settlor at the time of the transfer;

2. the taxation consequences of an income or capital interest to the beneficiary;

3. the possible attribution of income, losses, capital gains and capital losses of the trust to the contributor or settlor; and

4. the taxation of income, losses, capital gains and capital losses to the *inter vivos* trust, as distinct from a testamentary trust.

(a) Tax Consequences to the Contributor or Settlor

The first tax issue to consider is the tax treatment to the contributor or settlor on the making of the gift to the trust. A taxpayer who makes a gift *inter vivos*, or who disposes of property in a non-arm's length

---

[87] *Cock v. Cooke* (1866), L.R.1 P.D. 241 (Eng. Prob. Ct.). "It is undoubted law that whatever may be the form of a duly executed instrument, if the person executing it intends that it shall not take effect until after his death and it is dependant upon his death for its vigour and effect, it is testamentary."

[88] Manson J. in *Royal Trust Co. v. Lloyds Bank Ltd.* (1956), 7 D.L.R. (2d) 445 (B.C. S.C.), concerning a trust containing a power of revocation and reversionary interests arising on the settlor's death, regarding postponement of a beneficial interest until the settlor's death.

PART I — BASIC ESTATE AND TRUST PLANNING

transaction, for proceeds that are less than the fair market value of the property, is deemed to have received proceeds of disposition equal to the fair market value of the property gifted or disposed of to the trust, at the time of disposition, notwithstanding that a gift was made for no consideration or that a disposition occurred for inadequate consideration.[89]

In the case where a gift of capital property is made, there may be a realization of capital gains, capital losses, a terminal loss or a recapture of capital cost allowance resulting from the disposition. The recipient trust would be deemed by paragraph 69(1)(c) to have acquired the property at a cost equal to its fair market value.

This resulting tax treatment will not occur, for instance, if the asset transferred is not a capital asset that would normally attract such treatment. For example, the contents of a bank account can be transferred to an *inter vivos* trust without triggering capital gains or capital losses.

As an exception, property can be settled into an alter ego trust or a joint spousal or common-law partner trust without triggering gains or losses. This is discussed in additional detail in a later section in these materials.[90]

Although a gift of property is generally treated similarly under the Act, as to a sale at fair market value, there are situations in which an actual sale can create an alternative tax treatment. For instance, if the agreed sales price in a non-arm's length transaction exceeds the actual fair market value of the property, the transferee will be deemed to acquire the property at an amount not exceeding its fair market value, notwithstanding the agreed price. However, there is no compensating provision in the Act to reduce the contributor's or settlor's proceeds of disposition in such case. This occurrence can result in an unfortunate anomaly wherein the transferor pays an undue level of tax and there is no corresponding increase in the transferee's cost in the property for tax purposes.

---

89 Paragraph 69(1)(b).
90 See heading 5 of Chapter 2 entitled, "Alter Ego and Joint Spousal or Common-Law Partner Trusts."

CHAPTER 2 — TYPES OF TRUSTS AND BASIC PLANNING

In a situation where property is transferred in a non-arm's length transaction for an amount less than the fair market value of the property, paragraph 69(1)(b) deems the contributor's or settlor's proceeds of disposition to be equal to the fair market value of the property. The recipient trust, however, will acquire the subject property at a cost equal to the actual purchase price, as paragraph 69(1)(c) applies only in respect of property acquired by way of gift, bequest or inheritance.

It is clear that, as a general rule, paragraph 69(1)(b) will apply where a contributor or settlor makes a gift of property to an *inter vivos* trust for its intended beneficiaries. The contributor or settlor will be deemed to have received proceeds of disposition equal to the fair market value of the gifted property and the *inter vivos* trust will be deemed to have acquired the property at a cost equal to such fair market value.

(b) Tax Consequences of an "Interest" in the Trust to the Beneficiary

The second issue to consider is the tax position of the income or capital beneficiary. While it is clear that the trust, as an individual taxpayer, will acquire such property at fair market value by virtue of paragraph 69(1)(c), subsection 106(1.1) specifically provides that the cost to a taxpayer of an income interest in a personal trust, other than an interest acquired by the taxpayer from a person who was the beneficiary in respect of such interest immediately before its acquisition by the taxpayer, shall be deemed to be nil. Consequently, beneficiaries who acquire their interest by virtue of the creation of a personal trust cannot rely on the provisions of paragraph (69)(1)(c); such a beneficiary will generally acquire her interest at a cost of nil, except in cases where she has purchased her interest for some consideration from another beneficiary or where she has acquired her interest from another beneficiary by way of a gift.

A similar rule with respect to the cost of a capital interest in a trust, including a personal trust, is provided for in subsection 107(1.1). A beneficiary's capital interest in a trust will generally have a cost of nil, unless it was acquired by the taxpayer from a beneficiary who held the interest immediately before its acquisition by the taxpayer, or unless the

PART I — BASIC ESTATE AND TRUST PLANNING

taxpayer paid fair market value consideration in respect of the interest at the time of acquisition.

In most cases, a beneficiary who has a capital interest in a trust will, by virtue of subsection 107(1.1), have acquired that interest at a nil cost base. However, a subsequent disposition of a beneficiary's capital interest will not necessarily result in the realization of capital gains. Certain rules contained within the provisions of subsection 107(1) determine the adjusted cost base of a capital interest. These rules and others are described more fully in Chapter 6, dealing with capital distributions to beneficiaries.[91]

(c) Attribution

A third tax implication can result in the possibility of income attribution to the contributor or settlor of the trust. This, simply put, will occur if the settlor retains control over the trust property and its eventual destination. More specifically, income will be attributed back to the settlor on trust property if any one of the following conditions are present:

- the property, under the terms of trust, can revert to the settlor;[92]

- the settlor reserves the right to decide later who will receive property from the trust, maintaining control over the ultimate destination of income or capital; or

- under the terms of the trust, the first property cannot be disposed of except with the settlor's consent, or as directed by the settlor.

In order to avoid the attribution of income and gains, the settlor must be prepared to surrender control of the property when contributed or settled into the trust.

Income or loss from property transferred or loaned by an individual, either directly or indirectly to a trust to or for the benefit of that individ-

---

91 For commentary on this point see heading 1 of Chapter 6 entitled, "Capital Distributions to Beneficiaries."
92 Subsections 74.1(1) and 74.1(2).

CHAPTER 2 — TYPES OF TRUSTS AND BASIC PLANNING

ual's spouse or common-law partner or to certain minors, is attributed to the individual and not included in the income of the spouse, common-law partner or minor.[93] Taxable capital gains or allowable capital losses realized on the disposition of property transferred or loaned by the contributor or settlor of the trust to or for the benefit of that individual's spouse or common-law partner would also be attributed to the contributor or settlor.[94] In such case, attribution applies to income, capital gains or capital losses arising from the original property transferred or property substituted for it.

Even if the settlor does not maintain control over the trust property, income attribution can still apply if a portion of the trust property can revert to the settlor under the terms of the trust. This means that a settlor cannot be a capital beneficiary of the trust, otherwise such attribution will apply. Further, the trust should not be structured to allow some person, whether the settlor or not, to select capital beneficiaries on a discretionary basis. A right to appoint the settlor can result in the application of these attribution provisions.

Note, that there is no attribution of capital gains or capital losses in respect of property transferred to or for the benefit of minor beneficiaries of the trust, thereby providing an element of "capital gains splitting" for the minor beneficiaries of the trust. There is also no attribution if the individual contributor or settlor ceases to be a resident of Canada or ceases to be alive.

A second valuable exception to the income attribution rules arises on "second generation" income. While income earned directly on property transferred into the trust is subject to the income attribution rules, this income is sometimes referred to as "first generation" income. However, if first generation income is reinvested by retaining it in the trust, it then becomes capital at the end of the trust's taxation year. The income

---

93 Subsection 75(2).
94 Section 74.2. Note that in the case of a transfer or loan to a spouse or common-law partner, attribution ceases to occur once the spouse or common-law partners are legally separated, divorced and are living separate and apart. Attribution of capital gains or losses realized on such property can be avoided if a joint election is made between the transferor and former spouse or former common-law partner under subsection 74.5(3).

PART I — BASIC ESTATE AND TRUST PLANNING

on that income, sometimes referred to as "second generation" income, does not attract attribution to the settlor unless that attribution is a stock dividend.

(d) Taxation of Income, Losses, Capital Gains and Capital Losses

Certain *inter vivos* trusts created before June 18, 1971, are taxed at the personal marginal rates prescribed in section 117 at all levels of income.[95] *Inter vivos* trusts created after June 18, 1971, or those created before that date which have become "tainted" under subsection 122(2), are subject to federal and provincial taxes at a rate equal to the top marginal tax rate, excepting federal surtaxes, on all such trust income subject to tax.[96]

Income earned by an *inter vivos* trust, which is retained in the trust rather than being flowed through to a beneficiary, will be taxed at a high rate of tax. If income is paid or payable to a beneficiary for her benefit, it can be deducted from the trust's income. The trust is entitled to deduct income in respect of amounts eligible for the preferred beneficiary election,[97] and the provisions of the *Income Tax Act* also permit the deduction of income in respect of the payment or allocation of income to beneficiaries.[98]

2.4 Things You Need to Know

(a) Minimum Tax

Minimum tax generally applies to *inter vivos* trusts[99] with the exception of those trusts established prior to June 18, 1971, that, since that date,

---

[95] See also subsection 122(1).
[96] See Appendix C of Part VI entitled "Marginal Tax Rates" for a schedule detailing the various combined federal and provincial or territorial tax rates applicable to *inter vivos* trusts.
[97] See heading 5 of Chapter 4 entitled, "The Preferred Beneficiary Election."
[98] See heading 9 of Chapter 14 entitled, "Schedule 9 – Income Allocations and Designations to Beneficiaries."
[99] Paragraph 127.53(1)(c).

CHAPTER 2 — TYPES OF TRUSTS AND BASIC PLANNING

have been continuously resident in Canada and have not received any gifts and that, in the current taxation year, have not carried on any active business.[100]

3. Spousal Trusts

3.1 Summary

A qualifying spousal trust may be created during the life of a taxpayer or by the taxpayer's will. A qualifying spousal trust can also be established by court order in relation to an estate pursuant to dependants' relief legislation,[101] providing for the relief or support of dependants.

In order to qualify as a spousal trust, the trust must provide that the deceased taxpayer's spouse or common-law partner be entitled to receive all of the income of the trust during her lifetime, and that during the beneficiary spouse or common-law partner's lifetime, no other person can be entitled to receive or obtain the benefit of any of the income or capital of the trust.[102]

The major advantage of a qualifying spousal or common-law partner trust is that property can be transferred into the trust on a "rollover" basis. That is, the qualifying spousal or common-law partner trust is deemed to have acquired capital property at the contributor's cost for tax purposes and depreciable capital property at the undepreciated capital cost, for tax purposes, of the transferor.

The establishment of a qualifying spousal or common-law partner trust automatically provides a deferral for the taxation of capital gains and recaptured capital cost allowance until the beneficiary spouse or common-law partner dies. However, an election can be made under subsection 73(1) for the *inter vivos* transfer to be made at fair market

---

100 Paragraph 127.53(1)(b) and subsection 122(2). See also heading 12 of Chapter 14 entitled, "Schedule 12 – Minimum Tax" and heading 2 of Chapter 3 entitled, "Minimum Tax."
101 Subsection 248(9.1). See also M.N.R., Interpretation Bulletin IT-305R4, "Testamentary Spouse Trusts" (October 30, 1996), at paragraphs 5-8.
102 Paragraph 70(6)(b).

value; similarly subsection 70(6.2) provides a mechanism for the legal representative to opt-out of the automatic rollover provisions which apply for capital property bequeathed to a qualifying spousal or common-law partner trust within thirty-six months of death. In these circumstances, the election to "opt out" would result in the realization and taxation of any related capital gains or recaptured capital cost allowance inherent in the property at the time of transfer.

These "opting-out" alternatives should be considered where the transferor spouse has unutilized capital losses, non-capital losses or access to the $500,000 capital gains deduction, in respect of the property giving rise to the capital gain. Note, however, that subsection 70(6.2) is an "on/off" switch, and the election to opt out of the spousal rollover provision does not provide the legal representative with an ability to designate an amount between cost and fair market value. Where there are identical properties being transferred (such as marketable securities), it is possible to designate on some of the properties to achieve the desired tax effect. Where the subject property is not divisible (such as a building or section of land), the requirements under subsection 70(6.2) should be reviewed to ensure that a full election at fair market value creates the desired result for tax purposes.

Once a qualifying spousal or common-law partner trust is established, it remains in force until the trust property is fully distributed. This is the case even if the spouse or common-law partner decides to renounce or disclaim her interest in the trust property. On the death of the beneficiary spouse or common-law partner, the trust is deemed to dispose of its property for fair market value, and any deferral achieved on the rollover into the trust will be recognized at that time.

3.2 General Comments Relating to Spousal Trusts

(a) *Definition of Spousal Trust*

The terms "spouse" and "spousal trust" are generally taken to include a common-law partner or common-law partner trust. The income tax provisions treat one's legally married spouse in the same manner for tax

CHAPTER 2 — TYPES OF TRUSTS AND BASIC PLANNING

purposes as a "common-law partner." However, there is no actual definition of "spouse" in the *Income Tax Act*. The common-law definition of "spouse" includes one's legally married husband or wife.

A "common-law partner" of a taxpayer is defined in the Act as a person who cohabits in a conjugal relationship with the taxpayer and who:

- has cohabited throughout a continuous one-year period before that time; or

- is a parent of the taxpayer's child (*i.e.*, both individuals are parents of the same child).

The meaning of common-law partner is also extended to include a partner of the same sex.

Note also that a spousal or common-law partner trust can be either an *inter vivos* trust or a testamentary trust.

To qualify, both the settlor and the trust must be resident in Canada at the time the property is transferred to the trust. Interestingly, however, the spouse or common-law partner need not necessarily be resident in Canada to qualify as a beneficiary of the trust.

The main tax advantage obtained in utilizing a spousal trust is that property can be transferred into such trusts on a rollover basis. A special rule applies however, in respect of transfers of real property inventory. Real property inventory transferred to an *inter vivos* spousal trust does not qualify for rollover treatment, whereas such property does qualify if transferred to a qualifying spousal or common-law partner trust on a testamentary basis.

To qualify as a spousal trust all of the following requirements must be met:

- a spousal trust must be created by the testator's will. It cannot be created as a freestanding document outside of the will;

- the spouse or common-law partner must be entitled to all of the

PART I — BASIC ESTATE AND TRUST PLANNING

income from the trust during her lifetime (discussed in more detail below);

- no person other than the spouse or common-law partner can have any entitlement to the capital of the trust, during her remaining life;

- the assets bequeathed must "vest indefeasibly" in the trust within thirty-six months of death. The Act does not specifically define the term "vested indefeasibly." However, CRA has published commentary on their interpretation of "vested indefeasibly" for purposes of a "qualifying spousal trust";[103] and

- the testator must be a resident of Canada, immediately prior to death and the trust created by the will must have Canadian resident trustees.

To be entitled to all of the income, the spouse or common-law partner must have a legal right to enforce payment of the income from the trust. The trust will not qualify if the release of income is subject to a discretion on the part of the trustees.[104] The spouse or common-law partner can, however, retain and enjoy a discretion under the terms of the trust, and thereby leave income in the trust to be added to capital.[105] The mere existence of a discretion to pay income to any beneficiary other than the spouse or common-law partner, whether exercised or not, will disqualify the trust.[106]

---

103 See M.N.R., Interpretation Bulletin IT-449R, "Meaning of 'Vested Indefeasibly'" [Archived] (September 25, 1987), at paragraphs 1 and 2. This bulletin has been archived and should be used with caution. Refer also to M.N.R., Technical Interpretation 2003-0008285, "Spousal Trust – Entitlement – Payable" (September 23, 2003) discussing a spouse's enforceable right to income. See also M.N.R., Technical Interpretation 9203105, "Spousal Trust" (February 14, 1992).

104 *Peardon v. Minister of National Revenue* (1985), [1986] 1 C.T.C. 2083, 86 D.T.C. 1045, 1985 CarswellNat 486 (T.C.C.); M.N.R., Technical Interpretation 2002-0126775, "Spousal Trust" (May 3, 2002).

105 M.N.R., Technical Interpretation 2003-0014515, "Spouse's Discretion to Accumulate Income in Trust" (June 2, 2003).

106 M.N.R., Technical Interpretation 2002-0126775, *supra*, note 104.

CHAPTER 2 — TYPES OF TRUSTS AND BASIC PLANNING

(b) Qualifying Spousal Trust

The key advantage in establishing a "qualifying spousal trust" is that the usual deemed disposition rules do not apply in respect of assets transferred on death to a spouse, common-law partner or a qualifying spousal trust.

Where a deceased taxpayer transfers assets to a qualifying spousal trust as a consequence of death, the deceased is deemed to have disposed of the particular assets at her adjusted cost base (for non-depreciable capital assets) and at the undepreciated capital cost (for depreciable capital assets).[107] There are similar rollovers for inventory and other properties transferred on death to a spouse or a qualifying spousal trust.

A qualifying spousal trust as envisioned under subsection 70(6) must be created by a taxpayer's will, entitling the surviving spouse or common-law partner to receive and enjoy all of the income of the trust during her lifetime. A trust can also qualify for such treatment where a beneficiary of the trust renounces her interests in the trust, which would otherwise disqualify the trust as a qualifying spousal trust."[108] That is, the creation of a qualifying spousal trust is expressly recognized by statute, where the trust for the spouse or common-law partner directly results from a disclaimer, release or renunciation of any interest in the property, in favour of the spouse or common-law partner.

There are tax deferral and income-splitting opportunities, which can be utilized with a qualifying spousal trust. Generally, the advantages of utilizing a qualifying spousal trust are as follows:

- As mentioned earlier, a transfer to a "qualifying spousal trust" can achieve a complete rollover and deferral of tax on the death of the first spouse.

- A spousal trust is taxed as a separate individual. Income earned in a "qualifying spousal trust" is taxed at progressive rates, in the same manner as individuals are taxed on their personal returns. This per-

---

107 Subsection 70(6).
108 Subsection 70(6.1).

PART I — BASIC ESTATE AND TRUST PLANNING

mits the surviving spouse to continue to "income-split" investment income in the same manner as would have occurred prior to the death of the first spouse.

- Capital bequeathed on the death of the first spouse can be targeted to the residual beneficiaries (usually the children or grandchildren). This is also a strategy for preserving the estate capital, since the ability to encroach on capital would have to be approved by the trustees of the spousal trust.

- A spousal trust can be very useful in a potential second marriage situation. If the testator wishes to ensure that a portion of her wealth is transferred to children from a first relationship, the creation of a "qualifying spousal trust" provides a mechanism to eventually transfer this residual wealth, while still achieving an immediate tax deferral on a deemed disposition at death.

Also, aside from the tax deferral, a testator may not wish to transfer wealth to her children immediately; the "qualifying spousal trust" mechanism can serve both objectives.

When drafting a spousal trust, consideration should always be given to provide powers to the trustees to encroach on capital for the benefit of the spouse. For instance, capital property distributed to the spouse pursuant to the provisions of subsection 107(2) can be "rolled-out" at cost. The ability to do so can provide an opportunity to split future capital gains between the trust and the spouse, in respect of property originally settled on the trust.

Of course, such powers of encroachment also provide the trustees with the ability and flexibility to meet emergency cash needs of the surviving spouse.

(c) *Tainted Spousal Trust*

If a trust does not meet the test of a qualifying spousal trust, it may be a "tainted spousal trust." The term itself is not specifically defined in the Act. For instance if a trust created under the will provides for an income

CHAPTER 2 — TYPES OF TRUSTS AND BASIC PLANNING

or capital interest to a beneficiary, in addition to the spouse, the spousal trust becomes tainted.

There are means of "untainting" the trust. For instance, if the other beneficiary were to disclaim or "renounce" this interest and give up any claim to income or capital from the trust, the "tainted spousal trust" can be remedied.

There are also specific remedies set out in the Act, which provide for the trust to make payment of certain expenses outside of the normally permitted expenses of a "qualifying spousal trust."[109]

The most serious consequence of inadvertently creating a tainted spousal trust is that a capital gains tax will be triggered on death which might otherwise have been deferred had a properly constructed qualifying spousal trust been created.

Sometimes, however, a qualifying spousal trust may not be entirely satisfactory or necessary and the estate plan might call for a strategy to deliberately "taint" the spousal trust. Property, which is transferred to a qualifying spousal trust, will not be exempted from an ultimate deemed realization on the beneficiary spouse's death.

This may not be a desirable tax outcome, depending on the age of the beneficiary spouse and the likelihood for future appreciation of the subject property.

Some discretion may be required to determine which properties should go to a qualifying spousal trust and which properties might be

---

[109] Subsection 70(7) provides relief wherein a "tainted spousal trust" can be considered to be a qualifying spousal trust for purposes of the rollover of capital property under subsection 70(6). Where the payment of, or provision for payment of, certain testamentary debts results in the spousal trust becoming "tainted," subsection 70(7) permits such testamentary debts to be applied against property of the trust acquired from the deceased taxpayer, that is listed by the legal representative or executor. The election to do so must be made in the taxpayer's final return or within eighteen months of the date of death. See also M.N.R., Technical Interpretation 2002-016643A, "General Comments on 70(7)" (June 3, 2003).

PART I — BASIC ESTATE AND TRUST PLANNING

better transferred to another testamentary trust such as a tainted spousal trust. It is not uncommon for a will to also provide for the creation of a tainted spousal trust, and to give the executor or personal representative broad powers to determine which properties are best suited for each trust.

In such cases, very careful consideration must be given to the methods by which this might be achieved. One way this might be achieved is by creating a provision, which would divest the interest of the spouse to encroach on the capital of the trust in the event of remarriage, or to insert a provision, which would permit other persons to benefit from the capital of the trust. Other methods might include a direction to the trustees to pay only a specified portion of the trust income to the surviving spouse.

The creation of a tainted spousal trust (effectively just another testamentary trust) would permit a roll-out of the property at cost on the death of the spouse, thereby providing a further tax deferral.

4. Trusts for Minor Beneficiaries

4.1 Summary

A trust for minors is not recognized under the Act as a separate type of trust for income tax purposes, but the Act contains three provisions that afford specialized treatment to situations featuring minor beneficiaries. These are as follows:

1. Prior to a minor reaching age eighteen, property income from specific properties can be attributed to a related transferor under section 74.1 and excluded from the trust's and beneficiaries' income, if the transferor has transferred or loaned property to the trust.

2. Prior to a minor reaching age twenty-one, income can be attributed to a minor and deducted from the income of the trust where it is retained within the trust in circumstances to which subsection 104(18) apply.

CHAPTER 2 — TYPES OF TRUSTS AND BASIC PLANNING

3. The "kiddie tax"[110] can operate to tax split income, at the highest federal rate, in the hands of a beneficiary, who has not attained the age of eighteen.

"In-trust" accounts are taxed as trusts only if they satisfy the "three certainties."[111] Each situation should be scrutinized for that threshold issue before filing a T3 Return. When payments are made to minors, care should be taken to make sure that the terms of the trust authorize payments to a minor.

4.2 General Comments Relating to Trusts for Minor Beneficiaries

(a) Attribution to Non-Arm's Length Transferor under 74.1(2)

Where an individual transfers or loans property to a trust for the benefit of a person who is under the age of eighteen years, and that minor person does not deal at arm's length with the transferor or is a niece or nephew of the transferor, all income or losses from the property are deemed to be the income of the transferor under subsection 74.1(2). Such attribution occurs only while the transferor is resident in Canada, with respect to property transferred or loaned to the trust, directly or indirectly, and also to income or losses generated from substituted property.

CRA has issued a detailed Interpretation Bulletin dealing with attribution under 74.1(2) that should be consulted in conjunction with this material.[112]

---

110 Section 120.4. See also 4.2(c) of this chapter entitled "Kiddie Tax under Section 120.4" for discussion on this point.
111 See also 4.3(a) of this chapter entitled "Whether 'In-Trust Accounts' Qualify as Trusts," for commentary on this subject.
112 See M.N.R., Interpretation Bulletin IT-510, "Transfers and Loans of Property Made after May 22, 1985 to a Related Minor" (December 30, 1987).

PART I — BASIC ESTATE AND TRUST PLANNING

(i) The Minor

Attribution under subsection 74.1(2) occurs where the minor does not deal with the transferor at arm's length.[113] It also applies where the minor is a niece or nephew[114] of the transferor, persons not normally covered by the arm's length provisions of the Act. A minor for the purposes of this section of the Act is a person who is under the age of eighteen. The age of majority will differ from province to province and territory to territory but can be disregarded for the purpose of attribution under subsection 74.2(2).

Attribution to the transferor ends when the minor attains the age of eighteen years.

In order for these rules to apply, the minor must have a beneficial interest in the trust,[115] and it will be sufficient if she has a future interest under the trust, or one which is contingent on the occurrence of some future event or one which will not come into play without the exercise of a trustee discretion in her favour.[116]

(ii) The Transferor

Attribution under subsection 74.1(2) will not occur for any period of time in which the transferor is not resident in Canada, and will not occur following the death of the transferor.

---

113 Paragraph 74.1(2)(a). A parent and a child, or other descendant, natural or adopted, do not deal at arm's length. See M.N.R., Interpretation Bulletin IT-510, *ibid.* at paragraph 1. More generally see M.N.R., Interpretation Bulletin IT-419R2, "Meaning of Arm's Length" (June 8, 2004) (this can also extend to step-children or other dependant minors).
114 Paragraph 74.1(2)(b).
115 See M.N.R., Interpretation Bulletin IT-510, *supra*, note 112 at paragraph 2.
116 See M.N.R., Interpretation Bulletin IT-510, *supra*, note 112 at paragraph 1.

CHAPTER 2 — TYPES OF TRUSTS AND BASIC PLANNING

(iii) The Type of Income

Attribution takes place on property income generated by the contributed property or any substituted property. This includes dividends[117] and interest, as well as rents and royalties. It does not apply to any other kind of income that the minor may enjoy from the trust,[118] including business income (even if the contributed property is used in the course of that business[119]), or capital gains and losses,[120] or second generation income,[121] each of which is taxed in the trust or in the hands of the minor and not the transferor.

(iv) The Transfer Transaction and Type of Property

Attribution applies to any transfer into the trust,[122] including voluntary transfers of capital into a trust, such as gifts (where no consideration passes).[123] If the transferor receives consideration in return for the trans-

---

117 See M.N.R., Interpretation Bulletin IT-510, *supra*, note 112 at paragraph 22 (treatment of dividend tax credit).
118 Paragraph 74.3(1)(a).
119 See M.N.R., Interpretation Bulletin IT-510, *supra*, note 112 at paragraph 3. The exception to this rule is, of course, if attribution under subsection 75(2) applies, in which case business income or losses would be attributed to the contributor or settlor of the trust.
120 See M.N.R., Interpretation Bulletin IT-510, *supra*, note 112 at paragraph 19 (*inter vivos* transfers of farm property may give rise to a different result under section 75.1). This applies to the disposition of the property by the trust, which is to be contrasted to the earlier point when the property is initially inserted into the trust. Capital gains, recapture and losses may be triggered in the hands of the transferor at the point of the initial transfer to the trust.
121 See M.N.R., Technical Interpretation 9721325, "Attribution Rules and Transfer to a Trust" (October 27, 1997) (income generated on capitalized income, commonly called "second generation income" does not attract attribution).
122 *Romkey v. R.* (1999), 2000 D.T.C. 6047, 31 E.T.R. (2d) 245, 251 N.R. 303, 1999 CarswellNat 2598, [2000] 1 C.T.C. 390 (Fed. C.A.), leave to appeal refused (2000), 2000 CarswellNat 2423, 2000 CarswellNat 2424 (S.C.C.), at paragraph 17 ("transferred" to be interpreted broadly in the context of 74.1(2)); affirming 97 D.T.C. 719, 20 E.T.R. (2d) 37, [1997] 3 C.T.C. 2405, 1997 CarswellNat 619.
123 See M.N.R., Technical Interpretation 9830997, "Attribution – Minors" (April 8, 1999) (regardless of whether the gifts are Christmas gifts, or are considered "inconsequential" by the maker).

PART I — BASIC ESTATE AND TRUST PLANNING

fer, attribution under subsection 74.1(2) may still occur depending on the circumstances. Attribution will not occur if the consideration for the transfer represents the full fair market value of the property and is paid in full or, if not paid in full, is secured or evidenced by an appropriate loan at prescribed rates of interest.[124] Conversely, attribution does occur where the transfer is for inadequate consideration, or the consideration is unpaid and is not secured or evidenced with the appropriate indebtedness. It also will apply to property loaned by the transferor to the trust[125] unless the loan is a genuine loan,[126] bearing interest at the prescribed rate in effect at the time the loan was made.

An indirect transfer may occur and trigger subsection 74.1(2) attribution. Thus, attribution has been held to occur where a transferor enters into a series of transactions with the result that the value of the transferor's interest in a company, for instance, is reduced and, concurrently, the value of a beneficial interest in a trust held by the transferor's minor children increases.[127]

Attribution does not take place where the property settled into the trust is the proceeds of Canada Child Tax Benefit payments.[128]

(v) *Miscellaneous Points Relating to 74.1(2) Attribution*

Attribution occurs on substituted property, which is defined under paragraph 248(5)(a) to include an initial substitution for the property held, or property held after a chain of substitutions.[129]

---

124 Subsection 74.5(1). Also see M.N.R., Interpretation Bulletin IT-510, *supra*, note 112 at paragraph 16.
125 See M.N.R., Interpretation Bulletin IT-510, *supra*, note 112 at paragraph 2.
126 See M.N.R., Interpretation Bulletin IT-510, *supra*, note 112 at paragraph 17.
127 *Romkey v. R.*, *supra*, note 22; *Kieboom v. Minister of National Revenue*, [1992] 3 F.C. 488, [1992] 2 C.T.C. 59, 46 E.T.R. 229, 57 F.T.R. 11 (note), 145 N.R. 360, 1992 CarswellNat 308, 1992 CarswellNat 607, 92 D.T.C. 6382 (C.A.); and *Gehres v. R.*, 2003 TCC 471, 2003 D.T.C. 913, [2003] 4 C.T.C 2752, 2003 CarswellNat 2016 (T.C.C. [General Procedure]), at paragraph 5.
128 Subsection 74.1(2), containing an express exception. More generally see M.N.R., Technical Interpretation 9830997, *supra*, note 123; M.N.R., Technical Interpretation 9812245, "Social Insurance Number" (June 22, 1998) (reporting requirements for in-trust accounts funded with CCTB benefits).
129 See M.N.R., Interpretation Bulletin IT-510, *supra*, note 112 at paragraph 1.

CHAPTER 2 — TYPES OF TRUSTS AND BASIC PLANNING

The transferor and the trust are jointly liable for any increase in the Part I tax payable by the transferor as a result of attribution under subsection 74.1(2).[130]

Attribution under subsection 74.1(2) will not occur on any income that is taxed at top marginal rates in the hands of the minor under the "kiddie tax" rules[131] and may not occur where one of the main reasons for the transfer is to take advantage of subsection 74.1(2) and shift income taxes[132] to the minor.

A variation of a trust involving minor beneficiaries may, under certain circumstances, trigger attribution under subsection 74.1(2).[133]

(b) Pent Up Income Attributed to Minors Under 104(18)

Subsection 104(18) of the Act treats retained trust income as being payable to minor beneficiaries under some circumstances. Any beneficiary under the age of twenty-one years is considered to be a "minor" for this purpose. The intent of the section is that where the only reason that the income is not payable to a beneficiary is that she was a minor, then the income should be considered to be income payable to that beneficiary.[134]

Generally speaking, this section will result in the reduction of overall tax when it is available, particularly with an *inter vivos* trust. *Inter vivos*

---

130 M.N.R., Interpretation Bulletin IT-510, *supra*, note 112 at paragraph 24.
131 Subsection 74.5(13). The "kiddie tax" provisions are found at section 120.4. See 4.2(c) of this chapter entitled, "Kiddie Tax under Section 120.4" for a discussion of kiddie tax.
132 M.N.R., Interpretation Bulletin IT-510, *supra*, note 112 at paragraph 21 (by virtue of subsection 74.5(11)). Note, however, that subsection 160(1.2) provides that a parent will be jointly liable to the extent that the child is subject to "kiddie tax" under section 120.4.
133 Maria Hoffstein and Julie Yee, "Restructuring the Will and the Testamentary Trust: Methods, Underlying Legal Principles and Tax Considerations" (1993) 13 E.T.J. 42, at p. 96.
134 M.N.R., Department of Finance Commentary (Consolidated Explanatory Notes), "Trusts for Minors" (En June 20, 1996 [S.C. 1996, c. 21 (Bill C-36)]).

PART I — BASIC ESTATE AND TRUST PLANNING

trusts pay income tax at the top federal rate, and a beneficiary under the age of twenty-one will rarely have significant income of her own. The beneficiary may also have room in her personal amount that she can use to shelter portions of the income from tax. This is less of a consideration when dealing with a testamentary trust. While the same rules will apply, unless the testamentary trust is quite large and generates income in higher tax brackets, the tax rate for the trust and the beneficiary are often the same. However, to the extent that the trust's income is reported on the beneficiary's tax return, there will be an opportunity to take advantage of any unused personal amounts and tax credits available to the beneficiary. Where the applicable tax rate for the beneficiary would be higher than the applicable tax rate for the income if retained in the testamentary trust, it appears to be possible to override the application of subsection 104(18) by designating the income as trust income.[135]

Subsection 104(18) will apply and cause income to be taxed in the hands of the beneficiary and deducted from the income of the trust where each of the following requirements are met.

- The trust resides in Canada throughout the taxation year.[136]

- The income of the trust (including taxable capital gains) is not payable to the beneficiary in or before the end of the year and is, in fact, retained in the trust.[137]

- The beneficiary is less than twenty-one years old at the end of the year.[138]

- The beneficiary's right to income (including taxable capital gains)

---

135 M.N.R., Interpretation Bulletin IT-381R3, "Trusts – Capital Gains and Losses and the Flow-Through of Taxable Capital Gains to Beneficiaries" (February 14, 1997), at paragraph 17.
136 Subsection 104(18), preamble to the subsection.
137 Paragraph 104(18)(a); *Cole Trust v. Minister of National Revenue*, [1980] C.T.C. 3027, 81 D.T.C. 8, 1980 CarswellNat 515 (T.R.B.) at paragraph 16 (terms of trust must include a provision expressly requiring the retention of income in the trust pending a specified age. The mere fact that trustees decide not to pay income under a discretion is generally not sufficient, absent an express clause to that effect).
138 Paragraph 104(18)(b).

CHAPTER 2 — TYPES OF TRUSTS AND BASIC PLANNING

is vested by the end of the year and is vested by some reason other than by virtue of the exercise or the non-exercise of a discretionary power.[139] To have a vested right to income for the purposes of 104(18), the beneficiary must have an immediate fixed right of present or future possession of the income,[140] and the right to the future possession of the income means that this requirement is met even if the income cannot be paid out until the specified age or is, in fact, paid out earlier subject to a trustee's discretion that influences only the timing of the payment.[141] This requirement will not be met however if the trustees have a discretion to allocate income to one beneficiary to the exclusion of another,[142] or if some future event will affect the amount of the income entitlement, such as the birth or death of another beneficiary.[143] A discretion to encroach on and make payments of capital (as opposed to income) out of the trust will be irrelevant to the application of this requirement, even if it allows for the payment out of capital that stands in the trust as capitalized income from earlier years.[144]

- The beneficiary's right to enforce payment of the income is subject to the sole condition that the beneficiary survives long enough to attain some expressly specified age, which age is not to exceed forty years, and that right is subject to no other condition, other than attaining that age.[145] While the subsection only applies to income while the beneficiary is under twenty-one years of age, the terms of

---

139 Paragraph 104(18)(c).
140 M.N.R., Technical Interpretation 2002-0157725, "104(18)" (February 3, 2003).
141 M.N.R., Technical Interpretation 2002-0157725, *ibid.*; M.N.R., Technical Interpretation 9807495, "Trusts for Minors" (March 12, 1999).
142 M.N.R., Technical Interpretation 1999-0012305, "Payment by Discretionary Trust Benefit Minor" (June 5, 2000).
143 M.N.R., Technical Interpretation 9807495, *supra*, note 141 (see the comments relevant to "Scenario 2" – for an interest to be said to "vest" for the purposes of subsection 104(18), all individuals who are to have an interest in the trust must be in existence and ascertained, the size of each of their interests must be ascertained, and any conditions precedent must be satisfied other than the requirement that they attain the specified age set out in the trust).
144 M.N.R., Technical Interpretation 9702825, "Subsection 104(18) – Capital Encroachment" (June 23, 1997).
145 Paragraph 104(18)(d).

PART I — BASIC ESTATE AND TRUST PLANNING

the trust can impose any age under forty as the ultimate date for final entitlement to capital. A gift over to another beneficiary on the death of the initial beneficiary does not amount to a condition ousting the operation of subsection 104(18).[146]

If any of the above conditions are not met, then subsection 104(18) will not apply to deem the trust income to be that of the beneficiary.

Examples where CRA has taken the position that subsection 104(18) does apply, which would cause income attribution to the beneficiary, include:

- an *inter vivos* educational trust is established by friends and family for a child, following the death of her parent, on terms of trust under which the trustees were to accrue the income in each year, but also allowing net income to be used to pay for post secondary education for the child in years prior to the windup of the trust, and at that windup providing for the distribution of the remaining capital to the child at a specified age, and notwithstanding a term of trust providing that if the beneficiary were to die before attaining that age the capital was to be paid to an alternate capital beneficiary;[147]

- a testamentary trust is established having the minor nieces and nephews of the deceased as beneficiaries, dividing the capital into shares at the outset of the trust, one for each beneficiary, and holding those shares in trust until the beneficiaries reach age twenty-five, the income from each share to be added in each year to the capital of that share, subject to a discretion allowing the trustees to use the

---

146 M.N.R., Technical Interpretation 2002-0157725, *supra*, note 140.

147 M.N.R., Technical Interpretation 2002-0157725, *supra*, note 140 (the discretion was expressly characterized as a discretion as to the timing of payments of income, and not as a discretion as to entitlement to income); but see *Cole Trust v. Minister of National Revenue*, *supra*, note 137 (a contrary finding on other grounds in a factually similar case on a precursor formulation of the same subsection); and see *Alger v. Minister of National Revenue* [1972] C.T.C. 2227, 72 D.T.C. 1191, 1972 CarswellNat 226 (T.R.B.), considered and not followed in *Hall c. Quebec (Sous-ministere du Revenu)*, [1996] R.D.F.Q. 41, [1996] Q.J. No. 942, 1996 CarswellQue 350 (C.A.), leave to appeal allowed (1996), 206 N.R. 154 (note) (S.C.C.), reversed (1997), 1997 CarswellQue 1305, 1997 CarswellQue 1306, [1998] 2 C.T.C. 133 (S.C.C.).

CHAPTER 2 — TYPES OF TRUSTS AND BASIC PLANNING

income (or capital) from each share for the benefit of the respective beneficiary for whom the share was earmarked, and subject to a clause stipulating that if any beneficiary dies prior to age twenty-five and while their share or some portion of it remains in trust, then that share is to be divided among the shares of the surviving beneficiaries;[148] and

- an *inter vivos* trust is created for a sole beneficiary, and the trustees being obliged to accumulate the income for each year while the beneficiary is under the age of twenty-one, adding the income to the capital of the trust at the end of each year, but having the ability to make distributions from the capital of the trust, including capitalized income, but not allowing payments from current income in any given year.[149]

Examples where CRA has taken the position that subsection 104(18) does *not* apply and income will not be attributed to the beneficiary include:

- a trust is established for a group of minor beneficiaries but income is allocated at the discretion of the trustees among the various beneficiaries to be held, after allocation, within the trust in a series of segregated accounts and kept from the respective beneficiaries thereafter until age eighteen,[150] and

---

148 M.N.R., Technical Interpretation 9807495, *supra*, note 141 (being "Scenario 1") (the discretion to use income was, again, expressly characterized as attaching to the timing of payments and would not have any impact on the share of income that would accrue for the benefit of each beneficiary in a given year); but see *Cole Trust v. Minister of National Revenue*, *supra*, note 137 (a contrary finding on other grounds in a factually similar case on a precursor formulation of the same subsection); and see *Alger v. Minister of National Revenue*, *ibid.*, considered and not followed in *Hall c. Quebec (Sous-ministere du Revenu)*, *ibid.*

149 M.N.R., Technical Interpretation 9702825, *supra*, note 144 (on the principle that the possibility to encroach on the capital of the trust for the benefit of the beneficiary will not preclude the application of subsection 104(18) of the Act).

150 M.N.R., Technical Interpretation 1999-0012305, *supra*, note 142 (on the grounds that the income only vested with a given beneficiary by virtue of the exercise of the discretion of the trustee in that regard, contrary to paragraph 104(18)(c)).

PART I — BASIC ESTATE AND TRUST PLANNING

- a testamentary trust is established on a pooled basis, with the capital standing to the benefit of multiple minor beneficiaries, and the capital shares not divided until a future distribution date, and the share of capital and income therefore subject to increase or decrease with the birth of additional beneficiaries or the death of existing beneficiaries.[151]

(c) Kiddie Tax under Section 120.4

The "kiddie tax" rules are outlined in section 120.4 of the Act and came into effect on January 1, 2000. These provisions impose the highest rate[152] of federal tax on certain forms of income enjoyed by minors, termed as "split income" under the Act.[153] Split income includes:

- taxable dividends from private companies[154] received directly, or received through a trust or partnership,

- shareholder benefits or loans conferred on the minor by a private corporation, and

- income from a partnership or trust if the income is derived from the provision of goods[155] or services to a business carried on by a person related to the minor, or by a corporation where either

    o the minor is related to a person owning more than ten percent of the shares, or

---

151 M.N.R., Technical Interpretation 9807495, *supra*, note 141 (in "Scenario 2") (on the stated principle that the interest of each beneficiary in income would change with changes to the class of beneficiaries and could not be said to have vested if subject to future change).
152 Subsection 120.4(2).
153 Subsection 120.4(1), definition of "split income."
154 Dividends from corporations listed on prescribed stock exchanges are excluded along with dividends received from mutual fund corporations.
155 December 20, 2002, draft legislation proposes, in subsection 59(1), to change the wording from "goods or services" to become "property or services" in a bid to ensure that kiddie tax applies to rental and interest income. This change is discussed later in the text. See heading 5 of Chapter 10 entitled, "Line 05 – Other Investment Income."

CHAPTER 2 — TYPES OF TRUSTS AND BASIC PLANNING

○ the corporation is a professional corporation and the minor is related to a person who is a shareholder.

Based on the current wording of the Act, CRA has taken the position that kiddie tax does not apply to rental income.[156] That will change under proposed amendments, which will be retroactive to December 20, 2002, intended to make kiddie tax applicable to property income, including rental income. Even after the change, kiddie tax may not apply to rental income where the parent or other related person cannot be said to be carrying on a business in the circumstances.[157] Interest on loans made by trusts may also attract kiddie tax after the change.[158]

For the "tax on split-income" provisions to apply, the minor must be a resident of Canada throughout the year and must have a parent resident in Canada for at least part of the year.[159]

The high rate of tax applies to all split income. Also, since the personal amount does not apply, the only tax credits that are available are the dividend tax credit and credits for foreign source income.[160]

Kiddie tax does not apply to income from a property inherited from a parent[161] and, thus, will not apply to shares in a private corporation held in a testamentary trust following the death of a parent. It also does not apply to income from a property inherited from a parent or any other

---

156 M.N.R., Technical Interpretation 2000-0012635, "Split Income and Rentals" (June 20, 2000).
157 M.N.R., Technical Interpretation 2003-0044495, "Split Income" (December 17, 2003) ("However, if it is determined that the parent is carrying on a property management business that includes the collection and deposit of rents, and the trust earns income from property or services provided to or in support of this business, it is our view that such income would be considered split income.")
158 M.N.R., Technical Interpretation 2003-0181705, "Tax on Split Income" (March 3, 2003) (initial capital borrowed from related person); M.N.R., Technical Interpretation 2003-0039985, "Tax on Split Income – Kiddie Tax" (December 3, 2003) (initial capital borrowed from bank). See also heading 5 of Chapter 10 entitled, "Line 05 – Other Investment Income."
159 Subsection 120.4(1), definition of "specified individual."
160 Subsection 120.4(3).
161 Subsection 120.4(1), definition of "excluded amount," paragraph (a).

person if the minor is either engaged in post-secondary education[162] on a full-time basis or is disabled and eligible for the disability tax credit.[163]

Where a trust is fully discretionary and enjoys multiple forms of income, some of which would attract kiddie tax if paid out to a minor and some of which would not, then the trustees may be able to allocate different forms of income to different beneficiaries in such a way as to avoid the kiddie tax.[164] For example, the trust can avoid kiddie tax if the trustees are in a position to distribute dividend income from publicly traded corporations to a minor beneficiary and dividends from a private corporation to a beneficiary who has attained the age of eighteen.[165]

4.3 Things You Need to Know

(a) Whether "In-Trust Accounts" Qualify as Trusts

Parents or other family members frequently open bank accounts or investment accounts in their own name "in trust" for their children. The accounts are often opened with little in the way of formality.

The tax treatment to be afforded to income generated on those accounts hinges on whether a trust has been established or not. CRA has expressed its view on the topic on multiple occasions.[166] In summary, whether a trust has been established or not depends on a case-by-case

---

162 As defined in subsection 146.1(1).
163 Subsection 120.4(1), definition of "excluded amount," paragraph (b).
164 M.N.R., Advance Ruling 2001-0069213, "Limited Partnership; Call Option" (January 1, 2001).
165 M.N.R., Technical Interpretation 2001-0112945, "Distribution from a Trust" (March 19, 2002) (provided that the appropriate designation is made under subsection 104(19)).
166 M.N.R., Technical Interpretation 2002-017676A, "In Trust Accounts" (July 21, 2003) (the most recent and most comprehensive treatment on the topic including an extensive review of case law on the subject); M.N.R., Technical Interpretation 2001-0067745, "In-Trust Accounts for Minors" (March 27, 2001); M.N.R., Technical Interpretation 9829145, "How Are In-Trust Accounts Taxed?" (April 14, 1999); M.N.R., Technical Interpretation 9809755, "In-Trust Accounts" (February 23, 1999); M.N.R., Technical Interpretation 9717475, "In-Trust Accounts" (September 22, 1997).

CHAPTER 2 — TYPES OF TRUSTS AND BASIC PLANNING

basis analysis, focusing on whether the "three certainties"[167] are present. Where the documentation, words and conduct of the person or persons contributing the money demonstrate the intention to create a trust, and where the property forming the trust is clearly segregated and transferred as identifiable property at creation, and where the beneficiary of the purported trust is identified with sufficient certainty, then a trust relationship will be held to exist. Most problematic is the intent to create a trust. The strongest indicator of the intention to create a trust is often said to be a written trust agreement or declaration, which is rarely present when an in-trust account is established. Typically, at best, an account is opened with the words "in trust for (child's name)" endorsed on the account agreement, and that phrase itself is not sufficient to establish an intention to create a trust. In these circumstances, the conduct of the settlor becomes the key consideration. Where shares were issued to the grandfather endorsed "in trust" for his grandchildren, and taxes were filed each year as if a trust existed, and the proceeds of the sale of the shares were not used or enjoyed by the grandfather, a trust had been held to exist;[168] but where detailed instructions were received by the bank in which the purported settlor designated trustees, and primary and contingent beneficiaries, the trust was not found to exist where the settlor continued to control the funds as if they had never left his ownership.[169]

Once an in-trust account is characterized as a trust, it is taxed as a trust, and all of the provisions of the Act applicable to trusts and their beneficiaries apply. Where a trust does not exist, two other options exist for the proper characterization of the situation: first, the situation might be construed as a failed gift, in which case the contents of the in-trust account would still be owned by the purported settlor; second, the situation might be construed as an outright gift to the minor, with a non-binding effort to impose some conditions on its use, in which case the contents of the trust would be owned by the minor as the result of the gift.

---

167 See 1.4 of Chapter 1 entitled, "The Three Certainties."
168 *Blum v. R.*, (1998), [1999] 3 C.T.C. 2287, 99 D.T.C. 290, 1998 CarswellNat 1836 (T.C.C.).
169 *Gaskell v. Gaskell* (1828), 2 Y. & J. 504 (Exch.).

PART I — BASIC ESTATE AND TRUST PLANNING

Where doubt exists as to whether a trust exists or not, an opinion can be solicited from legal counsel. It is also possible to apply to the courts for a declaration as to whether or not a trust exists at law. Given the expense of court applications and the often nominal amounts that are held in informal in-trust accounts, this is rarely practical.

(b) Payments Made Outside Trustees' Discretion

A trust for a minor will often include the discretion to pay out income or capital, or both, for the minor. That discretion is almost inevitably created by the use of a collection of words, each with its own legal meaning,[170] describing the purposes for which the payments can be made, such as for the minor's "health, welfare and benefit," "maintenance and support,"[171] "benefit,"[172] "education," or "advancement."[173] Those words can be mixed and matched in various combinations. Payments made to a beneficiary outside of the legitimate scope of that meaning may be subject to attack.

5. Alter Ego and Joint Spousal or Common-Law Partner Trusts

5.1 Summary

An "alter ego trust" is created by an individual for her own benefit as beneficiary. A "joint spousal trust" is created by one or both members of a legally married couple, and a "common-law partner trust" is set up by one or both of two persons qualifying as common-law partners under the Act. To qualify as an alter ego, joint spousal or common-law partner trust, the following conditions must be met:

---

170 Marni M.K. Whitker, "Payments from Children's Trusts" (2000) 19 E.T.P.J. 109 (discussing various words and phrases).
171 Whitker, *ibid.* at p. 138 ("maintenance and support" including food, clothing and accommodations, but not extending to education).
172 Whitker, *supra*, note 170 at p. 132 ("benefit" construed liberally, and including payments that might benefit not only the minor but the minor's family).
173 Whitker, *supra*, note 170 at p. 131 ("advancement" denoting long-term promotion or betterment).

CHAPTER 2 — TYPES OF TRUSTS AND BASIC PLANNING

- The individual or individuals contributing the property into the trust must be sixty-five years of age or older.

- The individual (in the case of an alter ego trust) or the couple (in the case of a joint spousal or common-law partner trust) must be entitled to all of the income from the trust in each taxation year, up to their death.

- No person or persons other than those individuals specified above can be entitled to receive any of the income or capital from the trust while those individuals are living.

If the trust qualifies, capital property can be transferred to the trust on a tax-deferred rollover basis, and the twenty-one year deemed disposition rule pertaining to capital property of the trust does not apply. A settlor can opt out of transferring property into what would otherwise be a qualifying alter ego trust.

These forms of trusts are normally employed to pursue tax and estate planning objectives, including probate fee avoidance, confidentiality at death, the avoidance of claims under dependants' relief legislation, and tax jurisdictional shopping. These trusts are taxed as *inter vivos* trusts, and any subsequent or successor trusts created using the capital after the death of the initial beneficiaries will not qualify for treatment as a testamentary trust.

5.2 General Comments Relating to Alter Ego and Joint Spousal or Common-Law Partner Trusts

(a) Requirements for a Qualifying Alter Ego Trust

An alter ego trust must meet the following conditions:

- is a trust that was created after 1999 and is an *inter vivos* trust;[174]

---

174 Subparagraph 104(4)(a)(ii.1).

PART I — BASIC ESTATE AND TRUST PLANNING

- under the terms of the trust deed, the taxpayer alone is entitled to receive all of the income of the trust that arises before the taxpayer's death and no person except the taxpayer may, before the taxpayer's death, receive or otherwise obtain the use of any of the income or capital of the trust;[175]

- the person creating the trust must have attained the age of sixty-five years at the time the trust was created;[176] and

- the trust does not elect out of qualifying treatment as an alter ego trust.[177]

(b) Requirements for a Qualifying Joint Spousal or Common-Law Partner Trust

The following conditions must be present in order to meet the definition of a joint spousal or common-law partner trust:

- is a trust that was created after 1999 and is an *inter vivos* trust;[178]

- under the terms of the trust, the taxpayer or the taxpayer's spouse or common-law partner was, in combination with the spouse or common-law partner or the taxpayer, as the case may be, entitled to receive all of the income of the trust that arose before the later of the death of the taxpayer and the death of the spouse or common-law partner and no person could, before the later of those deaths, receive or otherwise obtain the use of any of the income or capital of the trust;[179] and

- the person creating the trust must have attained the age of sixty-five years at the time the trust was created.[180]

---

175 Clause 104(4)(a)(iv)(A).
176 Subparagraph 104(4)(a)(iv).
177 Subparagraph 104(4)(a)(ii.1). See 5.3(b) of this chapter entitled, "Opting Out Available for Alter Ego Trusts."
178 Subparagraph 104(4)(a)(ii.1).
179 Clauses 104(4)(a)(iv)(B) and (C).
180 Subparagraph 104(4)(a)(iv).

CHAPTER 2 — TYPES OF TRUSTS AND BASIC PLANNING

One spouse or common-law partner can contribute all of the property to the trust or both spouses or common-law partners can contribute property jointly to the same trust and still qualify for treatment as a joint spousal or common-law partner trust.[181]

An alter ego trust is able to opt out of the rollover that takes place at insertion, but that is not the case for a joint spousal or joint common-law partner trust.[182]

A joint spousal trust is established where the partners are legally married. A common-law partner trust is established where a couple meets the qualifying definition in the *Income Tax Act*, including same- and opposite-sex couples who have co-habited together in a conjugal relationship for a period of time of at least one year.

(c) Planning Opportunities

Alter ego, joint spousal, and joint common-law partner trusts are employed for a number of planning purposes, including probate avoidance, ensuring confidentiality, control of capital, incapacity planning, creditor-proofing, avoiding claims under dependants' relief legislation, and jurisdiction shopping.[183]

(i) Probate Avoidance

The most common reason for employing such trusts is to achieve a degree of probate reduction or avoidance.[184] Generally speaking, probate

---

181 M.N.R., Technical Interpretation 2001-0099055, "Joint Spousal Trust" (January 23, 2002).
182 Subparagraph 104(4)(a)(ii.1).
183 Carmen S. Theriault, "Alter ego and Joint Partner Trusts" (2002) 21 E.T.P.J. 345 (containing an excellent review of estate planning opportunities at pp. 356-367).
184 This strategy is generally effective only in those jurisdictions where probate rates are high, including British Columbia (1.4% of estate value in excess of $50,000.00), Nova Scotia (1.3% of estate value in excess of $100,000.00) and Ontario (1.5% of estate value in excess of $50,000.00). In provinces like Manitoba, Saskatchewan, New Brunswick, Newfoundland, Labrador and

PART I — BASIC ESTATE AND TRUST PLANNING

fees are levied by the provincial or territorial government in the province or territory of residence where an individual dies or, in the case of land, in the province or territory where the land is situate. Probate fees vary from jurisdiction to jurisdiction and only apply to property that cannot be passed at death to the ultimate beneficiary of the property without an order of probate from a court. Property for which an order of probate is required is commonly referred to as property that "passes through the estate." Some forms of property pass to the intended beneficiary and do so by operation of law or by other legal instrument that causes the ownership to pass to new owners without an order of probate. These assets are said to pass to beneficiaries "outside of the estate," without ever forming part of the estate. Conceived of in those terms, probate is an indirect tax or administrative charge, or "toll," that is paid on assets as they pass through the estate.

Strategies to avoid probate generally involve the placement of property into forms of ownership that ensure that such property passes outside of the estate. The objective is to transfer ownership of the property to the new owners on the death of the original owner without the requirement for an order of probate. These strategies include placing property into joint ownership (commonly implemented for property such as land or bank accounts), designating beneficiaries (other than the estate) for the proceeds of life insurance policies or registered investments, and implementing multiple will strategies in provinces such as Ontario. Also included among these strategies is the act of settling property into an alter ego or joint spousal or joint common-law partner trust, where legal ownership of the asset passes to the trustees. On the death of the settlor, or her spouse or common-law partner, as the case may be, the property remains in the trust and is governed by the terms of the trust. The terms

---

Prince Edward Island, the rates of probate are roughly one-half of those in the higher probate fee jurisdictions. The value of the assets placed into an alter ego trust in those jurisdictions will have to be exceedingly high, in the neighbourhood of $1,000,000.00 or $2,000,000.00, before probate savings will justify the cost and inconvenience of adopting this strategy. In still other provinces and territories, a small flat rate is charged by way of probate fees. Those include Alberta and the Northwest Territories ($400.00), the Yukon ($140.00) and Quebec ($87.00). In those jurisdictions, an alter ego trust, or a joint spousal or joint common-law partner trust will not be warranted from the perspective of probate avoidance.

CHAPTER 2 — TYPES OF TRUSTS AND BASIC PLANNING

of the trust may provide that the assets are to be distributed to the children of the settlor, or to a charity or that they be held in trust for another generation of beneficiaries. Regardless of their ultimate destination, an order of probate is not required on death and no probate fees need be paid.

(ii) Confidentiality

As noted above, property that is placed into an alter ego or joint spousal or joint common-law partner trust does not pass through the estate. Generally speaking, that means that it does not have to be disclosed as part of the inventory of assets of the deceased, typically filed with an application for probate. Hence, these forms of trusts can be used by families who wish to have a significant portion of their assets devolve outside of their estates and away from the public eye. The application for probate is typically a public document.

(iii) Control of Capital

Property can be placed into an alter ego, joint spousal, or joint common-law partner trust when an individual wishes to exercise control over the capital. The terms of the trust would, under those circumstances, place some restriction on the free access to capital of the trust. A restriction may, for instance, be structured with a view to ensuring that the capital will ultimately flow to children from a prior relationship or to a charity. It might also be structured with a restriction to ensure that the surviving spouse was not able to make the capital available to a new spouse or partner after the first of them passes away. The effectiveness of this strategy will vary from province to province, and it will be dependent upon the particular facts of each situation. Caution should be exercised in structuring such restrictions, otherwise a trust may invite a potential application to the courts for a variation of the terms or even dissolution of the trust.[185]

---

185 See 4.1 of Chapter 1 entitled, "The Rule in *Saunders v. Vautier.*"

(iv) Incapacity Planning

These forms of trusts can also be employed with a view to planning for incapacity. The settlor or settlors could place the property in the trust and arrange for a trust company, or other personal representative, to be appointed alongside them as a co-trustee or as an alternate trustee. In the event that the settlor later becomes incapacitated, there is already a co-trustee in place who has a track record with the assets, and their arrangement may allow for a more seamless transition. As a downside, individuals will also typically have property owned outside of the trust, and that property will not be subject to the control of the co-trustees. In that event, it will still be necessary to have a power of attorney in place to administer that outside property.

(v) Creditor-Proofing

These trusts can also be employed for the purpose of creditor-proofing, with a view to avoiding claims made by creditors should the settlor later fall on hard financial times. The effectiveness of this as a strategy may depend, in significant measure, on the timing and circumstances surrounding the establishment of the trust. If it is done at the last moment, with the creditors already pursuing the settlor, the transfer into the trust can potentially be set-aside under provincial and territorial laws dealing with fraudulent conveyances.[186]

(vi) Avoiding Dependants' Relief Legislation

Dependants' relief legislation in various provinces and territories across Canada allow a person to bring a claim against an estate if they were dependent on the deceased prior to death. Depending upon the jurisdiction, the claim is limited to a claim against the estate of the deceased and cannot attach any non-estate assets. Thus, in some jurisdictions a dependants' relief claim cannot attach to assets in an alter ego, joint spousal or common-law partner trust. The remarks made in the section

---

[186] For a general, albeit brief discussion on the use of trusts for asset protection, see Barry S. Engel, "Asset Protection Trusts: The Short Course" (1995), 15 E.T.P.J. 48.

CHAPTER 2 — TYPES OF TRUSTS AND BASIC PLANNING

5.2(b)(v) entitled "Creditor-Proofing" relating to fraudulent conveyances should be borne in mind, however.[187]

(vii) Jurisdiction Shopping

Another common use for these forms of trusts is in establishing a tax resident trust in a low income tax jurisdiction in Canada.[188] The idea is to secure access to lower tax rates. Some provincial and territorial income tax acts contain provisions setting out general anti-avoidance rules that may be applicable in such circumstances. For this strategy to work, it requires a structure that does not attract income attribution to the settlor under subsection 75(2).[189] Where tax residency is successfully established in another province,[190] and attribution rules do not apply, the income will be taxed in that province if retained in the trust or if paid or payable to the beneficiary, provided that an appropriate designation is made under subsections 104(13.1) and (13.2) of the Act.[191]

5.3 Special Features

(a) No Disposition at Insertion

When capital property is transferred into an alter ego, joint spousal or common-law partner trust, it is transferred on a tax-deferred basis.[192] Where the rollover rules apply, non-depreciable capital property will be

---

187 As examples in this context, consider: *Stone v. Stone* (1999), 46 O.R. (3d) 31, 29 E.T.R. (2d) 1, 1999 CarswellOnt 2980 (S.C.J.), affirmed (2001), 203 D.L.R. (4th) 257, 55 O.R. (3d) 491, 39 E.T.R. (2d) 292, 2001 CarswellOnt 2781 (C.A.) (spouse successful in setting aside conveyances intended to defeat her claim); *Hossay v. Newman* (1998), 22 E.T.R. (2d) 150, 5 C.B.R. (4th) 198, 1998 CarswellBC 1734 (S.C. [In Chambers]) (son unsuccessful in setting aside transfers into joint tenancy just prior to death of father).
188 As to the tax residency of a trust, see heading 1 of Chapter 3 entitled, "Tax Residency of a Trust."
189 See headings 1 and 2 of Chapter 5.
190 See heading 1 of Chapter 3 entitled, "Tax Residency of a Trust."
191 See heading 4 of Chapter 4 entitled, "Income Designations under 104(13.1) and 104(13.2)."
192 Subsections 73(1.01) and (1.02).

PART I — BASIC ESTATE AND TRUST PLANNING

deemed to have been disposed of by the individual for proceeds equal to the adjusted cost base to the individual of the particular property immediately before that time. Where the particular property is depreciable capital property of a prescribed class, the deemed proceeds on transfer will be equal to that proportion of the undepreciated capital cost to the individual immediately before that time, of all depreciable capital property of that class, is to the fair market value immediately before that time of the particular property, to the fair market value immediately before that time of all such property in that class.[193]

The transfer of property into the trust will qualify for the rollover where the following requirements are met, many of which parallel the requirements in subsection 104(4):

- The trust has to have been created after 1999.[194]

- Both the individual and the trust must be resident in Canada.[195]

- The trust must be an *inter vivos* trust.[196]

- The individual transferring property into the trust must have turned sixty-five years of age at the time the trust is created.[197]

- Under the terms of the trust,

    o in the case of an alter ego trust, the individual who contributed property to the trust is entitled to receive all the income of the trust that arises before the individual's death and no person except that individual may, before that individual's death, receive or otherwise obtain the use of any of the income or capital of the trust,[198] or

    o in the case of a joint spousal or joint common-law partner trust, either the individual or the individual's spouse or common-law

---

193 Subsection 73(1).
194 Paragraph 73(1.02)(a).
195 Subsection 73(1).
196 Subparagraph 104(4)(a)(ii.1).
197 Subparagraph 73(1.02)(b)(i).
198 Subparagraph 73(1.01)(c)(ii).

CHAPTER 2 — TYPES OF TRUSTS AND BASIC PLANNING

partner is, in combination with the other, entitled to receive all of the income of the trust that arises before the later of the death of the individual and the death of the spouse or common-law partner, and no other person may, before the later of those deaths, receive or otherwise obtain the use of any of the income or capital of the trust.[199]

(b) Opting Out Available for Alter Ego Trusts

The settlor can opt out of the rollover provisions which otherwise allow for the tax deferred insertion of property into an alter ego trust. The election to opt out under subsection 73(1) must take place for the taxation year of the settlor in which the property is contributed to the trust.

A variety of considerations are relevant in deciding whether the election to opt out should be made or not. The individual transferring property into the trust may wish to take advantage of the capital gains exemption on qualified farm property or shares in a qualified small business corporation. By triggering a capital gain, the settlor can take advantage of their capital gains deduction and bump the adjusted cost base of the property. The election is an all or none election and it cannot be made on an asset-by-asset basis as a collection of assets is inserted into the trust.

(c) No Deemed Disposition at Twenty-One Years

Where a trust qualifies as an alter ego, joint spousal or common-law partner trust, a deemed disposition of capital property within the trust every twenty-one years under subsection 104(4) of the Act does not occur.

In an alter ego trust, a deemed disposition of capital property takes place at fair market value at the date of death of the settlor.[200] In a joint spousal or common-law partner trust, the deemed disposition takes place

---

199 Clauses 73(1.01)(c)(iii)(A) and (B).
200 Subparagraph 104(4)(a)(iv).

PART I — BASIC ESTATE AND TRUST PLANNING

on the last-to-die of the two spouses or common-law partners.[201] In either situation, any resulting income or capital gains is subject to tax at the highest tax rate[202] payable by the trust under section 122 of the Act. If the property had been retained in the name of the settlor and never transferred into the trust, the income or the capital gains resulting would appear on the terminal return of the deceased and might be subject to lower rates of tax, a consideration which should be kept in mind when the trust is initially planned and established.

5.4 Things You Need to Know

(a) *Cannot Fund Testamentary Trust*

After the settlor of an alter ego trust has passed away, or after the second of the spouses or common-law partners has passed away in the case of a joint spousal or common-law partner trust, the terms of the trust may provide for the remaining trust property to be held as a continuing trust, or trusts, for the benefit of a second generation of beneficiaries. Those second generation trusts will not qualify as testamentary trusts and will be taxed on an ongoing basis as *inter vivos* trusts.[203]

The situation might be different if the terms of the trust directed that the capital from the trust was to be paid expressly into the estate of the deceased settlor (in the case of an alter ego trust), or into the estate of the second member to die (in the case of a joint spousal or common-law partner trust). That wording would add the capital to the estate, and it would therefore be governed by the will of the deceased and, arguably,[204] qualify the resulting trust established under the will as a testamentary trust. This form of structure would, however, thwart many of the planning objectives pursued in establishing an alter ego, joint spousal or common-law partner trust. Probate would be paid on the capital coming

---

201 Clauses 104(4)(a)(iv)(B) and (C).
202 Subsection 122(1), alter ego, joint spousal and common-law partner trusts being *inter vivos* trusts.
203 See 1.2(b)(viii) of Chapter 2 dealing with testamentary trusts and entitled, "Trusts Settled with Property from an *Inter Vivos* Trust."
204 CRA does not appear to have commented on this particular point.

CHAPTER 2 — TYPES OF TRUSTS AND BASIC PLANNING

into the estate, there would be no creditor-proofing and confidentiality would be lost.

(b) Attribution of Income to Settlor

The income from property held in an alter ego, joint spousal or common-law partner trust will be attributed back to the settlor where subsection 75(2) of the Act applies.[205] The commonly adopted terms of an alter ego trust will generally allow for reversion of capital to the settlor, spouses or common-law spouses, and attribution will be common but not mandatory. Such trusts should therefore be carefully drafted to avoid attribution under subsection 75(2) when one of the objectives of creating the trust is to allow for tax jurisdictional shopping as discussed above.

Subsection 74.2(1) may apply to joint spousal and common-law partner trusts and operate to attribute property income to the transferor, where property has been transferred directly or by way of a loan to the trust, directly or indirectly, for the benefit of the transferor's spouse or common-law partner.[206]

(c) Principal Residence Exemption

The principal residence exemption is available to personal trusts including alter ego, joint spousal and common-law partner trusts[207] and should be considered where the disposition of a house, summer home or other qualifying residence is made by the trustees.

For instance, on the death of a taxpayer, the taxpayer's principal residence will be deemed to be disposed of and the amount of the deemed proceeds will depend on whether the principal residence is bequeathed

---

205 See headings 1 through 4 of Chapter 5 (attribution occurring where there is a potential for reversion, retained control over the destination of property, or "gate keeping").
206 See M.N.R., Interpretation Bulletin IT-511R, "Interspousal and Certain Other Transfers and Loans of Property" (February 21, 1994), at paragraph 3.
207 See M.N.R., Interpretation Bulletin IT-120R6, "Principal Residence" (July 17, 2003), at paragraphs 2 and 7.

PART I — BASIC ESTATE AND TRUST PLANNING

to a surviving spouse, common-law partner trust[208] or to some other person.[209] Where the principal residence is disposed of in the former situation (spouse or qualifying spousal or common-law partner trust), subsection 70(6) will apply to deem the property to be disposed of with no gain or loss.[210]

When a principal residence is transferred to a spouse or a qualifying spousal or common-law partner trust, the transferee is deemed to have owned the property for those years it was owned by the deceased and to have occupied it for each year in which it was the deceased taxpayer's principal residence.[211] This provision ensures that the beneficiary spouse or qualifying spousal or common-law partner trust will be entitled to a "flow-through" of the principal residence exemption, on disposition, to which the deceased taxpayer spouse would have been entitled. To the extent that the surviving spouse or common-law partner ordinarily inhabits the property as her principal residence subsequent to the deceased's death, the full exemption on the principal residence will "flow-through" to the spouse, common-law partner or trust.[212]

After 1981, the Act provides that a family unit (taxpayer, spouse and minor children) can treat only one property as a principal residence for a given taxation year. Transitional rules apply where more than one principal residence was owned by members of a family unit prior to 1982. Prior to 1982, each spouse or common-law partner could own property which qualified as a principal residence. After 1981, only one of those properties can be designated in respect of those years of ownership thereafter. Consequently, on the non-eligible property, only that

---

208 Subsection 70(6), "Where transfer or distribution to spouse [or common-law partner] or spouse trust," provides for a rollover at the cost amount of the property at the time of death.
209 Subsection 70(5), "Capital property of a deceased taxpayer," provides for a disposition at the fair market value of the property at the time of death.
210 Subsection 70(6). See also M.N.R., Interpretation Bulletin IT-120R6, *supra*, note 207 at paragraphs 35-36. It may be advisable to elect under subsection 70(6.2) to transfer the principal residence to the spouse or qualifying spousal or common-law partner trust at fair market value, in order to take advantage of the principal residence exemption of the deceased taxpayer.
211 Subsection 40(4).
212 Paragraph a.1 of section 54, definition of "principal residence."

CHAPTER 2 — TYPES OF TRUSTS AND BASIC PLANNING

portion of the capital gain attributable to those years of ownership prior to 1982 will qualify for the principal residence exemption.

Therefore, even where subsection 40(4) deems the principal residence of the deceased spouse to be that of the beneficiary spouse or qualifying spousal or common-law partner trust for the entire period during which the particular property was a principal residence of the deceased, there is no restriction from the spouse or common-law partner from designating another property which they owned at December 31, 1981, as their principal residence for those years of ownership prior to 1982.

Part II
Taxation of Trusts and Beneficiaries

Chapter 3
Taxation of Trusts

1. Tax Residency of a Trust

The following factors (ranked in order of their importance and relevance) are generally considered to form the basic framework in determining the tax residency of a trust or estate within Canada:[1]

- *Residence of Managing Trustee* – If a trust has a trustee who is responsible for the management of the trust and the control of the trust assets (referred to as a "managing trustee"), the trust will generally be resident in the province or territory where the managing trustee resides.[2]

- *Residence of Preponderance of Managing Trustees* – If the trust has two or more managing trustees, and they live in the same jurisdiction, then the trust will be resident in that jurisdiction. If, however, they live in different jurisdictions and one trustee is seen to be dominant, handling the majority of the management and control, then the trust will generally be resident in the province or territory where the dominant trustee resides. If no one managing trustee is

---

[1] See generally M.N.R., Interpretation Bulletin IT-447, "Residence of a Trust or Estate" (May 30, 1980).

[2] See M.N.R., Interpretation Bulletin IT-447, *ibid.* at paragraph 1. See also M.N.R., Interpretation Bulletin IT-221R3, "Determination of an Individual's Residence Status" [Consolidated] (October 4, 2002) at paragraph 1. The commentary outlines criteria relevant in determining an individual's provincial residence which has application for the residency of an individual trustee.

PART II — TAXATION OF TRUSTS AND BENEFICIARIES

seen to be dominant, then the trust will be resident in the province or territory, if any, where the majority of the managing trustees reside.[3]

- *Location of Assets* – If the residence of the trust cannot be determined with reference to the factors outlined above, then the trust will generally be treated to be resident in the province or territory where the majority of the assets are located or where the rights of the trust are enforceable under provincial or territorial law.[4]

A person is said to be responsible for the management of the trust and control of the trust assets if they enjoy or exert responsibility over such things as banking, record keeping, business interests and property holdings of the trust. Management includes control over changes to the trust's investment portfolio, control over the trust's assets and the power to hire or fire advisors, including lawyers and accountants.[5]

A managing trustee (sometimes referred to as an "administrative trustee") can be expressly appointed under the terms of the trust, or the trust can contain a specific mechanism to appoint a managing trustee. Where this is the case and the trustee appointed for that purpose, in fact, discharges the duties of a managing trustee, then the residence of the trust will be the residence of that trustee. Where, however, a managing trustee is appointed in the trust document, but some other person is, in fact, engaged in the management and control of the trust, CRA may disregard the terms of the trust and take the position that the trust is resident in the jurisdiction where that person resides, even if he is not a trustee but is some other person, including a beneficiary or the settlor.[6]

Many trust documents do not expressly provide for the appointment of a managing trustee. Where that is the case, and if there is one trustee who does, in fact, manage the trust and control its assets, then the trust will be resident where the trustee resides. Where there are multiple trustees and all live in the same jurisdiction, then the determination is simple. If they live in different jurisdictions, then an analysis must be

---

3 See M.N.R., Interpretation Bulletin IT-447, *supra*, note 1 at paragraph 3.
4 See M.N.R., Interpretation Bulletin IT-447, *supra*, note 1 at paragraph 4.
5 See M.N.R., Interpretation Bulletin IT-447, *supra*, note 1 at paragraph 2.
6 M.N.R., Interpretation Bulletin IT-447, *supra*, note 1 at paragraph 5.

CHAPTER 3 — TAXATION OF TRUSTS

conducted to determine who is in fact engaged in the management of the trust and the control of its assets. The same basic framework should be followed, looking first for a dominant trustee and then, if necessary, to the preponderance of trustees. Where the document is not express in appointing a managing trustee, it might be possible to appoint one by having the group of trustees execute a document which delegates the role of managing trustee to one of them.[7]

The effort to manipulate tax residency and establish residency in a low-tax jurisdiction raises various anti-avoidance issues both in terms of federal and provincial income taxes.[8] Where the purported residence of a trust or estate appears to have been motivated by reasons of tax avoidance, CRA takes the position that it will not be governed by the factors discussed above and will consider "other factors" as potentially relevant.[9]

Where the management and control of a trust is exercised by a trust company, the province or territory of residence of the branch office of the trust company is the defining factor, regardless of the residence of the head office.[10]

It should also be noted that a trust resident outside of Canada that has discretionary powers to release income and capital to Canadian beneficiaries may be deemed to be a Canadian resident for tax purposes if it meets the requirements set out under subsection 94(1) of the Act.[11]

---

[7] The extent to which a trustee can delegate administrative and other powers to another person is not very well delineated. This is especially true in cases where the trust instrument does not expressly allow for it, and the delegation might be subject to challenge as a result. See D.W.M. Waters, *Law of Trusts in Canada*, 2nd ed. (Toronto: Carswell, 1984), at p. 706.
[8] David H. Sohmer, "Fundamental Issues in Shifting Income to Low-Tax Provinces" (2003) 22 E.T.P.J. 127.
[9] M.N.R., Interpretation Bulletin IT-447, *supra*, note 1 at paragraph 11.
[10] M.N.R., Interpretation Bulletin IT-447, *supra*, note 1 at paragraph 7.
[11] M.N.R., Interpretation Bulletin IT-447, *supra*, note 1 at paragraph 9.

PART II — TAXATION OF TRUSTS AND BENEFICIARIES

2. Minimum Tax

Trusts are subject to minimum tax imposed under Division E.1 of Part I of the Act unless a specific provision provides to the contrary.[12]

Minimum tax, however, does not apply to the following kinds of trusts in the following circumstances.

- Spousal trusts, whether *inter vivos* or testamentary, are not subject to minimum tax in the taxation year in which the spouse who is the beneficiary of the trust dies and, by passing away, causes a deemed disposition and reacquisition of property held in the trust.[13] In all other years, minimum tax will apply.

- Alter ego trusts are not subject to minimum tax in the taxation year in which the settlor dies and, by passing away, triggers the deemed disposition and reacquisition of property in the trust.[14] In all other years, minimum tax will apply.

- Joint spousal trusts or joint common-law partner trusts are not subject to minimum tax in the taxation year in which the second common law-partner or spouse dies and, by passing away, triggers the deemed disposition and reacquisition of property in the trust.[15] In all other years, minimum tax will apply.

- Minimum tax will never apply to a related segregated fund trust, or a mutual fund trust or a master trust.[16] These forms of trusts will not be subject to minimum tax, regardless of the year (unlike the trusts described immediately above that are free from minimum tax only in respect of the taxation year in which the triggering death occurs).

---

12 See for example M.N.R., Technical Interpretation 9903747, "Minimum Tax and Health and Welfare Trust" (June 14, 1999) (minimum tax provisions applicable to health and welfare trusts).
13 Subsection 127.55(e) and subparagraph 104(4)(a)(iii).
14 Subsection 127.55(e) and clause 104(4)(a)(iv)(A).
15 Subsection 127.55(e) and clauses 104(4)(a)(iv)(B) and (C).
16 Subsection 127.55(f).

CHAPTER 3 — TAXATION OF TRUSTS

Where minimum tax does apply, some but not all forms of trusts are entitled to take advantage of the $40,000 basic exemption. That exemption is available to:

- *inter vivos* trusts established prior to June 18, 1971, that, since that date, have been continuously resident in Canada and have not received any gifts, and that, in the current taxation year, have not carried on any active business,[17]

- testamentary trusts.[18]

Multiple trusts that qualify for the exemption but have the same settlor, as might be the case where multiple testamentary trusts are established under a person's will, are limited to a single exemption of $40,000.[19] The trusts may enter into an agreement in prescribed form[20] and file it with CRA, allocating that exemption among the trusts in whatever manner the trustees see fit.[21] If the agreement is not filed, and remains unfiled for thirty days following a request by the Minister that the agreement be filed, then CRA may allocate the exemption in any manner it wishes.[22]

3. Treatment of Income Generally

3.1 The General Rules Relating to Inclusion and Deduction of Income

A trust will generally be required to report and pay tax on its income in the same manner as any other individual. However, if income earned by a trust is paid or payable to a beneficiary during the year it will be taxed

---

17 Paragraph 127.53(1)(b) and subsection 122(2).
18 Paragraph 127.53(1)(b).
19 Subsection 127.53(2).
20 T3SCH6 (E) "Trusts' Agreement to Allocate The Basic Exemption From Minimum Tax."
21 Subsection 127.53(2).
22 Subsection 127.53(3).

PART II — TAXATION OF TRUSTS AND BENEFICIARIES

as the income of the beneficiary who received it[23] and will be deducted from the income of the trust.[24]

There are exceptions to those general rules, as well as special forms of trusts that have special rules applicable to the inclusion and deduction of income. Those exceptions and special types of trusts are dealt with in later sections.

3.2 Exceptions to the General Rules

The following are exceptions to the general rules relating to the inclusion and deduction of income:

- Designated income under subsections 104(13.1) and (13.2) will remain income of the trust notwithstanding that it is paid or payable to a beneficiary.[25]

- Income subject to a preferred beneficiary election is taxed in the hands of the beneficiary and deducted from the income of the trust notwithstanding that it is retained in the trust.[26]

- Income retained for beneficiaries under the age of twenty-one will in some circumstances be taxed in the hands of the beneficiary, notwithstanding that it is retained in the trust.[27]

- Benefits other than cash received by a taxpayer from a trust may be deemed to be income in the hands of the taxpayer, notwithstanding that no cash in fact changes hands.[28]

---

23 Paragraph 104(13)(a).
24 Paragraph 104(6)(b).
25 Subsections 104(13.1) and (13.2); and see heading 4 of Chapter 4 entitled, "Income Designations under 104(13.1) and 104(13.2)."
26 Subsection 104(12); and see heading 5 of Chapter 4 entitled, "The Preferred Beneficiary Election" for a full discussion.
27 Subsection 104(18); and see 4.2(b) of Chapter 2 entitled, "Pent Up Income Attributed to Minors under 104(18)" for a full discussion.
28 Subsection 105(1); and see heading 2 of Chapter 4 entitled, "Income in the Form of Benefits Conferred by the Trust" for a complete discussion.

CHAPTER 3 — TAXATION OF TRUSTS

- Outlays for the upkeep and maintenance of property maintained by the trust for the use of a beneficiary may be deemed to be income in the hands of the beneficiary notwithstanding that the outlays are not received by beneficiaries.[29]

- Foreign source income received by a Canadian resident trust and designated by the trustees to be beneficiary income may receive special treatment as beneficiary income.[30]

- Attributed income under subsection 75(2) is the income of the settlor and never becomes the income of the trust notwithstanding that the income may have been retained by the trust or paid out to beneficiaries.[31]

3.3 Special Kinds of Trusts Governed by Special Rules

There are special rules applicable to the inclusion and exclusion of income for certain types of trusts:

- employee trusts,[32]
- trusts governed by an employee benefit plan,[33]

---

29 Subsection 105(2); and see heading 3 of Chapter 4 entitled, "Income in the Form of Outlays for the Upkeep of Trust Property" for a discussion in this area.
30 M.N.R., Interpretation Bulletin IT-201R2, "Foreign Tax Credit – Trust and Beneficiaries" (February 12, 1996), at paragraph 1.
31 Subsection 75(2); M.N.R., Technical Interpretation 9411115, "Attribution" (April 28, 1994); and see heading 5 of Chapter 5 entitled, "Considerations Relating to Contributor" for commentary on this subject. While the income will not be income for tax purposes, it may still be income for trust law purposes: see also heading 5 of Chapter 1 entitled "The Relationship Between Tax Law and Trust Law".
32 Paragraph 104(6)(a), special rule as to deductions from trust income; however, this text does not deal separately with employee trusts. For information on this topic refer to M.N.R., Interpretation Bulletin IT-502SR, "Employee Benefit Plans and Employee Trusts" (May 31, 1991).
33 Paragraph 104(6)(a.1), special rule as to deductions from trust income; paragraph 104(13)(b), special rule relating to inclusion of income for beneficiary; more generally see M.N.R., Interpretation Bulletin IT-502SR, *supra*, note 32

PART II — TAXATION OF TRUSTS AND BENEFICIARIES

- trusts for religious congregations,[34]
- spousal and common-law partner trusts,[35]
- alter ego and joint partner trusts,[36] and
- amateur athlete trusts.[37]

(this text does not deal separately with trusts governed by employee benefit plans).

[34] Paragraph 104(6)(a.3), special rule as to deductions from trust income; this text does not deal separately with trusts for religious congregations.

[35] Subparagraph 104(6)(b)(ii), special rule as to deductions from trust income; also refer to commentary in heading 3 of Chapter 2 entitled, "Spousal Trusts."

[36] Subparagraphs 104(6)(b)(ii.1) and (iii), special rule as to deductions from trust income; also refer to commentary in heading 5 of Chapter 2 entitled, "Alter Ego and Joint Spousal or Common-Law Partner Trusts."

[37] Paragraph 104(13)(a), special rule as to inclusion of income for beneficiary; this text does not deal separately with amateur athlete trusts.

Chapter 4
Taxation of Beneficiaries

1. Determining Whether Income is Payable

Where the general rules apply, income will be taxable to the beneficiary if the income is "payable" to the beneficiary. Income is deemed under the Act not to be payable unless it is either paid to the beneficiary or the beneficiary is entitled to enforce payment of the income.[1] The beneficiary need not actually enforce payment or even try to enforce the payment. The determining factors include the beneficiary's absolute right to the income and the absence of any restriction, contractual or otherwise, as to its disposition, use or enjoyment.[2]

In determining whether the income of a trust has become payable to its beneficiaries, a distinction can be drawn between trusts where the distribution of income is discretionary and where the distribution of income is mandatory.

1.1 Discretionary Income Distributions

An income distribution is said to be discretionary where the terms of the trust do not force the income to be distributed or withheld but, instead, confer the authority on a person, normally the trustee or trustees, to make a distribution.

---

1 Subsection 104(24).
2 *Hall v. R.*, 2003 TCC 410, 2003 D.T.C. 779, [2003] 4 C.T.C. 2544, 2003 CarswellNat 1823 (T.C.C. [Informal Procedure]) at paragraph 6.

PART II — TAXATION OF TRUSTS AND BENEFICIARIES

Where a distribution of income is discretionary, income is payable to a beneficiary if the following conditions[3] are met:

- the trustees have exercised their discretion before the end of the trust's taxation year,[4]

- the exercise of discretion must have been irrevocable with no conditions attached to the beneficiaries' entitlement to enforce payment of the amount in the year,

- the allocation to each of the various beneficiaries, where applicable, must have been set (whether as a fixed percentage, or a fixed amount or "all" of the income), and

- the beneficiaries must have been advised of the trustees' decision during the taxation year.

In dealing with a discretionary trust, CRA has outlined recommendations and guidelines relating to the manner and proof of payment. CRA recommends that proof of the exercise of the discretion be in written form such as minutes of a trustees' meeting, or a signed resolution of the trustees.[5] Payment may be made in the form of a cheque. The cheque cannot be post-dated or subject to any condition, and it must be delivered to the beneficiary before the end of the taxation year, when the amount can be ascertained before the end of the trust's taxation year. Where the amount is not known until after the taxation year, perhaps due to administrative delays in obtaining financial information, the cheque should be delivered as promptly as possible after the amount can be quantified.[6] Payment may also be made in the form of a promissory note, with or without interest, provided that payment in that manner is either permitted by the terms of the trust, or permitted by the laws in

---

[3] See generally M.N.R., Technical Interpretation 9606227, "Amount Payable to a Beneficiary of a Discretionary Trust" (March 6, 1997).

[4] M.N.R., Interpretation Bulletin IT-286R2, "Trusts – Amount Payable" (April 8, 1988), at paragraph 5.

[5] M.N.R., Technical Interpretation 9606227, *supra*, note 3.

[6] M.N.R., Technical Interpretation 9606227, *supra*, note 3.

CHAPTER 4 — TAXATION OF BENEFICIARIES

effect in the province and the terms of the trust are silent on the point.[7] The note must be payable on demand and without restriction, and it should be delivered in the time frames and to the same persons as noted for the delivery of a cheque.[8]

1.2 Non-Discretionary Income Distributions

An income distribution is said to be non-discretionary where the trustees are expressly obliged under the terms of the trust to distribute income or to withhold income in some measure.

Where a trust provides that the income of the trust must be paid to a beneficiary, the income is generally payable at the time the payment must be made, regardless of whether the trustees fail to do so,[9] and regardless of whether the trustees decline to claim the deduction under paragraph 104(6)(b).[10] In terms of timing, where the terms of a trust provide that the income must be paid out to the beneficiaries, the income becomes payable when it becomes the property of the trust and does so notwithstanding that the calculation of the exact amount may be delayed until the following year due to administrative delays in obtaining financial information.[11]

Where, however, the amount cannot be ascertained during the taxation year and the reason is some contingency or event occurring after that time, then the income will not be payable.[12] In an estate, income

---

[7] M.N.R., Technical Interpretation 9606227, *supra*, note 3; M.N.R., Technical Interpretation 9529647, "Promissory Note – Discretionary Trust Amount Payable" (February 26, 1997).

[8] M.N.R., Technical Interpretation 9606227, *supra*, note 3; M.N.R., Technical Interpretation 9529647, *ibid*.

[9] *Brown v. R.*, [1979] C.T.C. 2190, 12 E.T.R. 1, 79 D.T.C. 201, 1979 CarswellNat 318 (T.R.B.), affirmed 1979 CarswellNat 285, [1979] C.T.C. 476 (Fed. T.D.).

[10] *Brown v. R.*, *ibid*.

[11] *Ginsburg v. Minister of National Revenue*, 92 D.T.C. 1774, 46 E.T.R. 188, [1992] 2 C.T.C. 2152, 1992 CarswellNat 370 (T.C.C.) (the taxpayer also attempted to disclaim the income by written waiver but it was still held to be payable to her); also see M.N.R., Technical Interpretation 9606227, *supra*, note 3.

[12] M.N.R., Technical Interpretation 9606227, *supra*, note 3.

PART II — TAXATION OF TRUSTS AND BENEFICIARIES

will be payable where the income stands in an estate and the only reason that the beneficiary is not able to claim and demand the income is the operation of the legal principal blocking such demands during the first twelve months of the administration of the estate.[13] Income will *not* be treated as payable where the income stands in an estate but the administration of the estate is not complete,[14] or if the estate or trust is not able to distribute income as a result of a protracted dispute.[15] However, the administrative position may be different relating to funds deposited with lawyers for safekeeping while a dispute is outstanding.[16]

If the trust document confers a power on the beneficiary to force the trustee to pay out income from the trust, the mere existence of that power will not make the income of the trust payable,[17] and, in similar fashion, a clause that confers a power on the beneficiary to amend the trust deed and, thereby, to allow access to income will not, by itself, make the income payable.[18] Where the beneficiary has a right to demand payment but that right is subject to the approval of a third party appointed under the terms of a trust, then income will not be payable.[19] In each of those

---

13 M.N.R., Interpretation Bulletin IT-286R2, *supra*, note 4 at paragraph 6. Generally, an executor or other personal representative is obliged to pay out the capital and the accrued income of an estate at such time as they are in a position to do so, and a legal presumption exists that the estate should be in a position to make that distribution when it reaches the one year mark. See the discussion appearing at 1.2(b)(vii) of Chapter 2 entitled, "An Estate" for commentary on administration and the executor's year.

14 *Hall v. R.*, *supra*, note 2 (income not payable while executors refusing to release estate until their fees settled and some assets still being called in, and not, at that stage, possible to wind up the estate and distribute the income and capital to the beneficiaries).

15 M.N.R., Technical Interpretation 9238487, "Trust Money in Dispute" (April 8, 1993) (estate locked in dispute over several years and not able to distribute income as a result; income properly taxed as trust income for each year the dispute drags on, but estate free to file a waiver with its T3 each year and seek reassessment after the dispute is over).

16 M.N.R., Technical Interpretation 9238487, *ibid.*

17 M.N.R., Interpretation Bulletin IT-286R2, *supra*, note 4 at paragraph 5 (beneficiaries having power to wind up trust and take income).

18 M.N.R., Interpretation Bulletin IT-286R2, *supra*, note 4 at paragraph 4 (but the amount may become payable when the power is exercised).

19 M.N.R., Interpretation Bulletin IT-286R2, *supra*, note 4 at paragraph 5 (but it would become payable after the beneficiary demand and third party approval were both made).

instances, however, the income would become payable upon the exercise of the relevant discretion, in the manner set out earlier at 1.1, "Discretionary Income Distributions."

There is some indication from CRA that income will not be payable where the terms of a trust stipulate that the income must be paid to the beneficiary but that the actual payment of the income is to be postponed for a fixed period of time, even if that period of time extends into the next taxation year.[20]

2. Income in the Form of Benefits Conferred by the Trust

The value of non-cash benefits that a trust confers on a taxpayer during the year may, under some circumstances, be added to the taxpayer's income pursuant to subsection 105(1) of the Act. The intent of the subsection is to ensure that the value of all benefits received or enjoyed by a taxpayer from or under a trust, other than capital distributions, are included in the taxpayer's income.[21]

Benefits conferred by a trust to a taxpayer under this subsection include the rent-free use of a vacant apartment where the apartment is not for personal use or enjoyment but for some other purpose[22] (the position is different, however, if the property is being put to personal use – see discussion below). The amount of income attributed to the taxpayer will, under such circumstances, be the fair market rental value

---

20 M.N.R., Technical Interpretation 2003-0008285, "Spousal Trust – Entitlement – Payable" (September 23, 2003) (considering a trust where the income was to be pooled for three year periods before release to the spouse, but CRA indicating that the specific wording of the particular trust document would be germane); but see *Hall v. R.*, *supra*, note 2 at paragraph 6 (pronounced four months prior to the date on the technical interpretations and suggesting what may be a contrary view).
21 M.N.R., Department of Finance Commentary (Consolidated Explanatory Notes), "Benefits Under A Trust" (En September 13, 1988 [S.C. 1988, c. 55 (C-139)]).
22 M.N.R., Technical Interpretation 2002-0118255, "Application of 75(2)" (June 10, 2002).

PART II — TAXATION OF TRUSTS AND BENEFICIARIES

that would have to be paid to secure the use of a comparable property, net of costs.[23]

Benefits that will *not* shift income from the trust to the taxpayer under this subsection include:

- scholarships, bursaries, fellowships, prizes or research grants paid for by the trust;[24]

- the right to use or live in a home or other residential dwelling owned by the trust, provided that the home qualifies as personal-use property[25] (The personal-use property of a trust will include property such as homes, cottages, boats, and cars, owned primarily for the personal use or enjoyment of a beneficiary of the trust or any person related to the beneficiary.[26] In a similar vein, the rent-free use of a property by a life tenant, when the property itself is being maintained by a trust, will not give rise to a subsection 105(1) benefit provided that the property would qualify as a principal residence of the life tenant if the life tenant owned the property.[27] Where subsection

---

23 M.N.R., Technical Interpretation 9238075, "Benefit from Trust" (March 31, 1993) (and note that where evidence as to fair market value is unavailable then the use of an imputed value approach has been suggested).
24 M.N.R., Interpretation Bulletin IT-75R4, "Scholarships, Fellowships, Bursaries, Prizes, and Research Grants and Financial Assistance" (June 18, 2003), at paragraph 40 (as those amounts must be included in calculating the income of the recipient under subparagraphs 56(1)(n)(i) or 56(1)(o)).
25 M.N.R., Technical Interpretation 2003-0047727, "Right of Use – Deemed Trust" (December 17, 2003); M.N.R., Technical Interpretation 9618885, "Third Party Payments and Rent Free Use of Trust Property" (September 22, 1997) (CRA taking the position that while such benefits would fall within subsection 105(1) as income, that they will *generally* not require those benefits to be included in the income if the benefits are relating to the rent-free use of personal-use property).
26 M.N.R., Technical Interpretation 9707305, "Rent Free Use of Trust Property" (September 22, 1997) (referring to the definition of personal-use property set out in section 54 of the Act).
27 M.N.R., Technical Interpretation 9514615, "Benefits to Life Tenant" (July 7, 1995); but see M.N.R., Technical Interpretation 9311945, "Benefits from a Trust" (September 16, 1993) (income may be attributed to the beneficiary if they enjoy continued use of the property, but the terms of trust do not give the beneficiary the right to use the property).

CHAPTER 4 — TAXATION OF BENEFICIARIES

105(1) is not applied by CRA in a situation dealing with personal-use property, an amount may still fall into beneficiary income on account of upkeep and maintenance under subsection 105(2));

- a settlement payment made from an estate to a child pursuant to a settlement agreement arising out of a dispute in connection with the estate;[28] and

- interest-free or low-interest loans from trusts to beneficiaries.[29]

Subsection 105(1) refers broadly to "taxpayers" and not more narrowly to "beneficiaries." Thus, CRA takes the position that an individual other than a beneficiary of the trust can have income attributed to her under subsection 105(1) if the individual receives benefits from the trust,[30] as where the settlor of a trust settles an apartment block into the trust and retains the right to the rent-free use of a vacant apartment from time to time.[31] Income will not, however, be attributed to the parent of a minor beneficiary when a trust pays or reimburses the parent for outlays for the child's benefit,[32] and income appears not to attribute under the same circumstances if the beneficiary is a disabled adult.[33] Whether the

---

28 M.N.R., Advance Income Tax Rulings 1999-0013123, "Distribution of Property from Trust" (January 1, 2001).
29 M.N.R., Technical Interpretation 9528037, "Benefit from a Trust – Loans" (February 26, 1996), also see *Cooper v. Minister of National Revenue*, 87 D.T.C. 194, [1987] 1 C.T.C. 2287, 1987 CarswellNat 402 (T.C.C.).
30 M.N.R., Technical Interpretation 9402515, "Application of Subsection 15(1) in a Specific Situation" (July 26, 1994).
31 M.N.R., Technical Interpretation 2002-0118255, *supra*, note 22.
32 M.N.R., Technical Interpretation 9618885, *supra*, note 27. ("It is our opinion that a taxable benefit under subsection 105(1) of the Act will not arise to the parent as a consequence of the trust (in accordance with the terms of the trust indenture or will) paying for the expenditures ... for the benefit of the child, including those that the parent would otherwise have been legally obligated to incur for the support, maintenance, etc., of the child pursuant to applicable provincial and/or federal statutes. However, payments made by the trust which meet the requirements outlined above will be included in the child's income.") See also M.N.R., Technical Interpretation 9707317, "Amounts Payable to Minor Beneficiaries and Taxable Benefits from a Trust" (August 26, 1997).
33 M.N.R., Technical Interpretation 9514457, "Special Purpose Trust and Taxable Benefit from a Trust" (June 30, 1995) (the authors defer prospectively to the position that is being developed by CRA, at the time, relating to minors).

PART II — TAXATION OF TRUSTS AND BENEFICIARIES

trust in question is a resident or non-resident of Canada for tax purposes does not appear to impact on the applicability of subsection 105(1) on a Canadian resident taxpayer receiving a benefit from the trust.[34]

3. Income in the Form of Outlays for the Upkeep of Trust Property

Amounts paid by a trust for the upkeep or maintenance of trust property may, under some circumstances, be included in the income of the beneficiary or life tenant pursuant to subsection 105(2) of the Act and will, in that event, be deductible from the income of the trust under paragraph 104(6)(b).

Subsection 105(2) will be applicable where the following conditions are met.

- The payment must be made by a trust.

- The payment must be made from the income of the trust and not from the capital of the trust.[35]

- The payment must be made for the upkeep or maintenance of property, or on account of taxes on that property.

- The terms of the trust must stipulate that the property shall be maintained for the use of a tenant for life or other beneficiary. Those terms have to be set out in the trust itself, not in some other contract or instrument.[36]

---

34 M.N.R., Technical Interpretation 9318775, "No or Low Interest Loan" (January 1, 1993).
35 Subsection 105(2), applying to ". . .an amount paid by a trust out of income of the trust. . .", and see M.N.R., Technical Interpretation 9514615, *supra*, note 27 (amounts paid out of income falling under 105(2) and amounts paid under capital potentially falling under 105(1)).
36 *Blackstien v. R.* (1997), 98 D.T.C. 3371, [1998] 1 C.T.C. 3269, 1997 CarswellNat 2297 (T.C.C.) at paragraph 6 (a marriage contract requiring that a property be maintained for the surviving spouse, for life, was not sufficient to ground the applicability of 105(2) on payments made by the estate to maintain

CHAPTER 4 — TAXATION OF BENEFICIARIES

When an amount qualifies, the whole of the amount paid out need not be included in the beneficiaries' income, only such amount as may be reasonable in the circumstances.[37] In the case of personal-use property, such as homes, cottages, boats and cars, CRA has adopted the policy that the use of such items will generally not be taxed as a benefit under subsection 105(1) as discussed earlier.[38] However CRA has been careful to repeatedly take the position that situations involving personal-use property may still give rise to income under subsection 105(2) to the extent that outlays have been made for maintenance, upkeep or taxes.[39]

Where a trust is *inter vivos* then the application of subsection 105(2) of the Act will generally be desirable, as the income will frequently be taxed at lower rates and with more deductions and credits available if taxed in the hands of the beneficiary. This may not be the case if the trust is testamentary, as there will be occasions where the applicable income tax rate in the trust will be lower than the rate on the income applicable to the beneficiary. Where subsection 105(2) does apply, and it would be more efficient to have the income taxed in the hands of the trust, the trustees can employ a designation under subsection 104(13.1) to have the income taxed in the trust.[40]

---

the property; this probably extends to life interests established by provincial and territorial statute in homestead and dower legislation).

37 Subsection 105(2), "such part of an amount...as is reasonable in the circumstances...."; see M.N.R., Technical Interpretation 2003-0047727, *supra*, note 25 (portion of upkeep in income when only portion of property used for personal residence).
38 See heading 2 in this Chapter 4 entitled, "Income in the Form of Benefits Conferred by the Trust."
39 See *e.g.* M.N.R., Technical Interpretation 9311945, *supra*, note 27 (will providing for life tenancy in home for spouse and for upkeep to be paid from estate income) and M.N.R., Technical News No. 11 (September 30, 1997) (at discussion under title "Taxable Benefit for Use of Personal-use Property").
40 M.N.R., Interpretation Bulletin IT-342R, "Trusts – Income Payable to Beneficiaries" (March 21, 1990), at paragraph 4; M.N.R., Technical Interpretation 9501395, "Spousal Trust – Subsection 104(13.1)" (May 2, 1995).

PART II — TAXATION OF TRUSTS AND BENEFICIARIES

4. Income Designations under 104(13.1) and 104(13.2)

Income paid out to a beneficiary of a trust is generally deducted from the income of the trust and included in the income of the beneficiary. As an exception, the Act contains provisions that allow income to be paid out to an individual while a designation is made under which the income is retained and taxed in the hands of the trust rather than the hands of the individual who actually received it.[41] The intent behind these subsections is described in detail in the following paragraphs.

Subsection 104(13.1) provides a mechanism for a trust to designate to its beneficiaries, their respective shares of that portion of the trust's actual income distributions which have not been deducted in calculating its income for the year. Such designated amounts are deemed not to have been paid or payable in the year by the trust for the purposes of subsections 104(13) and 105(2), with the result that such amounts will neither be deductible to the trust nor taxable in the hands of the beneficiaries.

Subsection 104(13.2) contemplates the situation where a trust has a non-capital loss carryforward from a prior taxation year and current taxable capital gains. In such circumstances, the trust may choose not to deduct the full amount to which it is entitled under subsection 104(6) in order to allow the non-capital loss carryforward to absorb the current taxable capital gain. The designation in subsection 104(13.2) allows the trust to designate in respect of its capital beneficiaries, their respective shares of the portion of the potential deduction under subsection 104(6) or, such amount used in the designation under subsection 104(13.1). Such amount designated under subsection 104(13.2) reduces the amount of taxable capital gains otherwise included in the beneficiary's income pursuant to subsection 104(21).[42]

---

41 Subsections 104(13.1) and (13.2).
42 M.N.R., Department of Finance Commentary (Consolidated Explanatory Notes), "Amounts deemed not paid" (En June 1988 [S.C. 1988, c. 55 (Bill C-139)]; see also M.N.R., Interpretation Bulletin IT-381R3, "Trusts – Capital Gains and Losses and the Flow-Through of Taxable Capital Gains to Beneficiaries" (February 14, 1997), at paragraph 18.

CHAPTER 4 — TAXATION OF BENEFICIARIES

Tax planning based on designations to retain income is employed for the most part in dealing with testamentary trusts. Since a testamentary trust is taxed under graduated tax rates, there will be occasions where income will be taxed at lower marginal rates in the trust, as opposed to including and having such income taxed at higher rates in the hands of an income beneficiary. Even where the tax rates are the same, there may still be an advantage gained in designating income as income of a testamentary trust, where doing so avoids the necessity of paying installment tax on the income if it were taxed in the hands of the beneficiary.

Less use is made of designated income in the case of *inter vivos* trusts. Such trusts pay income taxes at top federal and provincial marginal rates and, as a result, there is generally little reason to look for opportunities to tax income as trust income within the trust, rather than in the hands of the beneficiary on her T1 Return. The designated income provisions of the Act will still be useful however, where the *inter vivos* trust enjoys lower marginal tax rates than would apply to a beneficiary, as would be the case when the beneficiary resides in a high tax rate jurisdiction, such as Ontario, and the trust resides in a low tax rate jurisdiction, such as Alberta.

The use of income designations for pure income splitting has been sanctioned.[43] The Tax Court of Canada has also allowed taxpayers to amend returns, retroactively and without any time limitations, to take advantage of income designations and seek refunds.[44] However, CRA appears to take the continuing position that an income designation under the Act may be amended, filed late or revoked only in certain circumstances, as where an honest mistake was made, including situations where a taxpayer was not aware that the designation was available, or where a designation was filed that results in unintended tax consequences, and where remedial action is pursued by the taxpayer on a timely basis.[45] Notwithstanding the fact that the beneficiary actually

---

43 *Lussier v. R.* (1999), [2000] 2 C.T.C. 2147, 99 D.T.C. 1029 (Fr.), 2000 D.T.C. 1677 (Eng.), 32 E.T.R. (2d) 95, 1999 CarswellNat 1427, 1999 CarswellNat 2730 (T.C.C. [General Procedure]), at paragraphs 47 to 49.
44 *Lussier v. R.*, *ibid.*, at paragraphs 34 and 35.
45 M.N.R., Technical Interpretation 2000-0000385, "104(13.1) Designations" (September 29, 2000).

PART II — TAXATION OF TRUSTS AND BENEFICIARIES

receives the income and uses it for her own purposes, it is still taxed on the trust return if the subsection 104(13.1) designation is made.[46] A designation will not taint a spousal trust, even where the spouse is the sole trustee and beneficiary,[47] and regardless of whether the spousal trust is testamentary or *inter vivos*,[48] as the spouse's entitlement to the income is not altered in any of those circumstances by the trustee's decision to tax the income on the trust return. An income designation can still be used in the context of a spousal trust where the income has been capitalized in the trust by the spouse as a result of a written disclaimer of the income by the spouse.[49] When an estate is wound up in its first twelve months, and the income of the estate is otherwise treated as payable to the beneficiaries, designations under subsections 104(13.1) and (13.2) can be used to ensure that the income and taxable capital gains are taxed within the estate and not as income to the beneficiaries.[50] The designations appear to be available for income deemed to be income of beneficiaries under the age of twenty-one pursuant to subsection 104(18) of the Act.[51]

In terms of limitations, the designation is only available to a trust that is resident in Canada throughout the taxation year and is subject to Part I tax.[52] A designation is not possible in respect of a death benefit received by an estate or trust.[53] Also, the use of an income designation may interfere with other efforts to use the preferred beneficiary elec-

---

46 M.N.R., Technical Interpretation 9501395, *supra*, note 40.
47 M.N.R., Technical Interpretation 9501395, *supra*, note 40.
48 M.N.R., Technical Interpretation 9501395, *supra*, note 40 (dealing with a testamentary spousal trust); and M.N.R., Technical Interpretation 9230425, "Spousal Trust" (February 15, 1993) (dealing with an *inter vivos* spousal trust).
49 M.N.R., Technical Interpretation 9236345, "Spousal Trust and 104(13.1) Designation" (April 8, 1993); M.N.R., Technical Interpretation 9230425, *ibid*.
50 M.N.R., Technical Interpretation 9526815, "Executor's Year Passing Beneficial Ownership Estate" (May 24, 1996).
51 M.N.R., Interpretation Bulletin IT-381R3, *supra*, note 42 at paragraph 17. See also 4.2(b) of Chapter 2 entitled, "Pent Up Income Attributed to Minors under 104(18)" for additional commentary.
52 M.N.R., Interpretation Bulletin IT-342R, *supra*, note 42 at paragraph 4.
53 M.N.R., Technical Interpretation 9606825, "Death Benefit and 104(13.1)" (November 14, 1996).

CHAPTER 4 — TAXATION OF BENEFICIARIES

tion,[54] and while an income designation can be made when the beneficiary is a corporation, the income subject to the designation cannot be added to the corporation's safe income or safe income on hand.[55] An income designation cannot be made under subsection 104(13.2) for a non-resident beneficiary.[56] Part XII.2 of the Act[57] imposes a special tax on designated income, but only where the beneficiary is a member of a limited class of persons, primarily including non-residents and entities not subject to tax by virtue of subsection 149(1),[58] and not if the trust is a testamentary trust throughout the year (as Part XII.2 tax does not apply to testamentary trusts).[59]

Income designations under subsections 104(13.1) and (13.2) are not available to amateur athlete trusts, employee trusts, master trusts, related segregated fund trusts, retirement compensation arrangement trusts, trusts governed by deferred income plans, trusts governed by eligible funeral arrangements or cemetery care trusts.[60] If the trust is what is commonly called a "commercial trust" rather than a personal trust, then income designations under subsections 104(13.1) or (13.2) will reduce the adjusted cost base for the beneficiary's capital interest in the trust.[61]

After a designation has been made under subsections 104(13.1) or (13.2), and the tax on the income becomes payable by the trust, the beneficiary may agree to pay that tax liability for the trust, and that payment can be made by any one of the following methods:

- by reimbursing the trustee;

- by providing a cheque payable to the Receiver General; or

---

54 M.N.R., Interpretation Bulletin IT-394R2, "Preferred Beneficiary Election" (June 21, 1999), at paragraph 12.
55 M.N.R., Technical Interpretation 2003-0012075, "Safe Income and 104(13.1) Designation" (June 3, 2003).
56 M.N.R., Technical Interpretation 9708655, "Pre-1972 Spousal Trust – Deemed Disposition – 104(13.2)" (September 3, 1997).
57 Sections 210 through 210.2; also see M.N.R., Interpretation Bulletin IT-342R, *supra*, note 40 at paragraph 8.
58 Section 210.
59 Section 210.1(a).
60 Subsection 108(1), definition of "trust."
61 M.N.R., Interpretation Bulletin IT-342R, *supra*, note 40 at paragraph 5.

PART II — TAXATION OF TRUSTS AND BENEFICIARIES

- by receiving a net amount from the trustee reflecting the beneficiary's share of the income less the amount of the tax payable by the trust.[62]

Payment of that tax liability will not cause a testamentary trust to lose its status as a testamentary trust.[63] Further, for *inter vivos* trusts that were established before June 18, 1971, before top marginal rates became applicable to the income of such trusts,[64] the payment of taxes by the beneficiary will not amount to a gift that would otherwise have the effect of disqualifying them from grandfathering under the old rate structure.[65]

5. The Preferred Beneficiary Election

5.1 Summary

Until 1995, the preferred beneficiary election existed as a valuable tax planning mechanism, which allowed the trust to tax income in the beneficiary's hands without having to actually distribute the income from the trust.[66]

The election was generally available where a beneficiary was the settlor, spouse or former spouse of the settlor, or a child, grandchild or spouse of any such person. The Act provides for an extended meaning of the definition "child of the settlor"[67] to include:

- a person of whom the settlor is the natural parent, whether the child was born either in or outside of marriage;

---

62 M.N.R., Interpretation Bulletin IT-381R3, *supra*, note 42 at paragraph 19.
63 M.N.R., Technical Interpretation 9307775, "Election Under 104(13.1) – Trusts" (March 22, 1993); M.N.R., Technical Interpretation 9336735, "Testamentary Trust – IT-381R2" (February 23, 1994).
64 Subsection 122(2).
65 M.N.R., Interpretation Bulletin IT-381R3, *supra*, note 42 at paragraph 19; M.N.R., Technical Interpretation 9230425, "Spousal Trust" (February 15, 1993).
66 Subsection 104(12), amended by S.C. 1996, c. 21 s. 18(7) applicable to trust taxation years commencing after 1995.
67 Subsection 252(1). See also M.N.R., Interpretation Bulletin IT-394R2, *supra*, note 54 at paragraph 6.

CHAPTER 4 — TAXATION OF BENEFICIARIES

- a person wholly dependent upon the settlor for support, and who is presently, or was immediately prior to reaching the age of nineteen, under the custody and control of the settlor; and

- a child of the settlor's spouse, an adopted child of the settlor, or the spouse of a child of the settlor.

The preferred beneficiary election thereby allowed the trust to build and accumulate capital, while at the same time enjoying the tax rates at the marginal tax brackets of the beneficiaries, many of whom paid little or no tax on the designated trust income.

The Department of Finance determined that this income-splitting tool was being abusively employed and therefore introduced amendments in 1995 to curb the availability of the preferred beneficiary election.[68]

After 1995, the preferred beneficiary election is available only for a trust with a disabled beneficiary,[69] if the beneficiary is related to the settlor of the trust and the trust otherwise qualifies.

The beneficiary individual must meet the criteria listed, which is strictly interpreted and enforced by CRA.

- The individual must have a severe and prolonged mental or physical impairment.

- The effects of the impairment must be such that the individual's ability to perform a basic activity of daily living is markedly restricted or would be markedly restricted but for therapy that:

  ○ is essential to sustain a vital function of the individual,

  ○ is required to be administered at least three times each week for a total duration averaging not less that fourteen hours a week,

---

68 Subsection 104(14), amended by S.C. 1996, c. 21, s. 18(8), applicable to trust taxation years commencing after 1995.
69 See paragraphs 118.3(1)(a) and 118.3(1)(b).

PART II — TAXATION OF TRUSTS AND BENEFICIARIES

- ○ cannot reasonably be expected to be of significant benefit to persons who are not so impaired.

- A medical doctor (or in the case of certain specific impairments, specific other professionals as listed in subparagraphs 118.3(1)(a.2)(i) through (v)) must certify in prescribed form that the impairment is such that the individual's ability to perform a basic activity of daily living is markedly restricted (or would be but for therapy referred to above). The prescribed form must be filed with the Minister of National Revenue.

In addition, an avoidance rule in the definition of accumulating income in subsection 108(1) provides that in calculating the accumulating income, the trust must claim the greatest amount it is entitled to as a deduction for amounts paid to the other beneficiaries in computing its income for the year. This requirement prevents trusts that have a preferred beneficiary from distributing cash to other income beneficiaries (who may be in higher tax rates) without deducting those distributions from the trust income. This practice allows the additional income to form part of the trust's accumulating income available for the preferred beneficiary election.

In general, the rules in subsections 104(14) and (15) provide that the amount of a preferred beneficiary election must be in respect of the "allocable amount." In a testamentary trust or *inter vivos* discretionary trust, this can be up to all of the income of the trust. However, there are special rules to determine the allocable amount in the case of spousal trusts and, pursuant to recent amendments, alter ego trusts, joint spousal trusts, common-law partner and post-1971 common-law partner trusts.

Thus the use of the preferred beneficiary election in most trust circumstances is severely curtailed unless there are disabled beneficiaries. Many *inter vivos* trusts have been set up to allow the trustees to distribute income to various beneficiaries. These trusts permitted income to be divided (or sprinkled) among the beneficiaries. In such typical *inter vivos* trusts, the preferred beneficiary election has been eliminated. This then puts greater emphasis on the need for other alternatives and raises questions as to what one does with current discretionary *inter vivos* trusts which may be in existence.

CHAPTER 4 — TAXATION OF BENEFICIARIES

If a beneficiary suffers a disability that qualifies under the income tax definition indicated above, then the trust will be able to make a preferred beneficiary election in respect of that individual. In order to qualify, the beneficiary must be a "preferred beneficiary" as that term is defined in subsection 108(1). A preferred beneficiary of a trust for a particular taxation year is an individual who is resident in Canada at the end of the year, and who is:

- the settlor of the trust (generally the person who creates the trust);

- the spouse or common-law partner or former spouse or common-law partner of the settlor; or

- a child, grandchild or great grandchild of the settlor or spouse or common-law partner of any such person.

Where available, the purpose of the preferred beneficiary election is to allow income to be deducted from the trust and to be taxed on the tax return of the preferred beneficiary, notwithstanding that the income is retained in the trust and never becomes payable to the beneficiary. This situation can be a significant advantage with an *inter vivos* trust in which income would otherwise be taxed at the highest rates[70] and with a testamentary trust where the trust income is high enough to push the trust into higher tax brackets than the beneficiary. Care should be taken on a province-by-province and territory-by-territory basis to ensure that the notional income that is to be attributed to the beneficiary under the preferred beneficiary election will not unwittingly endanger the beneficiary's eligibility to income assistance or programming for the disabled.

Under the *Family Benefits Act* and Regulations,[71] eligibility depends on rather stringent liquid assets (financial property) and income tests. For a single person with a disability, only $3,000 in liquid assets is allowed a new applicant and only $3,300 for current recipients. Even where the person qualifies under the liquid assets test, most other types of income are deducted dollar-for-dollar from the monthly cheque.

---

70 Subsection 122(1).
71 R.S.O. 1990, c. F.2 and R.R.O. 1990, Reg. 366.

PART II — TAXATION OF TRUSTS AND BENEFICIARIES

5.2 Determining if the Preferred Beneficiary Election is Available

(a) Considerations Relating to Characteristics of Trusts

The preferred beneficiary election is generally available for personal trusts, but is not available for trusts such as amateur athlete trusts, employee trusts, master trusts, related segregated fund trusts, deferred income plan trusts and trusts commonly referred to as commercial trusts.[72]

The word "settlor" is defined under the Act in a way that will sometimes result in a trust that has no settlor for income tax purposes.[73] A preferred beneficiary election is not possible for a trust that has no settlor, which can occur in the case of an *inter vivos* trust that has more than one contributor, either at the outset (except in the case of a joint partner or joint spousal trust) or by later contribution.[74]

(b) Considerations Relating to Beneficiary

The beneficiary in question must suffer from a mental or physical handicap of a character sufficient to qualify under the definition of a preferred beneficiary.[75]

To qualify as a preferred beneficiary, the individual must also be either the settlor of the trust or must be related to the settlor of the trust.[76]

---

72 Subsection 108(1), definition of "trust." Also see M.N.R., Interpretation Bulletin IT-394R2, *supra*, note 54 at paragraph 2 for an expanded listing of trusts excluded from the application of the preferred beneficiary election. The trusts within the scope of this book have the preferred beneficiary election available to them.
73 Subsection 108(1), definition of "settlor."
74 M.N.R., Interpretation Bulletin IT-394R2, *supra*, note 54 at paragraph 5.
75 Subsection 108(1), definition of "preferred beneficiary." See M.N.R., Interpretation Bulletin IT-394R2, *supra*, note 54 at paragraphs 3 and 4.
76 Subsection 108(1), definition of "preferred beneficiary." See M.N.R., Interpretation Bulletin IT-394R2, *supra*, note 54 at paragraph 3.

CHAPTER 4 — TAXATION OF BENEFICIARIES

A beneficiary is generally considered related if she is the settlor's spouse or former spouse, child, grandchild or great grandchild, and will also be related if she is a spouse (but not a former spouse) of a child, grandchild or great grandchild of the settlor. The definition of child carries an extended meaning and includes a child of the settlor's spouse (whether adopted by the settlor or not), any child who is wholly dependent on the settlor and under the custody and control of the settlor (even if the child is neither the adoptive or biological child of the settlor), or a son-in-law or daughter-in-law.[77] The definition of spouse is also given an extended meaning and will include a common-law spouse, whether same- or opposite-sex, if cohabiting with the settlor in a conjugal relationship for a year or more, or whether cohabiting or not if they have a child together, natural or by adoption.[78]

The word "beneficiary" is defined broadly under the Act.[79] The preferred beneficiary election will be available if the beneficiary is a capital beneficiary of the trust regardless of whether she is an income beneficiary, if the beneficiary has an interest limited to a future right to income or capital from the trust, regardless of whether that future right is subject to some contingency that may or may not occur, or if the beneficiary's right to income is subject to a discretion that may or may not be exercised in her favour.[80] The allocable amount will be "nil" however, effectively making the preferred beneficiary election unavailable for a beneficiary who has a right to income that will not arise until the death of another beneficiary who has a capital interest in the trust but has no income interest in the trust.[81]

If a trust has multiple preferred beneficiaries, the trustees and the beneficiaries can make elections and divide the accumulated income in

---

77 See M.N.R., Interpretation Bulletin IT-394R2, *supra*, note 54 at paragraph 6.
78 See M.N.R., Interpretation Bulletin IT-394R2, *supra*, note 54 at paragraph 7.
79 Subsection 108(1), definition of "beneficiary," and see subsection 248(25). Also see M.N.R., Interpretation Bulletin IT-394R2, *supra*, note 54 at paragraph 16.
80 For an interesting, but somewhat dated analysis of CRA positions on this point, see Wolfe D. Goodman, "Revocable *Inter Vivos* Trusts" (1994) 13 E.T.P.J. 372, at pages 373-374.
81 M.N.R., Interpretation Bulletin IT-394R2, "Preferred Beneficiary Election" (June 21, 1999), at paragraph 16. See the discussion under the title "Calculating Beneficiary Income under the Preferred Beneficiary Election" at 5.3(b) of Chapter 4.

PART II — TAXATION OF TRUSTS AND BENEFICIARIES

any way they wish among some, all or none of those beneficiaries,[82] and the allocation of income by the trust can be inconsistent in doing so from year to year.[83] The elected amount does not have to be paid or become payable to any preferred beneficiary, now or in the future.[84]

5.3 Calculations Under the Preferred Beneficiary Election

(a) *Calculating the Deduction*

The deduction is calculated under subsection 104(12). The trust is entitled to deduct the total amount designated to beneficiaries,[85] subject to a maximum not exceeding the accumulating income of the trust for the year.[86]

The accumulating income[87] of the trust for the year is the income of the trust calculated while ignoring any of the adjustments described below which would otherwise be taken into account in determining the income of the trust for income tax purposes.[88]

---

82 M.N.R., Interpretation Bulletin IT-394R2, *ibid.* at paragraphs 15 and 21. Regulation 2800(3) currently suggests a forced allocation among the class of preferred beneficiaries but that regulation was in place to guide the operation of an earlier version of 104(15) and is based on and refers to former subparagraph 104(15)(c) removed from the Act by 1996 c. 21. Thus, the positions set out in the following documents no longer appear to be relevant: M.N.R., Advance Income Tax Ruling 9524483, "104(14)" (March 13, 1996); and M.N.R., Technical Interpretation 9314345, "Preferred Beneficiary Election" (September 17, 1993).
83 M.N.R., Interpretation Bulletin IT-394R2, *supra*, note 81 at paragraph 21.
84 M.N.R., Interpretation Bulletin IT-394R2, *supra*, note 81 at paragraph 21.
85 Paragraph 104(12)(a) (the total amount designated to beneficiaries being the amount calculated as the income of the beneficiaries in the next section of text. See 5.3(b) of this chapter entitled, "Calculating Beneficiary Income under the Preferred Beneficiary Election."
86 Paragraph 104(12)(b).
87 Subsection 108(1), definition of "accumulating income." More generally see M.N.R., Interpretation Bulletin IT-394R2, *supra*, note 81 at paragraphs 8 to 12.
88 Listed in paragraphs (a) and (c) of subsection 108(1), definition of "accumulating income."

CHAPTER 4 — TAXATION OF BENEFICIARIES

- *Alter Ego, Joint Spousal and Joint Partner Trusts* – Ignore any amounts that might be triggered by virtue of paragraphs 104(4)(a) and (a.1) on the death of the settlor of an alter ego trust or by the death of the surviving spouse or common-law partner in a joint spousal trust or a joint partner trust.[89]

- *Trust Holding NISA Account* – Ignore any amounts that might be triggered by virtue of subsection 104(5.1) on the death of the surviving spouse or common-law partner for a trust holding an interest in a NISA account.

- *Canadian Resource Property* – Ignore any amounts that might be triggered by virtue of subsection 104(5.2) for a trust holding Canadian resource property.[90]

- *PBE Deductions* – Ignore any amounts that might be deducted from the income of the trust by virtue of the proposed exercise of the preferred beneficiary election under subsection 104(12).

- *Capital Gains* – Ignore any amounts that might be triggered by virtue of subsection 107(4).[91]

- *NISA Receipts* – Ignore any amounts that might be included as a NISA receipt by virtue of subsection 12(10.2) except to the extent that subsection 12(10.2) applies to amounts paid to a trust to which paragraph 70(6.1)(b) applies and before the death of the spouse or common-law partner referred to in that paragraph.[92]

The calculation of accumulating income must also proceed as if the maximum deduction under subsection 104(6) were taken on account of income payable to beneficiaries during the year.[93] At least two impli-

---

[89] Also see M.N.R., Interpretation Bulletin IT-394R2, *supra*, note 81 at paragraph 10.
[90] Also see M.N.R., Interpretation Bulletin IT-394R2, *supra*, note 81 at paragraph 10.
[91] See generally M.N.R., Interpretation Bulletin IT-394R2, *supra*, note 81 at paragraphs 9 and 10.
[92] Also see M.N.R., Interpretation Bulletin IT-394R2, *supra*, note 81 at paragraph 11.
[93] Subsection 108(1), definition of "accumulating income" at paragraph (b).

PART II — TAXATION OF TRUSTS AND BENEFICIARIES

cations flow from this result. First, the use of the preferred beneficiary election will be inconsistent with the designation of income under subsection 104(13.1) of the Act.[94] Second, income deemed to be payable to a minor beneficiary under subsection 104(18) will reduce the accumulating income of the trust and limit the extent to which the preferred beneficiary election can be made.[95]

(b) Calculating Beneficiary Income Under the Preferred Beneficiary Election

The income to be included on the beneficiary's tax return is calculated under subsection 104(14). The amount of income to be included in the beneficiary's income will be such part of the accumulating income (discussed above) as may be jointly designated in the election, but is subject to a maximum in that it cannot exceed the allocable amount for the preferred beneficiary in respect of the trust for the year.[96]

The allocable amount for a preferred beneficiary is calculated under subsection 104(15). The allocable amount will be equal to the accumulating income of the trust, subject to two exceptions.

Certain kinds of trusts allow assets to be transferred into the trust without triggering capital gains. These include alter ego trusts, joint spousal and common-law partner trusts, post-1971 spousal and common-law partner trusts or trusts described in the definition of a "pre-

---

94 M.N.R., Interpretation Bulletin IT-394R2, *supra*, note 81 at paragraph 12. In other words, if income is designated under 104(13.1) it will reduce the amount of accumulating income available for the use of the preferred beneficiary election, and if all of the income were designated to the trust none would be available for the preferred beneficiary election.
95 M.N.R., Interpretation Bulletin IT-394R2, *supra*, note 81 at paragraph 8.
96 Subsection 104(14). Also see generally M.N.R., Interpretation Bulletin IT-394R2, *supra*, note 81 at paragraphs 13 to 16 (in theory, if there are multiple beneficiaries, each could have the whole or part of the allocable amount designated to their T1s, and thereby have allocable amounts totalling in excess of the accumulating income, but CRA points out that this is not advantageous as the deduction available to the trust will always be limited to the amount of the accumulating income of the trust).

CHAPTER 4 — TAXATION OF BENEFICIARIES

1972 spousal trust."[97] In each of these instances the triggering of gains is deferred until the later death of a beneficiary, the settlor in the case of an alter ego trust, or one of the spouses or the surviving spouse or partner in each of the other instances. If that beneficiary is alive at the end of the trust's taxation year, then the allocable amount is equal to the whole of the accumulating income of the trust.[98] This means that the preferred beneficiary election is freely available provided the beneficiary is alive for the whole of the year. If that beneficiary has passed away, whether the settlor of an alter ego trust or the surviving spouse or partner in each of the other instances, then the allocable amount is "nil."[99] This means that the preferred beneficiary election is not available in the year of death when capital gains would normally be triggered in the trust and thus cannot be used to export the gains from the trust to the terminal tax return of the deceased beneficiary.

Another exception occurs where the beneficiary's interest in the trust is solely contingent on the death of another beneficiary, and that other beneficiary has a capital interest in the trust and does not have an income interest in the trust. The allocable amount for the beneficiary will be "nil" under those circumstances.

5.4 The Mechanics of Making the Preferred Beneficiary Election

The election must be filed within ninety days of the end of the trust's taxation year.[100] Elections cannot be filed late, or be amended or revoked outside of that ninety day time frame except in circumstances considered to be outside of the control of the beneficiary and the trustee.[101] If the elections are filed late, they will be subject to a $100 penalty for each complete month overdue.[102] However, if elections are being made in connection with the capital gains exemption under subsections 110.6(25), (26) or (27), there may be an opportunity to file late on the

---

97 Subsection 108(1).
98 Subparagraph 104(15)(a)(i).
99 Subparagraph 104(15)(a)(ii).
100 Income Tax Regulations, Part XXVIII, Reg. 2800(2).
101 M.N.R., Interpretation Bulletin IT-394R2, *supra*, note 81 at paragraph 23.
102 M.N.R., Interpretation Bulletin IT-394R2, *supra*, note 81 at paragraph 24.

PART II — TAXATION OF TRUSTS AND BENEFICIARIES

preferred beneficiary election or amend or revoke an earlier election,[103] and in those circumstances any late filed preferred beneficiary election is deemed to have been made on time,[104] and a revoked preferred beneficiary election is deemed never to have been made.[105]

The election itself is made by filing two statements in prescribed form.[106] The forms must be signed by the preferred beneficiary or, if the beneficiary is unable to do so, by the legal guardian of the beneficiary's property.[107] Parents are normally the legal guardians of the property of their infant children by operation of provincial law. Where parents are joint legal guardians of a child's property, both should sign the election and if either parent refuses or fails to do so, the election may not be validly made.[108] One of the statements must be signed by the trustee or trustees of the trust or, if one trustee is authorized by the others to sign and file the election, then by the trustee designated for that purpose.[109]

Failure to file the election on time or in prescribed form is frequently the subject of litigation, which is usually lost by taxpayers.[110]

---

103 Subsection 104(14.01).
104 Paragraph 104(14.02)(b).
105 Paragraph 104(14.02)(b).
106 Income Tax Regulations, Part XXVIII, Reg. 2800(2). Also see M.N.R., Interpretation Bulletin IT-394R2, *supra*, note 81 at paragraph 18.
107 M.N.R., Interpretation Bulletin IT-394R2, *supra*, note 81 at paragraph 19.
108 M.N.R., Technical Interpretation 9726707, "Dispute Re Preferred Beneficiary Election" (October 31, 1997).
109 M.N.R., Interpretation Bulletin IT-394R2, *supra*, note 81 at paragraph 20.
110 *Muzich Family Trust v. Minister of National Revenue*, 93 D.T.C. 314, [1993] 1 C.T.C. 2330, 1993 CarswellNat 885 (T.C.C.); *Johnston Family 1991 Trust v. Minister of National Revenue*, [1999] 4 C.T.C. 75, 29 E.T.R. (2d) 256, 171 F.T.R. 57, 99 D.T.C. 5508, 1999 CarswellNat 1394 (T.D.); *McNabb Family Trust v. R.*, 98 D.T.C. 6385, [1998] 3 C.T.C. 264, 1998 CarswellNat 764 (Fed. T.D.); *McNabb Family Trust v. R.* (1997), [1998] 1 C.T.C. 330, 19 E.T.R. (2d) 231, 140 F.T.R. 160 (note), 221 N.R. 180, 1997 CarswellNat 1763, 98 D.T.C. 6001 (C.A.); *Muscillo v. R.*, 98 D.T.C. 1548, [1998] 2 C.T.C. 2896, 1998 CarswellNat 358 (T.C.C.).

CHAPTER 4 — TAXATION OF BENEFICIARIES

5.5 Miscellaneous Considerations in Employing the Preferred Beneficiary Election

A trust may allocate the net taxable gains (including those arising as a result of the twenty-one year deemed disposition rule) to a preferred beneficiary by making a designation under subsection 104(21).[111]

A trust may designate foreign source income to a preferred beneficiary under subsection 104(22).[112]

A trust may designate taxable dividends to a preferred beneficiary under the flow-through provisions pursuant to subsection 104(19).[113]

6. Non-Resident Beneficiaries

Paragraph 212(1)(c) of the Act imposes a Part XIII tax on payments to a non-resident beneficiary, equal to 25%[114] of all income from an estate or trust payable to that person as a beneficiary[115] under subsection 104(13).[116] Certain other amounts are included and there are also exceptions.[117] The Part XIII tax must be withheld by the trustees and remitted directly to the Receiver General.[118]

---

111 M.N.R., Interpretation Bulletin IT-394R2, *supra*, note 81 at paragraph 9; see also M.N.R., Interpretation Bulletin IT-381R3, "Trusts — Capital Gains and Losses and the Flow-Through of Taxable Capital Gains to Beneficiaries" (February 14, 1997), at paragraph 3.
112 M.N.R., Interpretation Bulletin IT-201R2, "Foreign Tax Credit – Trust and Beneficiaries" (February 12, 1996), at paragraph 1.
113 M.N.R., Interpretation Bulletin IT-524, "Trusts – Flow-Through of Taxable Dividends to a Beneficiary – After 1987" (March 16, 1990), at paragraph 1.
114 Paragraph 212(1)(c). See also M.N.R., Interpretation Bulletin IT-465R, "Non-Resident Beneficiaries of Trusts" (September 19, 1985), at paragraph 2.
115 See also commentary in heading 10 of Chapter 14 entitled, "Schedule 10 – Part XII.2 Tax and Part XIII Non-Resident Withholding Tax."
116 For a discussion of when income is "payable" to a beneficiary see heading 1 of Chapter 4 entitled, "Determining Whether Income is Payable."
117 For a detailed commentary by CRA see M.N.R., Interpretation Bulletin IT-465R, *supra*, note 114.
118 Subsection 215(1).

Chapter 5
Attributions to Contributor Under Subsection 75(2)

1. General Considerations

Where a trust receives property from a person, the income, loss, taxable capital gains or allowable capital losses on that property, while it is held by the trust, may in some circumstances be attributed to the contributor of the property pursuant to subsection 75(2).[1] Where attribution of income occurs, the income is not declared by the trust on the T3 or by the beneficiaries on their T1s, notwithstanding that the income might have been retained in the trust or paid out to the beneficiaries.[2] Where all of the income of the trust is attributed to the contributor, then a T3 should still be filed.[3]

While attribution will take place not just on income but on losses, taxable capital gains and allowable capital losses, the majority of material published on point deals with income.

---

1 See generally M.N.R., Interpretation Bulletin IT-369R, "Attribution of Trust Income to Settlor" (March 12, 1990).
2 M.N.R., Interpretation Bulletin IT-369R, *ibid.* at paragraph 10 (suggesting however that the rules may be different for non-resident beneficiaries); see also M.N.R., Technical Interpretation 9411115, "Attribution" (April 28, 1994).
3 M.N.R., T3 Trust Guide 2003 (T4013(E) Rev.03), at p. 2. This appears to be a change in position from M.N.R., Technical Interpretation 2001-0116045, "Trusts/First Nations/T3 Returns" (January 16, 2002) (suggesting that a T3 need not always be filed when all of the income is subject to 75(2), in at least some circumstances).

PART II — TAXATION OF TRUSTS AND BENEFICIARIES

Attribution will take place under subsection 75(2) in any one of three circumstances:[4]

1. where, under the terms of the trust, property may revert to the person who contributed it (discussed below under the heading "Potential Reversion under Subsection 75(2)");

2. where, under the terms of the trust, property may be distributed to beneficiaries determined by the contributor at a time after the trust was created (discussed below under the heading "Control over Destination"); or

3. where under the terms of the trust, property may only be disposed of with the consent of, or at the direction of, the contributor while alive (discussed below under the heading "Gate Keeping").

2. Potential Reversion under Subsection 75(2)

Attribution will occur under subparagraph 75(2)(a)(i) if the property may, under the terms of the trust, revert to the contributor. This will be the case where the terms of the trust expressly provide for the return of the property to the contributor if a future contingency occurs,[5] or where a discretionary power is given to a person to select future recipients of capital and that power includes the ability to return capital to the contributor.[6] It does not apply, and attribution by virtue of potential reversion will not occur, by means of a beneficiary's discretion to make secondary gifts of capital after the capital has been distributed to them from the

---

4 M.N.R., Interpretation Bulletin IT-369R, *supra*, note 1 at paragraph 3.
5 M.N.R., Interpretation Bulletin IT-369R, *supra*, note 1 at paragraph 3 (property reverting to contributor under terms of trust if the beneficiaries collectively predecease the contributor).
6 M.N.R., Technical Interpretation 2003-0050671E5, "Attribution of Property Transferred to a Trust" (April 5, 2004) (spouse of contributor to maintain power to select future capital beneficiaries – but note that situation would be recognized as different if terms of trust forbade the spouse from selecting the contributor when exercising the power). Also see M.N.R., Technical Interpretation 2002-0162855, "Powers of Appointment" (April 25, 2003).

CHAPTER 5 — ATTRIBUTIONS TO CONTRIBUTOR

trust.[7] A person is always free to make gifts, while living or by testamentary instrument, from capital that has vested in him as outright owner. Having received property as a capital distribution or "gift" from a trust, an individual is free to use his discretion in making a second gift to whomever he chooses.

What constitutes reversion? If the legal and beneficial ownership of the property is returned to the original contributor or settlor, such case clearly amounts to reversion. If even a small part of the property reverts, or if a lesser capital interest is subject to potential reversion, such as a right to use a portion of the property, then the income from the whole of the property may be subject to attribution.[8]

3. Control Over Destination

Attribution will occur under subparagraph 75(2)(a)(ii) if the property can, under the terms of the trust, pass to other persons who are selected or determined by the contributor at a time subsequent to the creation of the trust.[9] Control over destination does not apply and attribution will

---

7 M.N.R., Technical Interpretation 2002-0139205, "75(2) Arising as Consequences of a Will" (July 22, 2002), clarifying M.N.R., Technical Interpretation 2002-0116535, "Subsection 75(2) Arising as Consequences of a Will" (February 19, 2002) (scenarios "1" and "2" – terms of *inter vivos* trust providing that capital to be distributed to beneficiary's estate on his death, and the mere fact beneficiary would be free to have made gift in will to contributor not suggested as sufficient to ground 75(2) attribution). Note that a distinction may be drawn if the terms of the trust indicate that the capital is to be distributed from the trust to the persons who happen to be entitled to the beneficiary's estate under the beneficiary's last will and testament as, in that scenario, the assets never leave the trust before their ultimate destination is settled under a power of appointment.

8 M.N.R., Technical Interpretation 2002-0118255 "Application of 75(2)" (June 10, 2002) (contributor settling apartment block into trust, but retaining potential right to use one suite; CRA expressing the position that the right to use a unit "would constitute a 'capital interest' in the trust ... which could, in certain circumstances, lead to the application of 75(2)(ii)(a);" interestingly, CRA expresses the view that the income or loss from the whole of the block would be attributed to the contributor, even though only a small capital interest would be subject to capital reversion).

9 M.N.R., Technical Interpretation 2002-0116535, *supra*, note 7 (scenarios "3" and "4" – terms of *inter vivos* trust stipulating that capital, at death of last named beneficiary, to be distributed as set out in settlor's last will and testament).

PART II — TAXATION OF TRUSTS AND BENEFICIARIES

not occur where the capital beneficiaries are a fixed collection of persons, who do not include the contributor, and this will generally remain the case even if the contributor is a trustee who has the power to select the amount of capital that goes to each of the capital beneficiaries.[10]

4. Gate Keeping

Attribution will occur under paragraph 75(2)(b) if the terms of the trust put the contributor in a gate keeping role by providing that the property shall not be disposed of by the trust except with the contributor's consent or in accordance with the contributor's direction. This will normally be the case where the contributor is the sole trustee of the trust.[11] It will also occur where the terms of the trust provide that decisions are to be made by majority but that the contributor-trustee must be part of that majority or where the terms of the trust indicate that the contributor must consent to or ratify the decisions of the trustees.[12] This will generally not apply and income will not be attributed where the contributor is one of two or more trustees of the trust who individually cannot unilaterally exert the control necessary to give the consent or direction.[13]

---

10 M.N.R., Technical Interpretation 2003-0050671E5, *supra*, note 6 (beneficiaries under trust being named persons other than settlor and the terms of trust not being susceptible to modification in that regard).

11 M.N.R., Technical Interpretation 2001-0110425, "75(2) When Settlor is Sole Trustee" (June 20, 2002) (settlor being sole trustee of trust, but not a beneficiary and with no power to add beneficiaries, and no possibility of reversion, but in a position to determine the amount of income or capital to be paid to individual beneficiaries, on stated grounds that "Where the settlor is the sole trustee of the trust, none of the trust's property can be disposed of without the settlor's consent or direction"); M.N.R., Technical Interpretation 1999-0013055, "75(2)(B) Where Settlor is Sole Trustee" (June 20, 2002) (contributor other than settlor being sole trustee of trust, but not a beneficiary and with no power to add beneficiaries, and no possibility of reversion, but in a position to determine the amount of income or capital to be paid to individual beneficiaries). Both interpretations issued on the same day.

12 M.N.R., Technical Interpretation 1999-0013055, *ibid.*; also see M.N.R., Technical Interpretation 9407905, "Reversion of Trust Property" (June 6, 1994) (terms of trust providing that all decisions require a majority vote and two trustees appointed, one being the contributor).

13 M.N.R., Technical Interpretation 2003-0050671E5, *supra*, note 6 ("When the settlor is one of two or more co-trustees ... and there are no specific terms

CHAPTER 5 — ATTRIBUTIONS TO CONTRIBUTOR

5. Considerations Relating to Contributor

The person who contributes the property does not have to be the settlor of the trust in order for attribution to occur under subsection 75(2).[14]

Attribution to the contributor will occur whether the contributor is a corporation or an individual.[15] The rules remain the same if the contributor is an Indian Band.[16]

The contributor has some measure of continuing control over attribution under subsection 75(2) and can, in some circumstances, take steps to end the attribution of income and "cure" the trust. Where the contributor is the sole trustee and attribution occurs under the gate keeping provisions of paragraph 75(2)(b), that attribution will normally end when the contributor resigns as trustee.[17] Where the terms of the

---

outlining how the trust property is to be dealt with, but rather the property is subject to standard terms ordinarily found in trust indentures, we accept that paragraph 75(2)(a)(ii) will generally not be applicable."); M.N.R., Technical Interpretation 1999-0013055, *supra*, note 11 (attribution not occurring where contributor is one of many trustees and decisions are required to be unanimous); M.N.R., Technical Interpretation 9717815, "Settlor/Trustee and Majority Decisions" (November 19, 1997) (attribution not occurring where trustees' decisions to be made by majority and settlor-trustee is not required to be a part of the majority).

14 M.N.R., Interpretation Bulletin IT-369R, *supra*, note 1 at paragraph 11. That position was reiterated more recently in M.N.R., Technical Interpretation 1999-0013055, *supra*, note 11. In trust law, the person referred to as the settlor of the trust is normally the person who contributes the initial property into the trust at its inception. A person who makes a second settlement or contribution of property may not be properly referred to as a "settlor" of the trust but risks attribution nonetheless. See 1.2(b) of Chapter 1 entitled, "The Settlor."

15 Subsection 75(2), applying to "persons"; M.N.R., Interpretation Bulletin IT-369R, *supra*, note 1 at paragraph 9.

16 M.N.R., Technical Interpretation 2002-0152353, "First Nations Settlement – Trust" (January 1, 2003); M.N.R., Technical Interpretation 2002-0127663, "Taxation of Indian Trust" (January 1, 2002); M.N.R., Technical Interpretation 2001-0116045, "Trusts/First Nations/T3 Returns" (January 16, 2002); M.N.R., Advance Income Tax Ruling 2000-0036443, "Taxation of Indian Trust" (October 3, 2000); M.N.R., Advance Income Tax Ruling. 1999-0005513, "Public Body Perform Function of Government" (January 1, 2000).

17 M.N.R., Technical Interpretation 2001-0110425, *supra*, note 11; M.N.R., Technical Interpretation 1999-0013055, *supra*, note 11.

PART II — TAXATION OF TRUSTS AND BENEFICIARIES

trust provide for the possible return of the property to the contributor and attribution occurs under the potential reversionary provisions of subparagraph 75(2)(a)(i), then that attribution will normally end when the contributor renounces any right to the reversion of the property and the terms of the trust are varied to extinguish the right of potential reversion in the future.[18]

Attribution does not occur or will end when the contributor dies.[19] Since the settlor of a testamentary trust is, by definition, a deceased person, subsection 75(2) will never apply to a testamentary trust.

The residency of the contributor of the property is also a consideration. Attribution only occurs during periods of time in which the contributor is a resident of Canada, and attribution will end as of the date of emigration,[20] if the contributor ceases to be a resident of Canada, and attribution will commence when the contributor becomes a resident of Canada.[21]

6. Factors Relating to Property

Where an original property or substituted property is sold, thereby generating proceeds of disposition, attribution will occur on any income or loss generated by the investment of the proceeds or any other non-business use of the proceeds.[22]

---

18 M.N.R., Technical Interpretation 2002-0118255, *supra*, note 8 (see "Scenario 2A" and note other possible tax consequences of variation).
19 Subsection 75(2), closing words state that attribution will take place during the "existence of the person" that contributed the property; also see M.N.R., Technical Interpretation 9815227, "Attribution to Settlor" (August 7, 1998) (attribution ending as of the date of death). Where the contributor is a corporation, the corporation will no longer be "in existence" and attribution will presumably end as of the date the corporation is dissolved.
20 M.N.R., Technical Interpretation 9815227, *ibid.*
21 See generally M.N.R., Interpretation Bulletin IT-369R, *supra*, note 1, at paragraph 4 (also noting that the residency of the contributor at the time of the contribution is not relevant, just during the year that the income under consideration becomes income of the trust); also see M.N.R., Technical Interpretation 2000-0052505, "Trust Becoming Resident in Canada" (October 23, 2001).
22 M.N.R., Interpretation Bulletin IT-369R, *supra*, note 1 at paragraph 7 (giving

CHAPTER 5 — ATTRIBUTIONS TO CONTRIBUTOR

Attribution will occur on income generated on both the property originally received by the trust from the contributor and on income generated on property substituted within the trust for the original property.[23]

7. Considerations Relating to Type of Income

The type of income or loss is significant in determining whether attribution will occur. Attribution does not occur on business income[24] or on losses from a business, even if the business operates with some or all of the property received from the contributor.[25] Attribution does not occur on "second-generation income" that arises where the property or its replacement property is invested and creates income (referred to as "first-generation income"), which first-generation income is invested, thereby creating second-generation income.[26] Attribution does occur on property income or losses[27] and on taxable capital gains and allowable capital losses from the actual or deemed disposition of the property or substituted property.[28]

---

example "if the property received from a person is a building which is subsequently disposed of for $100,000, yielding a taxable capital gain of $20,000, not only will the taxable capital gain attribute to that person but also so attributable will be any non-business income earned on the $100,000 proceeds").

23 Paragraph 75(2)(a); M.N.R., Interpretation Bulletin IT-369R, *supra*, note 1 at paragraph 3.
24 *Fraser v. Minister of National Revenue*, [1991] 1 C.T.C. 314, 41 F.T.R. 255, 91 D.T.C. 5123, 1991 CarswellNat 385 (T.D.), affirmed (1995), 190 N.R. 232, 95 D.T.C. 5684, 104 F.T.R. 319 (note), 1995 CarswellNat 1843 (C.A.).
25 M.N.R., Interpretation Bulletin IT-369R, *supra*, note 1 at paragraph 5.
26 M.N.R., Interpretation Bulletin IT-369R, "Attribution of Trust Income to Settlor" (March 12, 1990), at paragraph 6 (giving example "if the property received from a person is money which is deposited by the trust into a bank account, the interest on the initial deposit will attribute to [the contributor]... but the interest on the interest left to accumulate in the bank account will not attribute"). See also M.N.R., Technical Interpretation 2002-0127085, "No Double Taxation of Income Attributed" (April 2, 2002).
27 M.N.R., Technical Interpretation 2002-012676A, "Attribution of Net Profit Interest Royalty Income" (February 7, 2003), subsection 75(2) applying to royalty income from oil and gas property, provided that the income is property income).
28 M.N.R., Advance Income Tax Ruling 2002-0152353, *supra*, note 16 at ruling

PART II — TAXATION OF TRUSTS AND BENEFICIARIES

8. Miscellaneous Points Relating to Subsection 75(2) Attribution

Attribution to the contributor will occur whether the trust receives the property directly or indirectly from the contributor.[29]

Attribution does not occur as a result of a genuine loan made to a trust provided that the terms of the loan are outside of and independent from the terms of the trust.[30]

Where the transfer of property into the trust is not at arm's length, subsection 160(1) may apply to the trust and to the contributor at the same time as subsection 75(2). When that situation occurs, the contributor and the trust will be jointly and severally liable for certain taxes.[31]

Where a taxable capital gain is attributed to a person under subsection 75(2), he is eligible to claim the capital gains deduction under section 110.6 to the same extent as if he had realized the gain directly.[32]

The trustees of a trust to which subsection 75(2) applies may be in a position to "cure" the trust and end the attribution. A trust to which subsection 75(2) applies might be cured by varying its terms[33] or by

---

"D" (gains and losses triggered by deemed disposition included). See more generally the wording of 75(2) and M.N.R., Interpretation Bulletin IT-369R, *supra*, note 26.

29 Subparagraph 75(2)(a)(i); for an example of a brief analysis of when a gift might be direct or indirect see M.N.R., Technical Interpretation 9624905, "Attribution on Trust Property Gifted from Beneficiary, Indirect" (December 4, 1996).

30 M.N.R., Interpretation Bulletin IT-369R, *supra*, note 26 at paragraph 1; see also M.N.R., Technical Interpretation 9811115, "Attribution and Genuine Loan" (July 6, 1998). For an example where this may not work see M.N.R., Technical Interpretation 2000-0012557, "75(2) On Transfer of Shares to Trust" (July 17, 2000).

31 M.N.R., Interpretation Bulletin IT-369R, *supra*, note 26 at paragraph 12 (including the formula for the calculation of those taxes).

32 M.N.R., Interpretation Bulletin IT-369R, *supra*, note 26 at paragraph 8 (also see subsection 74.2(2)).

33 M.N.R., Technical Interpretation 2002-0118255, *supra*, note 18 (however other tax consequences of variation should be considered).

CHAPTER 5 — ATTRIBUTIONS TO CONTRIBUTOR

transferring the property in question to a second trust to which subsection 75(2) does not apply.[34]

Where the provisions of subsection 75(2) apply to a trust, the tax deferred "roll-out" provisions available under subsection 107(2), which are discussed in the next chapter, may not be available to the trust unless certain requirements are met.[35]

Where attribution has taken place under subsection 75(2), the trust can pay the taxes on behalf of the contributor and the trust appears able to do so without adverse tax consequences.[36]

---

[34] M.N.R., Technical Interpretation 2001-0067955, "Application of 75(2) and 107(4.1) to a Trust" (January 3, 2002) (other tax consequences and GAAR should be considered).

[35] Subsection 107(4.1); see paragraphs (c) and (d). Note also that subsection 107(4.2) was added by draft legislation released December 20, 2002, in respect of property distributed by the trust after December 20, 2002, to a beneficiary.

[36] M.N.R., Technical Interpretation 9411115, "Attribution" (April 28, 1994). A different conclusion might be drawn and the situation should be looked at carefully when dealing with a spousal trust, or an alter ego or joint partner trust.

Chapter 6
Dispositions of Trust Property

1. Capital Distributions to Beneficiaries

The manner in which a capital distribution from a trust is taxed differs depending on the type of trust. Where a distribution of capital arises from a personal trust, which is not a qualified spousal or common-law partner trust, the distribution will not create a realization of gains or losses. On the contrary, a final distribution from a spousal or common-law partner trust can be subject to tax on the deemed realization of trust property. This is outlined below.

1.1 Spousal or Common-Law Partner Trusts

Note that where the beneficiary is a spouse or common-law partner, trust property can "roll-out" to the spousal beneficiary at the adjusted cost base of the property,[1] unless the distribution is made in satisfaction of

---

1 Paragraph 106(2)(b). When the spouse or common-law partner dies there is a deemed disposition of trust assets at fair market value. However, a "post-1971 spousal trust" cannot deduct under paragraph 104(6)(b) the amount of any taxable capital gains arising in the year from deemed dispositions of trust property which occurs on the day on which the spousal or common-law partner dies, or when property is distributed to a beneficiary other than the spouse or common-law partner during her lifetime. See M.N.R., Interpretation Bulletin, IT-385R2 "Disposition of an Income Interest in a Trust" (May 17, 1991) at paragraphs 11 and 12. However, subsection 110.6(12) provides some relief in permitting the spousal or common-law partner trust to utilize the unused capital gains exemption of the

PART II — TAXATION OF TRUSTS AND BENEFICIARIES

the spouse or common-law partner's income interest in the trust,[2] which could occur as a result of death.

An exception to the rule in paragraph 106(2)(a) is contained under subsection 106(3), if capital is distributed to a spouse or common-law partner beneficiary in satisfaction of their income interest in the trust. This might occur, for example, if the trust was being terminated during the life of the spouse or common-law partner beneficiary, and the trust property is being distributed to other capital beneficiaries in proportion to their respective values of their interests in the trust, in addition to the distribution being made to the spouse or common-law partner. In such circumstances, the trust is deemed to have disposed of its property for fair market value and all of the beneficiaries are deemed to have acquired their respective shares of such property at a cost equal to that amount.

If trust property is distributed to a beneficiary other than the spouse or common-law partner, the distribution will be subject to a realization of gains or losses at the fair market value of the property at the time of distribution.[3]

Subsection 107(4) effectively provides that such trust realizations will be subject to tax, otherwise it would be possible to avoid the deemed realizations, which are intended to occur on the death of the spouse or common-law partner.

However, the general rules will continue to provide for a "roll-out" of the trust property for distributions of capital to a spouse or common-law partner beneficiary. Difficulties can arise when there is a question whether a discretionary distribution of capital made to the spouse or common-law partner was made in partial satisfaction of the beneficiary's income interest in the trust.

A trustee's exercise of power to encroach on capital appears to give the beneficiary a capital interest in the trust, with the result that a distri-

---

deceased spouse or common-law partner. See also M.N.R., Interpretation Bulletin IT-381R3, "Trusts – Capital Gains and Losses and the Flow-Through of Taxable Capital Gains to Beneficiaries" (February 14, 1997), at paragraphs 17 and 18.
2 Subsection 106(3).
3 Subsection 107(4).

CHAPTER 6 — DISPOSITIONS OF TRUST PROPERTY

bution can be regarded as having been made in partial satisfaction of that capital interest and not as compensation for the disposition of an income interest.

This is typically the view taken by practitioners in concluding that the exception contained within subsection 106(3) does not apply and there would be no corresponding realization on such a distribution.

1.2 Personal Trusts Other than a Spousal or Common-Law Partner Trust

A capital distribution by a personal trust, other than a spousal or common-law partner trust, to one or more resident Canadian beneficiaries results in a disposition of the property for trust purposes. However, subsection 107(2) provides that when a personal trust makes a capital distribution to a resident Canadian beneficiary, it is deemed to dispose of the property for proceeds equal to the cost of the property to the trust.

For non-depreciable capital property, the cost is the adjusted cost base of the property to the trust. Depreciable capital property is deemed to be disposed of at its undepreciated capital cost for tax purposes. The mechanics of subsection 107(2) generally provide that no tax recognition event occurs when assets are distributed from a trust to one or more beneficiaries, in satisfaction of their capital interest in the trust.

A resident Canadian beneficiary is deemed to have acquired property at the trust's adjusted cost base for non-depreciable capital assets and at the undepreciated capital cost for depreciable capital assets, received as a distribution in respect of which the beneficiary held a capital interest.[4]

---

4 Paragraph 107(2)(b). The beneficiary will acquire the property at the same adjusted cost base of the trust unless the beneficiary has an adjusted cost base in respect of her capital interest in the trust. In this case, the beneficiary is deemed to acquire the property at a cost equal to the greater of its adjusted cost base to the trust and the adjusted cost base of the beneficiary's capital interest in the trust. This provision is intended to ensure that a beneficiary, who has, for example, purchased her capital interest for an amount greater than the cost of the property in the trust, will acquire the property at a cost equal to the purchase price paid

PART II — TAXATION OF TRUSTS AND BENEFICIARIES

Specifically, the capital beneficiary is deemed to have acquired depreciable capital property at its original cost to the trust and is deemed to have deducted the cumulative capital cost allowance which the trust deducted.

In this manner, capital gains and recaptured capital cost allowance on the property will not be realized for tax purposes until the beneficiary ultimately disposes of the subject property.

An exception to these rules occurs when subsection 75(2) applies to the trust.[5] In this situation, property distributed by the trust to a beneficiary is deemed to be disposed of for proceeds equal to its fair market value at the time of disposition.[6]

A second exception to the "roll-out" rules occurs when a trust resident in Canada distributes property, including certain types of taxable Canadian property, to a non-resident beneficiary in satisfaction of all or part of the non-resident beneficiary's capital interest in the trust. The trust is deemed to have disposed of such property for proceeds of disposition equal to the fair market value of the property at the time of the disposition.[7] This provision ensures that gains, which accrue in the trust while the property is owned in Canada, do not escape Canadian tax. This rule does not apply to property that is a share of the capital stock of a non-resident-owned investment corporation.

The table in Figure 6.1 serves to summarize the general rules relating to distributions of trust capital.[8]

---

for the capital interest, thereby relieving the beneficiary from potential double taxation on the disposition of the actual property.

5 Subsection 107(4.1) applies, with the result that a tax deferred "roll-out" under subsection 107(2) does not occur. Subsection 107(4.1) was amended by draft legislation released December 20, 2002, in respect of property distributed by a trust to a beneficiary after December 20, 2002.

6 Subsection 107(2.1).

7 Subsection 107(5).

8 Refer to commentary at 13.10 of Chapter 9 entitled, "Distribution to Beneficiary."

CHAPTER 6 — DISPOSITIONS OF TRUST PROPERTY

Figure 6.1
Distribution of Trust Capital – General Rules

Type of Trust	Beneficiary	Tax Recognition Event	
		Contribution of Property to Trust	Distribution of Property to Beneficiary
INTER VIVOS Spousal or common-law partner trust	Spouse or common-law partner	NO	NO
	Other beneficiary (not a spouse or common-law partner)	NO	YES
Alter ego trust	Settlor	NO	YES
Joint spousal or common-law partner trust	Settlor or common-law partner	NO	YES
TESTAMENTARY Qualifying spousal or common-law partner trust	Spouse or common-law partner	NO	YES
"Tainted" spousal or common-law partner trust	Spouse or common-law partner	YES	NO
Other personal trust	Other beneficiary (not a spouse or common-law partner)	YES	NO

2. Deemed Realizations

On specified dates during the existence of a trust, the trust is deemed to have disposed of its capital property, land inventory and Canadian and foreign resource properties, and to have reacquired such properties at their respective fair market values at the date of deemed disposition.[9]

If a deemed realization occurs, the trust may be subject to tax on the resulting capital gains and recaptured capital cost allowance on the deemed disposition of its property.

---

9 Subsections 104(4) to 104(5.2).

PART II — TAXATION OF TRUSTS AND BENEFICIARIES

2.1 Deemed Realizations at Twenty-One Years

Personal trusts are subject to a deemed realization every twenty-one years, specifically:

- for a spousal or a common-law partner trust, at the time of the spouse or common-law partner's death and every twenty-one years thereafter; and

- for all other personal trusts (excepting alter ego and joint common-law partner trusts), every twenty-one years, commencing the later of January 1, 1972, and the date the trust was created.

Note that there is a deemed realization of trust assets on the death of the settlor of an alter ego trust and on the last-to-die of a joint spousal or joint common-law partner trust.

Also note that the twenty-one year deemed disposition does not occur in a trust under which all interests have vested indefeasibly[10] at the time the deemed disposition would otherwise occur, other than those trusts listed in subparagraphs (g)(i) to (vi) of the definition of trust in subsection 108(1).[11] Interests will fail to vest indefeasibly and the twenty-one year rule will apply, where income interests shift among a pool of beneficiaries as they die, or a remainder interest in the trust may become effective in the future.[12]

---

10 For useful commentary on the meaning of vested indefeasibly see M.N.R., Interpretation Bulletin IT-449R, "Meaning of 'Vested Indefeasibly'" [Archived] (September 25, 1987), at paragraphs 1 and 2. Since M.N.R. Interpretation Bulletin IT-449R has been archived, the reader is also directed to M.N.R. Technical Interpretation 9926255, "Spousal Trust Entitled to Receive All In" (January 6, 2000) for additional commentary on the meaning of enforceability of payment in context of a qualified spousal trust.
11 M.N.R., Technical Interpretation 2000-0038195, "Indefeasible Vesting of Interest in Trust" (November 7, 2001).
12 M.N.R., Technical Interpretation 9802615, "21-Year Deemed Disposition Rule" (December 9, 1998).

CHAPTER 6 — DISPOSITIONS OF TRUST PROPERTY

Effective planning for a deemed realization is critical. A variety of options and considerations are available[13] when a deemed realization is in the offing.

- *Roll-outs* – A deemed realization at fair market value can produce a significant tax liability, as might be the case if a cottage property is held in a trust but no liquid assets are available in the trust to pay the taxes. This can force the sale of the non-liquid assets to generate funds necessary to pay taxes. To avoid this, many personal trusts will arrange to distribute appreciated trust property to the capital beneficiaries of the trust on a tax-deferred "roll-out" basis,"[14] prior to the deemed realization date. For this to work, the terms of the trust have to give the trustees the power to distribute the capital of the trust to the beneficiaries. In terms of actual wording, that power can be expressed in a variety of ways, including the power "to encroach on capital," or "to advance capital," or to "make capital distributions." As long as the power is there, the property can be rolled out to the beneficiaries and the deemed realization can be avoided. A roll-out cannot be made on a tax neutral basis if the distribution of capital property was financed by a liability of the trust that was incurred as part of a plan to avoid taxes on a deemed realization.[15]

- *Variations* – What if the terms of trust do not allow for the release of capital assets to beneficiaries? The beneficiaries or the trustees can seek to vary the terms of the trust to allow for the capital distribution. In some jurisdictions in Canada, that variation can be achieved with the simple concurrence of the beneficiaries, provided they are all adults and have the necessary mental capacity, while in other jurisdictions that amendment cannot be conducted without

---

13 For a detailed discussion of these options and of this topic in general see Wolfe D. Goodman, "Deemed Realization on the 21st Anniversary of a Trust" (paper presented to the CBA (Ontario) September 12, 2000, as part of program "Tax, Trusts and Estates: When Worlds Collide").
14 Subsection 107(2), "Distribution by personal trust."
15 Paragraph 104(4)(a.2). For commentary see Rosanne T. Rocchi, "Estate Planning & Litigation: Recent Developments of Importance" (Canadian Legal Lexpert Directory, LEXD/2001-25).

PART II — TAXATION OF TRUSTS AND BENEFICIARIES

judicial approval.[16] To be certain of the result, any variation has to be successfully arranged and the property transferred to the beneficiaries prior to the deemed realization date. Realization of any pent up capital gains is then deferred until the capital beneficiary disposes of the property. The beneficiary may be in a position to realize the gain at lower marginal rates than would have been possible in the trust, particularly if an *inter vivos* trust is involved.

- *Transfer to an Intervening Holding Company* – There may be occasions where the trustees are reluctant to put the property into the hands of the capital beneficiary, as might be the case, for example, in dealing with a spendthrift trust (where the trust is put in place to protect a beneficiary from her poor financial judgement). In this situation, a solution might be for the trustees to incorporate a company and then transfer the capital asset to the corporation on a tax-deferred basis, pursuant to the provisions of subsection 85(1), in exchange for two classes of shares.[17] One class of shares would be preferred voting shares, with nominal paid-up capital and redemption amount. Those shares would be retained by the trustees allowing them to maintain control of the company and, thereby, the capital assets held by the company. The second class of shares would be non-voting equity shares. That latter class of shares would, after issuance to the trustees, be rolled out to the beneficiary as a capital distribution on a tax-deferred basis prior to the deemed realization date. When the realization date occurs, only the preferred voting shares would be held by the trustees and would be subject to a deemed disposition and reacquisition.[18] Arguably, these preferred shares would have little or no value and a deemed realization would result in little or no tax payable by the trust. The trustees would

---

16 See the discussion dealing with variations at 4.1 of Chapter 1 entitled, "The Rule in *Saunders v. Vautier*."
17 Goodman, *supra*, note 13 at p. 10 (also reviewing more elaborate variations on the same theme, as well as a series of other solutions involving corporate structures to work around deemed realizations in differing situations).
18 This type of structure has passed the muster with CRA: M.N.R., Advance Income Tax Ruling 2003-002169C, "Variation and 21 year rule" (January 1, 2003); M.N.R., Advance Income Tax Ruling 1999-0013143, "21 Year Rule – Trusts" (January 1, 2000); and M.N.R., Advance Tax Ruling 2000-0022483, "21 Year Rule" (January 1, 2000).

CHAPTER 6 — DISPOSITIONS OF TRUST PROPERTY

remain free, at a later date, to distribute the preferred voting shares to the beneficiary as the situation warranted.

- *Rolling Out a Remainder Interest* – Where a trust holds land or an interest in real property for the benefit of a life income beneficiary, and the trust provides that the land is then to be given to a capital beneficiary or beneficiaries, the deemed realization at twenty-one years might be avoided by having the trustees transfer a legal remainder interest into the names of the second generation of capital beneficiaries,[19] causing title to that remainder interest to issue in the names of those beneficiaries at the appropriate land titles office. The legal life interest would issue in the names of the trustees and be retained in the trust for the benefit of the life income beneficiary. When the deemed realization occurs, the life interest retained in the trust would have little or no fair market value. It may, in fact, depreciate over time.

- *Weathering the Twenty-One Year Deemed Disposition* – There will be situations where it is preferable to avoid any roll-out and retain the capital assets intact in the trust. This might, for example, be the case where a testamentary trust is in place and is being used to hold a pool of investments with a view to income splitting. Investment strategies can be adopted to minimize the capital gains exposure at the deemed realization date, perhaps by dint of frequent dispositions to harvest gains piecemeal over time or by the selection of investments that are geared to generate forms of income other than capital gains. This type of planning has to be done years in advance. In terms of drafting, a flexible windup date will often be preferable to a mandatory wind up just prior to twenty-one years.

When does the clock start to run on the twenty-one years? Generally, this will occur when the trust is constituted, being the date on which the three certainties are present and assets are initially settled into the names of the trustees. This date may or may not be clear, particularly when

---

19 See M.N.R., Technical Interpretation 1999-0013475, "Distribution from Trust to Avoid 104(4)" (February 29, 2000) (suggesting this solution); Goodman, *supra*, note 13 at p. 15 (giving commentary); and Rocchi, *supra*, note 15 (additional commentary).

PART II — TAXATION OF TRUSTS AND BENEFICIARIES

dealing with some testamentary trusts.[20] Some wills are structured such that a clear transfer occurs to demark the passage of assets from executors or administrators to trustees, so that the moment on which the trust comes into existence is clear and is corroborated with a distinct paper trail. Other wills simply leave the executors or administrators holding the property and shifting roles to become trustees at such time as the estate is fully administered. The moment demarking the transfer may be unclear. In that event, the counsel of greatest prudence would be to select the date of death as the date when the twenty-one years commenced. Where a slightly later date is preferred or required, a historical review of the estate records and the T3 Return may allow for the identification of a later date. Properly speaking, the date ought to coincide with the end of an earlier tax year, as the windup date of the estate is the mandatory close of the estate's first tax year.[21] Where an estate gives rise to a trust, it might be advisable in the administration of the estate to carefully mark the date that the estate ends and file a final T3 Return, seeking a clearance certificate,[22] to create a clear start date for the newborn trust.

Where the deemed realization date is unavoidable and tax is payable on a deemed disposition of the trust property, the trust can elect to pay the tax arising from the deemed realization in up to ten annual installments. Interest at the prescribed rate will apply on the outstanding balance. The trust should make this election[23] on Form T2223 and file at the Tax Services Office no later than the day the T3 Return is due, for the taxation year of the trust, which includes the deemed realization.

2.2 Deemed Realization on Emigration

A deemed realization will also occur where a trust emigrates. A trust which ceases to be a Canadian resident trust is also deemed to have disposed of its trust property for proceeds equal to the fair market value

---

20 Goodman, *supra*, note 13.
21 See generally M.N.R., Interpretation Bulletin IT-179R, "Change of Fiscal Period" (May 28, 1993), at paragraphs 2-5. Also see M.N.R., Interpretation Bulletin IT-286R2, "Trusts – Amount Payable" (April 8, 1988), at paragraph 6.
22 See heading 7 of Chapter 7 entitled, "Clearance Certificates" for commentary on this point.
23 Subsection 159(6.1).

CHAPTER 6 — DISPOSITIONS OF TRUST PROPERTY

of the property at the date the trust ceased to be a resident of Canada and to have reacquired the property, at the same value immediately thereafter.

These rules do not apply in respect of certain properties, including:

- real property situated in Canada, Canadian resource property or timber resource property;

- property of a business carried on by the trust through a permanent establishment in Canada, including capital property, eligible capital property and property considered inventory of the business;

- pension or other similar rights or amounts; and

- payment out of a NISA Fund 2.

A trust which ceases to be a resident of Canada any time after 1995 must file Form T1161, "List of Properties by an Emigrant of Canada," listing each property owned by the trust at that time.

The trust or beneficiary can defer payment of tax resulting from the deemed disposition by providing acceptable security to CRA.

2.3 Deemed Realization on Certain Amendments

An amendment to a trust that varies the capital and income interests of beneficiaries may, in some circumstances, amount to a disposition of that interest and trigger unanticipated tax consequences.[24]

---

[24] Maria Hoffstein and Julie Yee, "Restructuring the Will and the Testamentary Trust: Methods, Underlying Legal Principles and Tax Considerations" (1993) 13 E.T.J. 42, at pp. 95-98. The amendment of a trust to allow for the interposition of a holding company to avoid the 21-year deemed realization has been held not to be a "disposition" triggering capital gains: M.N.R., Advance Income Tax Ruling 2003-002169C, *supra*, note 18 and M.N.R., Technical Interpretation 9727793, "21-Year Deemed Disposition Rule" (January 1, 1998).

PART II — TAXATION OF TRUSTS AND BENEFICIARIES

2.4 Trust Transfers or Mergers

Where one trust transfers assets to another, or two trusts are merged, subsection 104(5.8) of the Act is intended to ensure that the transfer or merger does not extend or defeat deemed realizations otherwise occurring in the trust or trusts under the Act.

In such cases, the deemed realization date of the second trust becomes the *earliest* of the following dates:

- the deemed realization date for the first trust as if the transfer had not occurred;

- the deemed realization date for the second trust as if the transfer had not occurred;

- the day of the transfer if the transfer occurred on a rollover basis, for example where the first trust was:

    o a spousal or common-law partner trust, and the beneficiary spouse or common-law partner is still alive at the time of the transfer;

    o a joint spousal or common-law partner trust, and the settlor or beneficiary spouse or common-law partner is still alive at the time of the transfer; or

    o an alter ego trust, and the settlor is still alive at the time of the transfer.

Note that the last condition does not apply with respect to a transfer between two trusts of the same type. For example, a transfer of trust property from a spousal trust to another spousal trust will not automatically result in a deemed realization on the date of transfer. However, the deemed realization of the trust property would still apply on the earlier date on which either trust would otherwise have been subject to the deemed realization.

Part III
Filing Requirements and Administration by CRA

Chapter 7
General

1. Who Should File?

It is the responsibility of the trustee, executor, administrator, liquidator or other personal representative to file the required T3 Return in respect of the ongoing activities of the trust. The requirement to file, as summarized below, reflects the administrative comments outlined in the CRA T3 Guide. There is a specific requirement to file where the trust (in any one or more circumstances):

- has tax payable;

- disposed of or was deemed to dispose of capital property,[1] or would be liable to report a taxable capital gain;

- is a non-resident trust throughout the year and disposed of taxable Canadian property;

- is a deemed resident trust;[2]

- holds property subject to subsection 75(2);[3]

- has provided a benefit of more than $100 to a beneficiary for upkeep,

---
1 Refer to heading 2 of Chapter 6 entitled, "Deemed Realizations."
2 Refer to heading 12 of Chapter 9 entitled, "Deemed Resident."
3 Refer to heading 1 of Chapter 5 entitled, "General Considerations."

PART III — FILING REQUIREMENTS AND ADMINISTRATION

maintenance or taxes for property maintained for the beneficiary's use and enjoyment;[4] or

- receives income, gain or profit that is allocated to beneficiaries, and any one of the following conditions are met:

    o the total income exceeds $500;

    o the income allocated to any one beneficiary exceeds $100; or

    o one or more of the beneficiaries is a non-resident of Canada.

A T3 Return may not be required to be filed in the case of a trust with low income (below $500), if all of that income is paid or payable to Canadian resident beneficiaries, is deducted from the trust's income for the year leaving it with a taxable income of "nil", and no one beneficiary is allocated more than $100 in income.[5]

In the case of a deceased taxpayer, it is the responsibility of the personal representative of the deceased, in his capacity as executor, administrator or trustee, to file a T3 Return. However, CRA has stated that where the estate assets are distributed immediately after death, or if the estate did not earn any income before the distribution of assets to the beneficiaries, the filing of a T3 Return may not be required.[6] In these circumstances, the personal representative can merely account for the distribution by giving each beneficiary a statement reflecting the proportionate allocation of estate assets to the beneficiaries. In other circumstances, an estate may not come into existence for tax purposes. This will occur where all of the property of the deceased is owned jointly with other persons or passes directly to beneficiaries by beneficiary

---

4 Refer to headings 2 and 3 of Chapter 4, respectively entitled, "Income in the Form of Benefits Conferred by the Trust" and "Income in the Form of Outlays for the Upkeep of Trust Property" for commentary on this subject.
5 See subsection 150(1.1) for the statutory exceptions to filing a return.
6 But see comments at 1.2(b)(vii) of Chapter 2 entitled, "An Estate" and remarks dealing with estates at 1.2 of Chapter 4 entitled, "Non-Discretionary Income Distributions." Generally speaking, it is not possible to distribute estate assets immediately, as there is inevitably some lag-time while an Order of Probate or Administration is sought.

CHAPTER 7 — GENERAL

designations. Ownership of those assets passes to the intended recipients by operation of law and does not pass through the estate. Income on those assets is never estate income.

The T3 Return includes an income tax return and an information return, which reports amounts allocated and designated to beneficiaries. There may be a requirement to file both types of forms, depending on whether amounts were paid or allocated by the estate or trust to beneficiaries.

2. Where to File

The tax residency of the trust determines where the T3 Return is to be filed.[7]

The T3 Trust Income Tax and Information Return together with the T3 Summary and Supplementaries can be filed at the CRA Taxation Centre serviced by the trust's province or territory of residence. CRA prefers that the T3 Return, T3 Summary and related documents be filed at the Ottawa Technology Centre for trusts resident in Canada.[8] The filing address is:

> Ottawa Technology Centre
> Canada Revenue Agency
> Ottawa, Ontario K1A 1A2

You can contact CRA at 1-800-959-8281 for information about resident trusts.

3. How to File

The T3 Return, T3 Summary and related Supplementaries can be filed in the following formats:

---

7 See commentary at heading 1 of Chapter 3 entitled, "Tax Residency of a Trust."
8 See also heading 1 of Chapter 8 entitled, "Filing Information."

PART III — FILING REQUIREMENTS AND ADMINISTRATION

- paper return, summary and slips, or
- magnetic media.

3.1 Paper Return, Summary and Slips

The T3 Return can be prepared using the prescribed forms that are printed by CRA or pre-approved computer software (customized) forms. If filing more than 500 slips, see "Filing on Magnetic Media" at 3.2. If the trust designs and issues its own customized forms, it must obtain written approval from CRA. For more information, see Information Circular 97-2, "Customized Forms." Do not staple the T3 Summary and slips to the T3 Return.

3.2 Filing on Magnetic Media

If the trust has a taxation year-end of December 31, and it prepares and files more than 500 slips (the total number of T4, T4A, T4A-NR, T4RIF, T5, T5008, T4RSP, NR4, and T3 slips), it must do so on magnetic tape, cartridge, CD-ROM or diskette. If the trust completes less than 500 slips, it can use a computerized system to generate them. In such case, CRA prefers that the T3 slips and T3 summary be filed on magnetic media disk.

If the trust completes and files more than 500 slips (the total number of T4, T4A, T4A-NR, T4RIF, T5, T5008, T4RSP, NR4, and T3 slips), it must do so using magnetic media. In this case, send CRA the tape, cartridge, CD-ROM or diskette on or before the filing deadline. Do not send a paper copy of the summary or slips. For technical specifications, visit the CRA website at www.ccra.ga.ca/magmedia.

For more information about this method of filing, you can call CRA at 1-800-665-5164 or if you prefer, you can write to:

>   Magnetic Media Processing Unit
>   Ottawa Technology Centre
>   Canada Revenue Agency
>   Ottawa, ON K1A 1A2

CHAPTER 7 — GENERAL

Note: The magnetic media program is undergoing a redesign. In 2004, tapes, diskettes, and CD-ROMs will be accepted in the current format and the new XML format. Starting in 2005, only CD-ROMs in the new XML format will be accepted.

4. Filing Requirements and Deadlines

The filing requirements for an estate or trust depend on the trust's taxation year-end.

The deadline to file the T3 Return, T3 and NR4 Summaries, and T3 and NR4 Supplementaries is no later than ninety days subsequent to the trust's taxation year.[9] Payment of any balance arising on the T3 Return is due ninety days after the trust's taxation year.

Note that the requirement to file T4, T4A and T4A-NR slips issued by the trust is the last day of February after the calendar year in which the trust made the payment.

CRA's current policy is to recognize the date of the postmark on the envelope or the delivery date of a courier service as the date on which the return was filed. If the required filing date falls on a Saturday, Sunday or a Statutory holiday, the filing deadline will be extended to the first working day after the required filing date.

5. Interest and Penalties

CRA assesses interest on unpaid amounts and on the total amount of any penalties assessed. Interest is charged at the prescribed rate of interest in effect, from the date the unpaid amount is due until the date of payment.

A late filed T3 income tax return is subject to a penalty of 5% of the unpaid tax plus one per cent of the unpaid tax for each month that the return is late, to a maximum of twelve months.[10]

---

9 Paragraph 150(1)(c).
10 Subsection 162(1).

PART III — FILING REQUIREMENTS AND ADMINISTRATION

In the event that a "Demand to File" has been issued by CRA, the penalty on the late filed T3 Return increases to 10% of the unpaid tax plus 2% of the unpaid tax for each month that the return is late, to a maximum of twenty months.[11]

Penalties can also apply to the preparation and filing of T3 slips, if the trustee does not make a reasonable effort to obtain the identification number of the recipient. This number will be either the social insurance number (SIN) or the business number (BN) of the recipient. Unless the trustee makes a reasonable effort to get this information, he will be liable to a $100 penalty each time he does not provide the SIN or BN on the information slip.[12]

If the person or partnership does not have a SIN or BN, the following rules apply:

- the person or partnership must apply for the number within fifteen days of the request to do so (the SIN from any Human Resources Development Canada Office and the BN from CRA); and

- once the person or partnership has received the number, they have fifteen days to give it to the trustee.

Persons or partnerships who, for any reason, do not comply with these requirements are liable to a penalty of $100 for each failure to give their SIN or BN. A beneficiary may indicate that a SIN or BN has been applied for, but has not yet been received, or the beneficiary may refuse to provide the number. In these cases, do not delay in completing the information slip beyond the filing deadline. If you have not received the SIN or BN by the time you prepare the T3 slip, enter "nil" in Box 12.

Also, you cannot knowingly use, communicate or allow a SIN or BN to be communicated, other than as required or authorized by law, without the written consent of the individual taxpayer or partnership. Any person who does so is guilty of an offence, and liable on summary conviction to a fine, imprisonment or both.

---

11 Subsection 162(2).
12 Subsection 162(6).

An information return or T3 supplementaries that are filed late are subject to a penalty of $25 a day for each day late, with a minimum penalty of $100 to a maximum of $2,500 for *each* failure to comply. This penalty can apply notwithstanding that there is no income tax payable by the trust.[13]

If you are filing more than 500 slips in a calendar year, the trust is required to file these in electronic format. The penalty for failure to do so can result in a fine of up to $2,500 per slip. Failure to file a return or slip as required can result in conviction and imprisonment for a period of up to twelve months, plus a fine ranging from a minimum of $1,000 to a maximum of $25,000.

There are also penalties that will apply if, due to culpable conduct, you prepare income tax or information returns, forms or certificates on behalf of another person and these documents include representations that are false statements or omissions. The penalty is the greater of $1,000 or 50% of the tax avoided or refunded as a result of the falsification or omission.

In the event that penalties or interest is assessed, the personal representative can apply to CRA to cancel or waive all or a portion of the assessed amounts.[14]

6. Liability of Trustees and Personal Representatives

It is the responsibility of the trustees and/or the personal representative to discharge all outstanding liability for income taxes of the estate or trust. Should the trustees or the representative distribute the assets of the estate without obtaining an income tax clearance certificate from CRA, they (and not the beneficiaries) will be strictly liable for any and all taxes, interest and penalties payable.[15] For this reason, application for a

---

13 Subsection 162(7).
14 For more information see M.N.R., Information Circular 92-2, "Guidelines for the Cancellation and Waiver of Interest and Penalties" (March 18, 1992).
15 Subsection 159(3).

PART III — FILING REQUIREMENTS AND ADMINISTRATION

clearance certificate should always be obtained prior to any final distribution to beneficiaries.

Similarly, it is the responsibility of the trustees or the personal representative to file all information and income tax returns on time to avoid interest and penalties.

7. Clearance Certificates

A clearance certificate represents a confirmation from CRA that all taxes, interest and penalties payable by the taxpayer have either been paid or have been secured to the satisfaction of the Minister. An executor or the personal representative of an estate or trust should always obtain a clearance certificate from CRA by filing in prescribed form, prior to distributing property under his control.[16]

In reality, the application for a clearance certificate and the filing of a final T3 Return can create a circular problem, since all taxes must be paid and all returns must be filed and assessed prior to the issuance of a clearance certificate by CRA. There are at least two practical solutions.

First, the personal representative can establish a scheme of distribution as of a certain date chosen by the representative. The date chosen for the distribution should be a date prior to the date on which the clearance certificate request is made. A final T3 estate income tax return for the taxation year ending on the "chosen date" should then be prepared and filed with all taxes calculated and paid as if the distribution and termination of the estate had occurred on the chosen date. Once the final T3 Information and Income Tax Return is assessed, the personal representative should complete and file prescribed Form TX19 requesting the issuance of a clearance certificate.[17] The request for a clearance certificate can also be made simultaneously when filing the return, and this might be appropriate in cases where the personal representative wishes to save time.

---

16 Subsection 159(2); See also M.N.R., Information Circular 82-6R2, "Clearance Certificate" (May 19, 1999).
17 See M.N.R., Information Circular 82-6R2, *ibid*.

CHAPTER 7 — GENERAL

CRA will issue a final clearance certificate on Form TX21 only when:

- the estate or trust has filed the final return and CRA has assessed all required returns; and

- all amounts of tax for which the estate or trust is liable have been either paid or adequately secured.

Upon receipt of Form TX21, the personal representative or trustee can make a final distribution of the remaining property. CRA considers the date chosen by the personal representative as being the actual date of distribution for taxation purposes. In effect, the personal representative holds the estate property on behalf of the beneficiaries and the beneficiaries are directly liable for tax on any income earned after the "chosen date".

As a second solution, the personal representatives might distribute the whole of the estate except for a "tax hold-back." The tax hold-back represents an amount that is withheld on a worst case scenario to represent additional funds that might be due to the Receiver General on any conceivable reassessment. The tax hold-back must be in a form that does not generate income (a solicitor's trust account can be employed for that purpose in jurisdictions where interest on those accounts accrues to the lawyer's governing body). Thus, the income earning assets are distributed, the estate tax return is filed along with the appropriate cheque to pay the taxes, and whatever funds or property that remain do not garner further income. If additional taxes are payable, they are paid from the tax hold-back. The tax hold-back is distributed among the residual beneficiaries of the estate after the final taxes have been paid and the clearance certificate is in hand. This strategy works well and keeps things simple, but it may not be appropriate if the tax hold-back is a significant amount and the loss of income on the hold-back deprives the beneficiaries of more than an inconsequential sum.

Chapter 8
Administration

1. Filing Information

The T3 Return, together with related documents, as well as the T3 Summary and related supplementaries should be filed as follows:

Trusts Resident in Canada

>Ottawa Technology Centre
>Canada Revenue Agency
>Ottawa, Ontario K1A 1A2

Non-resident Trusts and Deemed Resident Trusts

>International Tax Services Office
>Canada Revenue Agency
>Ottawa, Ontario K1A 1A8

CRA's administrative policy is to permit the T3 Return to be filed at either the local district taxation office or the Taxation Centre for the jurisdiction of the estate or trust. CRA will accept a T3 Return filed at either the district taxation office or the Taxation Centre serving the area and then forward it on to Ottawa for processing and assessment.

PART III — FILING REQUIREMENTS AND ADMINISTRATION

The T3 Information and Income Tax Return can be delivered by hand or by courier to the Taxation Centre or the local tax services office, although CRA prefers that the return go to Ottawa.

2. Assessments and Reassessments

CRA will generally process a T3 Return in four months. The trustee, executor, liquidator, administrator or other personal representative of the trust will receive a Notice of Assessment for the trust confirming or varying the assessment of tax reported on the T3 Return as filed. The assessment will contain the trust's account number assigned to it by CRA. This account number is to be referenced in all future correspondence with CRA.

CRA can reassess the return or make additional assessments of tax, interest or penalties within the following time frames:

- three years from the date of mailing of the original Notice of Assessment, or a notice that no tax was payable for the taxation year; or

- six years from the date of mailing of the original Notice of Assessment, to permit a carryback of certain deductions, including a loss or an unused investment tax credit.[1]

The normal three year reassessment period does not apply where there is evidence of a misrepresentation because of neglect, carelessness, culpable conduct or fraud in either filing the T3 Return, related documents or in supplying information as required by the Act.

The normal three year reassessment period can also be waived where CRA receives from the trust, a duly completed prescribed Form T2029 "Waiver in Respect of the Normal Reassessment Period," provided that the form is filed with the Tax Services Office prior to the expiry of the normal reassessment period. To revoke a waiver previously filed, it is

---

1 See M.N.R., Information Circular 92-3, "Guidelines for Refunds Beyond the Normal Three Year Period" (March 18, 1992).

CHAPTER 8 — ADMINISTRATION

necessary to file Form T652 "Notice of Revocation of Waiver." The revocation takes effect six months after filing Form T652.

3. Notice of Objection

If the estate or trust receives a Notice of Assessment (or Reassessment), which differs from the T3 Return as filed, the trustee, executor, liquidator, administrator or other personal representative (or a duly authorized representative of any one of those parties) can file a Notice of Objection with CRA, outlining the facts and reasons stating why CRA has improperly assessed taxes, interest and penalties.

The Notice of Objection should be filed in prescribed Form T400A within the statutory time limits. The right to do so is generally ninety days from the date of mailing of the Notice of Assessment (or Reassessment).

However, certain legislative amendments passed in late 1991 extend this right (for testamentary trusts only) to the later of ninety days from the date of mailing of the Notice of Assessment (or Reassessment) or one year from the due date of the T3 Return.[2]

In addition, the "extended period" for filing a Notice of Objection applies only in respect of ordinary income taxes and surtaxes, not in respect of minimum taxes.

Failure to file a Notice of Objection within the prescribed time frame precludes the right to appeal against CRA's assessment or reassessment.[3]

---

[2] See commentary at 1.4(b) of Chapter 2 entitled, "Opportunity to Seek Reassessments."
[3] See also M.N.R., News Release 97-107 for more information on filing a Notice of Objection.

Part IV
Preparing the T3 Trust Information and Income Tax Return

Chapter 9
Completing the Information Return

1. Name of Trust

Enter the full legal name of the trust. The same exact legal name should be used on all returns and correspondence for the trust. If the legal name is longer than sixty characters, CRA will modify the name to satisfy their "computer field" requirements.

A corporation or a flesh and blood person has a clearly defined legal name. The same cannot be said for a trust.[1] To determine the full legal name of the trust, begin by looking at the trust agreement, trust indenture, last will and testament or other document creating the trust and determine whether it contains an express clause naming the trust.[2] In many cases, there will be no clause naming the trust. When working with an estate, the solution is normally to complete this line by inserting "Estate of [full name of deceased shown in order of probate or administration]."[3] In cases where a single, longer-term trust is established to hold estate assets after the administration of the estate proper is complete,[4] it is commonly acceptable to refer to the testamentary trust as the "Estate of [full name

---

1 Unlike corporations and flesh and blood persons, a trust is not a legal entity. See 1.1 of Chapter 1 entitled, "Trusts as Relationships."
2 For example, "This trust will be called the 'John Doe Family Trust'. . ."
3 For example, "Estate of John David Doe."
4 See 1.2(b)(vii) of Chapter 2 on Testamentary Trusts entitled, "An Estate" for additional commentary on this point. See also M.N.R., Technical Interpretation 9526815 "Executor's Year Passing Beneficial Ownership Estate" (May 24, 1996).

PART IV — T3 TRUST INFORMATION & TAX RETURN

of deceased]" into the indefinite future, although technically a misnomer because the estate itself is wound up and ends. Where multiple trusts are set up under a will, or a trust is set up in a document other than the will, such as a trust agreement, and each trust is not expressly named, then a proper legal name should be selected by the trustees for the purpose of filing the T3 and for ease of reference. There are no hard and fast rules for selecting that name and the name does not have to be cleared or registered with any provincial or territorial government.

2. Name of the Trustee, Executor, Liquidator or Administrator

Enter the name of the trustee, executor, liquidator, administrator, or other personal representative who will be the contact person for the estate or trust. CRA will forward correspondence for the trust in care of the individual listed in this field.

3. Mailing Address

Enter the mailing address for the trust. CRA might modify the mailing address to accommodate Canada Post's requirements. If the mailing address for the trust is the same as the prior taxation year, check the box "YES" on the jacket of the T3 Return. If the address changed in the year, check "NO" and list the address shown on the prior year T3 Return.

4. Trust Account Number

Enter the trust's account number assigned by CRA. The account number will appear on the Notice of Assessment for the trust. If this is the first year filed, write "nil" in this space. CRA will assign an account number as a course of assessing the return.

Once the trust is assigned an account number, be sure to reference this number on all future correspondence and returns submitted to CRA on behalf of the trust.

CHAPTER 9 — COMPLETING THE INFORMATION RETURN

5. Telephone Numbers

Enter the telephone number for the trustee, executor, liquidator or administrator appearing on the T3 Return and also the telephone number for the mailing contact person, if different.

6. Residence of Trust

Enter the province or territory for which the trust was resident in respect of the taxation year being filed.

A trust, as a separate taxpayer, will be resident in one province or territory, just like a living person. The tax residence of a trust is important since different provinces have different provincial rates, thereby creating varying tax results depending on the jurisdictional residency of the trust.

As a general rule, a trust is resident where the trustee or trustees who manage its day-to-day affairs are resident. Where all of the trustees reside in the same province or territory, and they have not delegated the management of the day-to-day affairs to an outsider, simply insert the province or territory where the trustees reside. If the trustees reside in different provinces, territories or countries, or if they have delegated the day-to-day affairs of the trust to an outsider, whether that delegation takes place in fact (in the case of a settlor who still exerts control over the trust assets) or takes place in writing (in the case of a custodial arrangement), the tax residency of the trust will have to be determined in relation to other factors.[5]

If the trust became or ceased to be a resident of Canada in the year, indicate the date of entry or departure on the T3 Information Return.[6]

---

5 See heading 1 of Chapter 3 entitled, "Tax Residency of a Trust" for commentary on determining the residency of a trust.
6 See also commentary at 2.2 of Chapter 6 entitled, "Deemed Realization on Emigration" for a discussion of the taxation consequences on ceasing to be a resident of Canada and also Chapter 9, heading 12 entitled, "Deemed Resident" and 13.11, entitled "Additional Contribution of Property," commenting on circumstances when a non-resident trust is deemed to be resident.

PART IV — T3 TRUST INFORMATION & TAX RETURN

7. Type of Trust

7.1 Testamentary Trust

Generally speaking, a testamentary trust is one that arises as a result of the death of an individual[7] and has not lost that status through any subsequent disqualifying event.[8]

Report the date of death for the testator and the Social Insurance Number (SIN) of the deceased, where indicated. If the testamentary trust constitutes a qualifying spousal trust or a common-law partner trust, check the box.

To qualify as a spousal trust or a common-law partner trust all of the listed requirements must be met.

- A spousal trust must be created by the testator's will. It cannot be created as a freestanding document outside of the will.

- The spouse or common-law partner must be entitled to all of the income from the trust during his or her lifetime.

- No person other than the spouse or common-law partner can have any entitlement to the capital of the trust, during their remaining life.

- The assets bequeathed must vest indefeasibly in the trust within thirty-six months of death. The act does not specifically define the term "vested indefeasibly," however, CRA has published commentary on their interpretation of vested indefeasibly, for purposes of a qualifying spousal trust.[9]

---

[7] Subsection 108(1), definition of "testamentary trust."
[8] See Chapter 2 at 1.2(a) entitled, "Definition of Testamentary Trust" and also 1.2(b) entitled, "Qualifying and Non-Qualifying Testamentary Trusts."
[9] M.N.R., Interpretation Bulletin IT-449R, "Meaning of 'Vested Indefeasibly'" [Archived] (September 25, 1987), at paragraphs 1 and 2. However, as M.N.R., IT-449R has been archived by CRA, the reader should also refer to M.N.R., Technical Interpretation 2003-0008285 "Spousal Trust – Entitlement – Payable"

CHAPTER 9 — COMPLETING THE INFORMATION RETURN

- The testator must be a resident of Canada immediately prior to death and the trust created by the will must have Canadian resident trustees.

7.2 *Inter Vivos* Trust

An *inter vivos* trust[10] is, in common terms, a trust which is created by a living person. Under the *Income Tax Act*, an *inter vivos* trust is defined as a personal trust that does not qualify as a testamentary trust.[11] This means that a trust that is established by virtue of an individual's will is taxed as an *inter vivos* trust if it fails to qualify as a testamentary trust or if it loses that characterization and is disqualified.[12]

For tax purposes, when a settlor transfers property into an *inter vivos* trust, the transfer of these assets will result in a disposition for tax purposes, which could create a tax liability. Generally, there is no tax deferred rollover into an *inter vivos* trust, except for certain *inter vivos* trusts, which are specifically defined as an "alter ego trust" or a "joint spousal trust" or "common-law partner trust."

Indicate the date for which the *inter vivos* trust was created. This date may or may not be the effective date stated on the trust agreement or indenture that brings the trust into existence. The creation date will be the first date on which the "three certainties" are present[13] and property has been settled into the trust by transferring it to the trustees.[14] If a trust agreement or indenture is in place, but no property is transferred into the trust until some later date, the effective date on which the trust comes

---

(September 23, 2003) and M.N.R., Technical Interpretation 2002-0126775, "Spousal Trust" (May 3, 2002) for recent commentary.
10 See heading 2 of Chapter 2 entitled, "*Inter Vivos* Trusts" for a more comprehensive discussion of the types of *inter vivos* trusts and basic tax planning relating to the use of *inter vivos* trusts.
11 See commentary at 1.2(b) of Chapter 2 entitled, "Qualifying and Non-Qualifying Testamentary Trusts."
12 See 1.4(a) of Chapter 2 entitled, "Loss of Status as a Testamentary Trust."
13 See 1.4 of Chapter 1 entitled, "The Three Certainties."
14 A more detailed discussion dealing with determining the start date of a trust is set out at 2.1 of Chapter 6 entitled, "Deemed Realizations at Twenty-One Years."

PART IV — T3 TRUST INFORMATION & TAX RETURN

into existence will generally be the date on which the initial settlement of property is transferred to the trustees, even if that date is later than any "effective date" stipulated in the documentation itself.

Check the box, which defines the type of *inter vivos* trust. If none of the boxes apply, check the "other *inter vivos*" box.

8. Taxation Year

Indicate the taxation year applicable by reporting the first day, month and year for which the taxation year commenced and the last day, month and year for which the taxation year ended.

Note that all *inter vivos* trusts must report their taxation years on a calendar year basis (December 31 year end).[15] A testamentary trust can report on a non-calendar year basis, and, provided the first taxation year does not exceed twelve months from the date of death, the personal representative of the estate or the trustee of the trust can select the closing date for the first taxation year.[16]

The legal representative can therefore choose, for the first fiscal period, a taxation year of less than twelve months. This decision might be made, for instance, to minimize the amount of income taxable to the estate or trust, or its beneficiaries, for that first taxation year. In some cases, the personal representative may choose to report on a calendar year basis. It is not uncommon for the fiscal year to also be based on the twelve month period commencing from the date of death. Once a taxation year is established, it cannot be changed without application and approval from CRA.[17]

---

15 Subsection 104(2) and subparagraph 249.1(1)(b)(i.1).
16 Subsection 104(23).
17 Paragraph 104(23)(a). For a comprehensive discussion of issues relating to the beginning and end of taxation years for testamentary trusts, see 1.3(b) of Chapter 2 dealing with testamentary trusts entitled, "Flexible Year End." See also M.N.R., Interpretation Bulletin IT-179R "Change of Fiscal Period" (May 28, 1993), at paragraph 4.

CHAPTER 9 — COMPLETING THE INFORMATION RETURN

If this is the first year of filing, check the box "YES," otherwise check "NO." If this is the first year of filing attach a copy of the trust document or will to the T3 Return, together with a list of assets held at the date of death. If the trust filed for a prior taxation year, indicate the day, month and year for which a T3 Return was last filed.

9. Amended Return

If you are filing an amended return, check the box "YES," otherwise check "NO."

10. Final Return

If this is the final return of the trust check the box "YES," otherwise check "NO."

The legal representative should establish a scheme of distribution in anticipation of the final taxation year and should apply for a clearance certificate from CRA.[18]

If this is the final taxation year of the estate or trust, involving the wind-up and complete distribution of estate or trust assets, state the "chosen date."

11. Official Language

Please check either the English or French alternative so that CRA can respond in the preferred official language.

12. Deemed Resident

There can be circumstances where a trust, which is otherwise resident in another country, is also considered to be resident in Canada for tax

---

18 Refer to commentary in heading 7 of Chapter 7 entitled, "Clearance Certificates."

PART IV — T3 TRUST INFORMATION & TAX RETURN

purposes.[19] In such case, the trust is considered to be a "deemed resident trust" for Canadian tax purposes.

A trust is considered to be a deemed resident trust if either of the following conditions exist:

- a resident of Canada transferred property to the trust and either holds or retains a beneficial interest in the trust or is related to a person who holds such an interest. Note that for purposes of this rule, the meaning of "related" is extended to include an aunt, uncle, nephew or niece of the contributor or transferor; or

- the beneficiary acquired an interest in the trust by way of purchase, gift or inheritance from a Canadian resident who previously transferred or contributed property to the trust.

A trust will be considered to be a deemed resident of Canada if it acquired property from a person who is resident in Canada, or if any of the beneficiaries are resident in Canada and a contribution was made by a resident or former resident of Canada.[20]

---

19 Subsection 94(1). Note that substantial amendments have been made to section 94(1), as introduced by the "Notice of Ways and Means Motion – Taxation of Non-Resident Trusts and Foreign Investment Entities – October 2002" (re-introduced October 30, 2003). The scope and extent of these amendments are substantial. The practitioner should carefully review these legislative amendments to ascertain whether a non-resident trust may in fact be considered to be a "deemed resident trust" for Canadian tax purposes under newly legislated section 94(1). As an example, a Canadian resident taxpayer may transfer assets to a Bahamian trust for asset protection purposes. An obvious question will arise as to whether or not such trust is Canadian resident for income tax purposes and whether or not there is a requirement to file a return. While such trusts will often be subject to the attribution provisions of subsection 75(2), CRA would take the position that the trust, nonetheless, has a requirement to file as a "deemed resident trust." The amendments to section 94(1) apply to taxation years commencing after 2002. See also 13.11 of this chapter entitled "Additional Contribution of Property," for a further discussion of circumstances in which a trust can be considered to be a "deemed resident trust."

20 Paragraph (a) of subsection 94(1), definition of "resident contributor."

CHAPTER 9 — COMPLETING THE INFORMATION RETURN

13. Other Information Required

Page two of the T3 Return lists eleven questions which must be answered, either by checking the box "No" or "Yes." The following commentary outlines the technical taxation aspects pertaining to each question; each item is addressed with a summary discussion of the related information and a statement recapping the CRA question.

13.1 Multiple Trusts

CRA Question 1

Is the trust one of a number of trusts created from contributions by the same individual? If yes, attach a list of the names, addresses, and account numbers of the other trusts.

Commentary

CRA can, in certain circumstances, invoke ministerial discretion to tax multiple trusts as a single trust.[21] In so doing, all of the income earned by all of the trusts included by this provision would be taxable in aggregate, as if it was earned by a single trust. This is only a concern where the trusts are testamentary in nature and would each be taxed separately at progressive rates.

For instance, if one settlor establishes two or more trusts, for the benefit of the same beneficiary, or the same group or class of beneficiaries, it would seem that absent any special or mitigating circumstances all of the trusts would be taxed as though they were a single trust.

There are many factors to be considered in determining whether this provision would actually apply.[22]

---

21 Subsection 104(2).
22 For a more detailed discussion on this topic see 1.4(f) of Chapter 2 entitled, "Separate Taxpayer Status for Multiple Testamentary Trusts."

PART IV — T3 TRUST INFORMATION & TAX RETURN

13.2 Change in Ownership

CRA Question 2

For any trust (other than a unit trust) did the ownership of capital or income interests change since 1984? If yes, state the year, and if during this taxation year, attach a statement showing the changes.

Commentary

A disposition of a capital or an income interest in a personal trust can represent a change of ownership that creates a taxable event for both the trust and the beneficiary.

For instance, a payment in satisfaction of a beneficiary's income interest in the trust might result in the trust realizing a taxable capital gain or an allowable capital loss, even though the actual amount of the payment may not be taxable to the beneficiary. However, in circumstances where an *inter vivos* personal trust is terminated by virtue of the consent of all beneficiaries, a disposition could result in a taxable realization of a beneficiary's income interest in the trust.[23] Note that CRA does not consider a disclaimer, release or surrender of a life income interest in an estate or trust to be such a disposition.[24]

Similar tax treatment under paragraph 106(2)(a) could result if a beneficiary disposed of his income interest in a trust to another income beneficiary or to a capital beneficiary. Where such transactions are contemplated, it is generally advisable to ensure that any payment made to an income beneficiary in satisfaction of his income interest in the trust is structured to occur as a distribution from the trust, rather than a payment from one of the other beneficiaries of the trust.

Generally, where property is distributed to a capital beneficiary in satisfaction of a capital beneficiary's interest in the trust, the distribution

---

23 Paragraph 106(2)(a).
24 M.N.R., Interpretation Bulletin IT-385R2, "Disposition of an Income Interest in a Trust" (May 17, 1991).

CHAPTER 9 — COMPLETING THE INFORMATION RETURN

occurs on a tax-deferred basis and there is no tax recognition event. The trust property is considered to be disposed of on a "rollover" basis; that is, the capital beneficiary is deemed to acquire the capital property of the trust at the cost amount of the property to the trust on the date of distribution.

The practitioner should be advised therefore, that there can be a dramatically different tax treatment for income versus capital beneficiaries of a personal trust.

13.3 Terms of the Trust Amended or Varied

CRA Question 3

Were the terms of the trust amended or varied since June 18, 1971? If yes, state the year, and if during this taxation year, attach copies of the documents effecting these changes.

Commentary

Certain inter *vivos trusts* created before June 18, 1971, are taxed at the personal marginal rates prescribed in section 117 of the Act.[25] Consequently, where the terms of the trust (which was in existence on June 18, 1971) are amended or varied, the trust becomes "tainted"[26] and subject to federal and provincial taxes at the top marginal tax rates, excepting surtaxes, on all trust income.

Where there has been an amendment or variation of the terms of a pre-June 18, 1971, *inter vivos* trust, a statement outlining the nature of the change and the relevant date should be prepared and attached to the T3 Return.

---

25 See also subsection 122(1).
26 Subsection 122(2).

PART IV — T3 TRUST INFORMATION & TAX RETURN

13.4 Continuously Resident in Canada

CRA Question 4

Has the trust continuously resided in Canada since it was established (or since June 18, 1971, if it was established before that date)?

Commentary

A trust that ceases to be resident in Canada at any time during a taxation year is deemed to have disposed of all its property for proceeds equal to the fair market value of such property, at that time, and to have reacquired the property at that value, immediately thereafter. The deemed disposition, which occurs as a result of the trust ceasing to be resident in Canada, can obviously create an extremely onerous tax result.

For taxation years commencing after 1995, a trust that holds property having a fair market value in excess of $25,000 at the time it ceases to be resident in Canada must file with it's T3 Income Tax Return for that taxation year, Form T1161, "List of Properties by an Emigrant of Canada" listing each property that the trust owned at the time it ceased to be a resident of Canada.

A trust can defer payment of the resulting tax liability from the deemed disposition by providing acceptable security to CRA.

13.5 Additional Capital Contributed

CRA Question 5

Did the trust receive any additional capital property by way of a gift since June 18, 1971? (Do not include the original property settled on the trust.) If yes, state the year, and if during this taxation year, attach a statement giving details.

CHAPTER 9 — COMPLETING THE INFORMATION RETURN

Commentary

A subsequent contribution of capital to a trust can result in adverse tax consequences. For instance, in the case of a testamentary trust created after November 12, 1981, a subsequent contribution of property to the trust, other than a contribution resulting from the individual's death, will effectively cause the trust to lose its testamentary status. Since the trust would no longer be considered testamentary, it would, by default, be considered to be *inter vivos*.[27] Note, however, that a contribution or "gift" to a trust should be distinguished separately from a purchase of an asset at fair market value or the making of a loan for adequate consideration and with reasonable terms.

When a subsequent contribution is made to a personal *inter vivos* trust by another individual, or any number of other individuals, and the aggregate fair market value of those subsequent contributions exceeds the fair market value of the contribution made by the original settlor, the original contributor becomes disqualified as the settlor of the trust. To the extent that the fair market value of such subsequent contributions exceed the fair market value of the contributions by the original individual, the trust is considered to have no settlor.[28] A disqualified settlor can create serious tax consequences with respect to the status of the trust.

A disqualified settlor can remedy this status by making additional contributions to the trust so that the aggregate fair market value of these contributions exceeds the aggregate fair market value of all other contributions made to the trust.

13.6 Incurred a Non-Arm's Length Debt

CRA Question 6

Did the trust borrow money or incur a debt in a non-arm's length transaction since June 18, 1971? If yes, state the year, and if

---

27 Subsection 108(1), definition of "testamentary trust" at paragraph (b). See also 1.4(a) of Chapter 2 entitled, "Loss of Status as a Testamentary Trust" for more information on this point.
28 Subsection 108(1), definition of "settlor" at paragraph (b).

PART IV — T3 TRUST INFORMATION & TAX RETURN

during this taxation year, attach a statement showing the amount of the loan, the lender's name and the lender's relationship to the beneficiaries.

Commentary

If an *inter vivos* trust, which was in existence and created before June 18, 1971, incurs a debt or any other obligation to pay an amount to a non-arm's length person, such debt can have the effect of nullifying the favourable tax treatment afforded *inter vivos* trusts that were established prior to June 18, 1971. Such trusts are subject to the graduated rates of taxation, rather than the top marginal rates applicable to post-June 18, 1971, *inter vivos* trusts. A trust is not considered to have incurred a debt or obligation for such purposes, where the trust acquires property or assets at fair market value in exchange for the debt or obligation incurred.

A debt or obligation of the trust arising as an amount payable to a beneficiary of the trust, who deals not at arm's length with the trust, can result in the loss of the trust's favourable tax status, unless the debt or obligation is discharged within a "reasonable time," normally by the end of the taxation year following the year the debt became payable by the trust. CRA publishes more detailed commentary on this matter and the practitioner should refer to this source.[29]

13.7 Election to Defer the Deemed Realization Day

CRA Question 7

In any previous taxation year, did the trust use Form T1015 to elect to defer the deemed realization day?

---

29 M.N.R., Interpretation Bulletin IT-406R2 "Tax Payable by an *Inter Vivos* Trust" (May 11, 1990), at paragraphs 9-12.

CHAPTER 9 — COMPLETING THE INFORMATION RETURN

Commentary

An election[30] to defer the deemed realization day was previously available where there was an "exempt beneficiary" of the trust. Where such an election was made, a tax-free distribution of trust property under subsection 107(2) could be made only to an exempt beneficiary. Consequently, any deemed realization would have been deferred until the day following the death of the trust's last-surviving exempt beneficiary.

However, new subsection 104(5.3) placed a limitation on this deferral, with an effective realization date of January 1, 1999. If there were still exempt beneficiaries alive on January 1, 1999, there would have been a deemed realization on that date, even if the deferral election under subsection 104(5.3) was made. Note that if a "pre-1972 spousal trust"[31] made such an election, on prescribed Form T1015, the trust will not be eligible to claim any unused portion of the beneficiary spouse's capital gains deduction. If the subsection 104(5.3) election was not made, then a pre-1972 spousal trust can still qualify for the capital gains deduction on any eligible capital gains arising on the death of the beneficiary spouse.

13.8 Income Payable to Beneficiaries

CRA Question 8

Does the will, trust document, or court order require the payment of trust income to beneficiaries?

Commentary

Where the terms of the document that establish the estate or trust require the payment of income to beneficiaries, the estate or trust is required to include all income that is paid or payable for the taxation year as income to be taxed in the hands of the beneficiaries and not that of the estate or

---

30 Subsection 104(5.3).
31 Subsection 108(1), definition of "pre-1972 spousal trust."

trust.[32] A trust which is subject to this provision can deduct from its income in the taxation year such parts of its income and net taxable capital gains as is payable in the year to the beneficiaries.[33]

13.9 Transfer from Non-Grandfathered *Inter Vivos* Trust

CRA Question 9

Did the trust receive, after December 17, 1999, any property as a transfer from a non-grandfathered *inter vivos* trust where the beneficial ownership of the property did not change as a result of the transfer? If yes, state the year, and if during this taxation year, attach a statement giving details.

Commentary

Generally, when a personal trust distributes property to a beneficiary, in satisfaction of the beneficiary's capital interest in the trust, the roll-out of the property occurs on a tax-deferred basis.[34]

However, the Act imposes a special rule designed to prevent the avoidance of the twenty-one year deemed realization date through the use of transfers to another trust.[35]

This rule applies where a trust transfers property to another trust on a "rollover" basis, and the twenty-one year deemed realization rule applies in respect of the transferor trust. When this occurs, the first deemed realization date for the transferee trust, after the date of transfer, is the earliest of the following dates:[36]

---

32 Subsection 104(13). See also M.N.R., Interpretation Bulletin IT-286R2 "Trusts – Amount Payable" (April 8, 1988), at paragraph 2. For more detailed commentary on the tax treatment of trust income, refer to heading 1 of Chapter 4 entitled, "Determining Whether Income is Payable."
33 Paragraph 104(6)(b).
34 Subsection 107(2).
35 Subsection 104(5.7).
36 Paragraph 104(5.8)(a).

CHAPTER 9 — COMPLETING THE INFORMATION RETURN

- the deemed realization date for the first trust as if the transfer had not occurred;

- the deemed realization date for the second trust as if the transfer had not occurred;

- the date of the transfer if the transfer occurred on a rollover basis, where the transferee trust was a:

    - spousal or common-law partner trust and the beneficiary spouse or common-law partner is alive at the time of the transfer;

    - a joint spousal or common-law partner trust, where the settlor or beneficiary spouse or common-law partner is alive at the time of the transfer; or

    - an alter ego trust, where the settlor is alive at the time of the transfer.

An automatic "deemed realization" does not occur when there is a transfer between two trusts of the same type. For example, a transfer of trust property from one spousal trust to another will not automatically result in a deemed realization on the date of transfer. In such case, the twenty-one year rule will still apply on the earlier date on which either trust would otherwise have been subject to the deemed realization.

13.10 Distribution to Beneficiary

CRA Question 10

Did the trust distribute assets other than cash to a beneficiary during the taxation year? If yes, attach a statement giving a complete description of the property, the name and address of the beneficiary to whom the property was distributed, and the date the property was distributed. If the beneficiary is an individual, also state the beneficiary's social insurance number.

PART IV — T3 TRUST INFORMATION & TAX RETURN

Commentary

A distribution "in kind" of trust property, including capital property and depreciable capital property, generally occurs on a tax-deferred roll-out basis. An exception to this rule exists in respect of distributions from a qualifying spousal or common-law partner trust following the death of the spouse or common-law partner, or to a person other than the spouse or common-law partner during the spouse or common-law partner's lifetime. Also, a distribution of trust property to a non-resident beneficiary is excluded from "rollover" treatment.

A distribution of trust property that is not accorded rollover treatment will result in a deemed disposition of the property to the trust at fair market value at the time of distribution. Any capital gains, recaptured capital cost allowance or resulting income would be subject to tax within the trust.

For this reason any distribution of property in kind from a "qualifying spousal or common-law partner trust" will generally trigger a tax recognition, unless the distribution is made *inter vivos* to the spouse or common-law partner.[37] Note that an opposite tax treatment occurs for a "tainted spousal trust," wherein a capital distribution of property in kind to a resident Canadian beneficiary is deemed to "roll out" at cost,[38] thereby deferring the tax recognition of gains or losses until the recipient beneficiary ultimately disposes of the property.

Where a personal trust makes a distribution of trust property (in kind) to a beneficiary in respect of any portion of the beneficiary's capital interest in the trust, a statement outlining the particulars of the property distributed and the recipient beneficiary must be prepared and attached to the T3 Return for the taxation year of the estate or trust in which the distribution is made.

The following information should appear on the statement:

---

37 See also commentary in at 1.1 of Chapter 6 entitled, "Spousal or Common-Law Partner Trusts."
38 Paragraph 107(2)(b). See also 1.2 of Chapter 6 "Personal Trusts Other than a Spousal or Common-Law Partner Trust."

CHAPTER 9 — COMPLETING THE INFORMATION RETURN

- the date of distribution;

- a description of the property, including a legal description for real estate where applicable;

- the fair market value of the property at the date of distribution;

- the cost amount of the property to the trust; and

- the name, address and social insurance number (if relevant) of the individual recipient beneficiary.

13.11 Additional Contribution of Property

CRA Question 11

Did the trust receive any additional property by way of a contribution (as defined in the Glossary of the guide[39]) since June 22, 2000? If yes, state the year and, if during this taxation year, attach a statement giving details.

Commentary

This question is aimed at and related to the provisions of new section 94 of the Act, which deals with non-resident trusts. For the most part, the requirement for there to be a Canadian resident beneficiary of the trust for section 94 to apply has been dropped. What is relevant is that there be a Canadian resident contributor. Any person who therefore has contributed property to the trust and is resident in Canada may be liable for the trust's tax.

A "contribution" generally refers to a transfer or loan of property to a non-resident trust, including:

---

39 For purposes of this question, the CRA T3 Guide defines a contribution to be a transfer or loan of property, other than an arm's length transfer by a particular entity, to a non-resident trust including a series of transfers or loans that results in a transfer or loan to a non-resident trust and any transfer or loan made by an entity as a result of a transfer or loan involving the non-resident trust.

PART IV — T3 TRUST INFORMATION & TAX RETURN

- a new series of transfers or loans that results in a transfer or loan to the non-resident trust; and

- a transfer or loan made by an entity as a result of a transfer or loan involving the non-resident trust.

A "resident contributor"[40] to a trust at any time is an "entity" who is both resident in Canada and a contributor to the trust.

If a non-resident trust is considered to have a Canadian "resident contributor," the trust is deemed to be resident in Canada[41] for purposes of determining its taxable income and, consequently, its taxes payable under Part I of the Act.

The test for determining whether an entity is a "resident contributor" for purposes of subsection 94(1) is based on a reference to time. Therefore, if the person who was a resident contributor of the trust subsequently becomes a non-resident of Canada, then that person would, at that subsequent time, cease to be a resident contributor of the trust. Ceasing to be a deemed resident trust can invoke significant tax consequences, since the trust will be deemed to have disposed of all its assets immediately before that time.[42]

Also, the definition of resident contributor contains a sixty month exemption[43] for immigrants to Canada, and also an exemption for inbound *inter vivos* and testamentary trusts, providing that the person contributing property to the trust has not been resident in Canada for more than sixty months during his lifetime.

A resident contributor does not include an individual who contributed to an *inter vivos* trust prior to 1960 while a non-resident.[44]

---

40 Subsection 94(1), definition of "resident contributor."
41 Paragraph 94(3)(c) provides that paragraph 128.1(1)(a) will apply to deem a year-end of the trust at that time and to permit a step-up in the cost base of the trust's property.
42 Subsection 94(5), ceasing to be deemed resident.
43 Paragraph (a) of subsection 94(1), definition of "resident contributor."
44 Paragraph (b) of subsection 94(1), definition of "resident contributor."

CHAPTER 9 — COMPLETING THE INFORMATION RETURN

The new rules in subsection 94(1) are generally applicable with respect to trust taxation years commencing after 2002, where there is either a Canadian resident contributor or a Canadian resident beneficiary.

The term "resident beneficiary" is somewhat more complicated in operation than "resident contributor."

Under old subsection 94(1), an individual who was previously resident in Canada for sixty months or more could set up a non-resident trust, provided that they had not been a resident of Canada for the immediately preceding eighteen months. Under subsection 94(1), a similar exemption applies in limited circumstances. The eighteen month period has been extended to sixty months for transfers or contributions occurring after June 22, 2000. This test now looks to both the past and future "non-resident time" of a contributor to determine whether or not a trust is a deemed resident of Canada.

For transfers prior to June 23, 2000, the period of non-residency remains at only eighteen months. Also, where the trust arises as a consequence of the death of the individual, the period of non-residency is shortened to eighteen months before the contribution.

PART IV — T3 TRUST INFORMATION & TAX RETURN

Figure 9.1
T3 Trust Income Tax and Information Return
(Page 1 of 4)

At the date of publication, the 2004 T3 Trust Income Tax and Information Return and Schedules were not available. These will be sent to you as and when they become available from CRA.

CHAPTER 9 — COMPLETING THE INFORMATION RETURN

Figure 9.1 (continued)
T3 Trust Income Tax and Information Return
(Page 2 of 4)

Other required information

	No	Yes
1. Is the trust one of a number of trusts created from contributions by the same individual? If yes, complete Schedule 6 and attach a list of the names, addresses, and account numbers of the other trusts.	☐	☐
2. For any trust (other than a unit trust), did the ownership of capital or income interests change since 1984? If yes, state the year, and, if during this taxation year, attach a statement showing the changes. _____	☐	☐
3. Were the terms of the trust amended or varied since June 18, 1971? If yes, state the year, and, if during this taxation year, attach copies of the documents effecting these changes. _____	☐	☐
4. Has the trust continuously resided in Canada since it was established (or since June 18, 1971, if it was established before that date)?	☐	☐
5. Did the trust receive any additional capital property by way of gift since June 18, 1971? (Do not include the original property settled on the trust). If yes, state the year, and, if during this taxation year, attach a statement giving the details. _____	☐	☐
6. Did the trust borrow money, or incur a debt, in a non-arm's length transaction since June 18, 1971? If yes, state the year, and, if during this taxation year, attach a statement showing the amount of the loan, the lender's name, and the lender's relationship to the beneficiaries. _____	☐	☐
7. In any previous taxation year, did the trust file Form T1015 to elect to defer the deemed realization day?	☐	☐
8. Does the will, trust document, or court order require the payment of trust income to beneficiaries?	☐	☐
9. Did the trust receive, after December 17, 1999, any property as a transfer from a non-grandfathered inter vivos trust where the beneficial ownership of the property did not change as a result of the transfer? If yes, state the year, and, if during this taxation year, attach a statement giving details. _____	☐	☐
10. Did the trust distribute assets other than cash to a beneficiary during the taxation year? If yes, attach a statement giving a complete description of the property, the name and address of the beneficiary to whom the property was distributed, and the date the property was distributed. If the beneficiary is an individual, also state the beneficiary's social insurance number.	☐	☐
11. Did the trust receive any additional property by way of a contribution (as defined in the Glossary of the guide) since June 22, 2000? If yes, state the year, and, if during this taxation year, attach a statement giving details. _____	☐	☐

Step 2 – Calculating total income – See lines 01 to 20 in the guide.

- Taxable capital gains (line 21 of Schedule 1) .... 01 •
- ▲ Pension income .... + 02 •
- ▲ Actual amount of dividends from taxable Canadian corporations (line 1 of Schedule 8) .... + 03 •
- ▲ Foreign investment income (line 4 of Schedule 8) .... + 04 •
- ▲ Other investment income (line 10 of Schedule 8) .... + 05 •

	Gross		Net	
Business income (Form T2124)		96	+	06 •
Farming income (Form T2042, Form T1163, or Form T1164)		97	+	07 •
Fishing income (Form T2121)		98	+	08 •
Rental income (Form T776)		99	+	09 •

- NISA Fund 2 .... + 10 •
- (Includes _____ NISA Fund 2 payments received while the beneficiary spouse or common-law partner is, or was, alive, or received by a communal organization) •
- Deemed realizations (line 42 of Form T1055) .... + 11 •
- ▲ Other income (specify and attach any information slips received)

_____ +
_____ +
                         = ► + 19 •

▲ Add lines 01 to 19. This is the trust's **total income**. = ► _____ 20

187

PART IV — T3 TRUST INFORMATION & TAX RETURN

Figure 9.1 (continued)
T3 Trust Income Tax and Information Return
(Page 3 of 4)

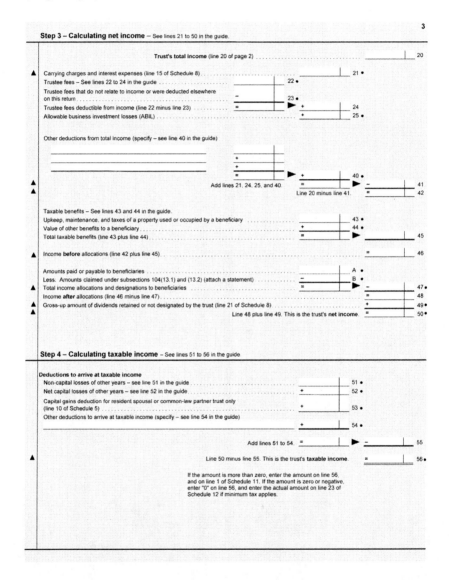

CHAPTER 9 — COMPLETING THE INFORMATION RETURN

Figure 9.1 (continued)
T3 Trust Income Tax and Information Return
(Page 4 of 4)

Step 5 – Summary of tax and credits – See lines 81 to 100 in the guide.

Tax:

Total federal tax payable (line 37 of Schedule 11, or line 55 of Schedule 12)		81
Provincial or territorial tax payable (from the applicable provincial or territorial form)	+	82
Part XII.2 tax payable (line 12 of Schedule 10)	+	83
Add lines 81 to 83. **Total taxes payable.**	=	▶ 84

Credits:

Tax paid by instalments		85
Total tax deducted	+	86
Transfer to Quebec:		
Refundable Quebec abatement (line 38 of Schedule 11, or line 56 of Schedule 12)	+	87
Refundable investment tax credit [Form T2038(IND)]	+	88
Capital gains refund (Form T184)	+	89
Part XII.2 tax credit (box 38 of T3 slip)	+	90
Other credits (specify) _____	+	91
Add lines 85 to 91. **Total credits.**	=	▶ — 93
Refund or balance owing – Line 84 minus line 93.	=	94

If the result is negative, you have a **refund**.
If the result is positive, you have a **balance owing**.

We do not refund or charge a difference of $2 or less.

Amount enclosed 95

Payment: Attach a cheque or money order payable to the Receiver General. Do not mail cash.

Refund code
(see the guide for details) [ ] 100

Name and address of person or company (other than trustee, executor, liquidator, or administrator) who prepared this return.

Certification (by trustee, executor, liquidator, or administrator)

I, (please print) _____

certify that the information given on this T3 return and in any documents attached is, to the best of my knowledge, correct, complete, and fully discloses the income from all sources.

Postal code | Telephone
( )

Authorized person's signature

Position or title

Privacy Act – Personal Information Bank number RCT/P-PU-015.

Date

Printed in Canada

Chapter 10
Calculating Total Income

1. Line 01 – Taxable Capital Gains

Enter the taxable capital gains of the trust as calculated on Line 21 of Schedule 1. Schedule 1 should report the disposition, deemed or actual, of all capital property owned by the trust in the taxation year. Capital gains dividends received by the trust should be reported on Line 10 of Schedule 1 and will form part of the taxable capital gains reported on this line.

If the amount calculated on Schedule 1 results in a net capital loss, do not enter any amount on Line 01. A trust cannot deduct net capital losses in the year from other sources of income nor can the trust allocate any losses to its beneficiaries.[1] The allowable capital loss is included in the trust's net capital loss for the taxation year, and that amount becomes subject to the net capital loss carryover provisions contained within paragraph 111(1)(b) and the related rules in section 111 of the Act.

1.1 General Rules

The general rule in calculating a capital gain or loss is that the amount of the gain or loss is the difference between the proceeds of disposition

---

[1] See M.N.R., Interpretation Bulletin IT-381R3, "Trusts – Capital Gains and Losses and the Flow-Through of Taxable Capital Gains to Beneficiaries" (February 14, 1997), at paragraph 10. See also heading 2 of Chapter 12 entitled, "Line 52 – Net Capital Losses of Other Years" for a discussion on utilizing such losses.

PART IV — T3 TRUST INFORMATION & TAX RETURN

received in respect of the property and the aggregate of the adjusted cost base (ACB) of the property and the expenses or costs of disposition. The Act specifically excludes from the definition of a capital gain or loss the following:

- property, the disposition of which gives rise to income from a business, property or an adventure in the nature of trade,[2] and
- eligible capital property.

The ACB of a property is generally the amount paid to acquire the property. However, for certain kinds of property, there can be adjustments, which must be made to the original cost to arrive at the ACB for tax purposes.[3]

Costs of disposing of a property can include:

- an agent's or broker's commission;
- legal costs relating to the sale of the property;
- surveyor costs;
- transfer taxes; and
- registration fees.

The actual term "disposition"[4] is defined in the Act to include any event entitling a taxpayer to "proceeds of disposition." While not exhaustive, this list can include proceeds from:

- the sale of property;
- compensation for stolen property;

---

2 Subsection 248(1), "business" defined. See also M.N.R., Interpretation Bulletin IT-459 "Adventure or Concern in the Nature of Trade" (September 8, 1980) and M.N.R., Interpretation Bulletin IT-218R "Profit, Capital Gains and Losses From the Sale of Real Estate Including Farmland and Inherited Land and Conversion of Real Estate from Capital Property to Inventory and *Vice Versa*" (September 16, 1986).
3 Paragraph 53(2)(a); subsection 127.2(8), and subsection 127.3(6), deductions in computing ACB. See also M.N.R., Interpretation Bulletin IT-456R "Capital Property – Some Adjustments to Cost Base" (July 9, 1990), at paragraphs 10-13 and subsections 40(3), 52(1), 53(1) additions in computing ACB; see also M.N.R., Interpretation Bulletin IT-456R at paragraphs 2-5.
4 Subsection 248(1), "disposition" defined.

CHAPTER 10 — CALCULATING TOTAL INCOME

- compensation for property lost or destroyed;
- compensation for expropriated property;
- the redemption or cancellation of shares, bonds and other securities;
- mortgage settlements and foreclosures;
- transfers of property by the trust; and
- the settlement or extinguishing of a debt.

1.2 Reserve for Proceeds Not Due

If the proceeds from a sale of capital property are not all receivable in the year of sale, a portion of the capital gain can be deferred and realized in a subsequent taxation year.[5] Note that you must complete Schedule 2, "Reserves on Dispositions of Capital Property." The reserve claimed at the end of the taxation year should be entered on Line 14 of Schedule 1 to calculate the net capital gain reportable for the trust's taxation year.

The amount of the capital gain, which can be deferred for tax purposes, must be "reasonable," based on the amount of the proceeds not payable at the end of the taxation year. A reasonable reserve would be:

$$\frac{\text{Capital gain}}{\text{Proceeds of disposition}} \times \text{Proceeds not payable until after the end of the taxation year} = \text{reserve}$$

For dispositions occurring after November 12, 1981, the reserve is effectively restricted to a maximum of five years, with a minimum recognition of 20% of the capital gain in the year of disposition and an additional minimum 20% realizable in each successive taxation year.

---

5 Subparagraph 40(1)(a)(iii), calculation of gain, loss or reserve and M.N.R., Interpretation Bulletin, IT-236R4, "Reserves – Disposition of Capital Property" [Archived] (July 30, 1999) (See General comments in paragraphs 1-5). See also the various restrictions on claiming reserves contained in subsection 40(2). Be aware that CRA has archived M.N.R., Interpretation Bulletin IT-236R4. The reader is also directed to M.N.R., Technical Interpretation 912081, "Promissory Notes and Reserves" (August 21, 1991). CRA's position with respect to the acceptance of promissory notes and reserves under subparagraph 40(1)(a)(iii) is that a promissory note is assumed to be received as conditional payment unless the agreement between the parties clearly indicates that the note has been accepted as absolute payment.

PART IV — T3 TRUST INFORMATION & TAX RETURN

Note that a trust can only claim a reserve on the portion of sale proceeds which is "not payable" until after the end of the taxation year. The fact that an amount is not collected is not sufficient to consider the amount "not payable." Accordingly, where the terms of a sale require that the amount be paid to the vendor, and the amount is simply not collected, a reserve is not available for the uncollected amount under subparagraph 40(1)(a)(iii). Similarly a reserve would not be available, in respect of a demand note which is payable to the vendor upon execution of the transaction, unless the terms of payment are "qualified." For instance, a reserve might be available where payment is only due a fixed number of days subsequent to the demand for payment on the note.

A reserve, which is claimed at the end of one taxation year, must be included in income in the following year. A new reserve would be calculated based on the proceeds not due at the end of that taxation year, with the provision that a minimum of 20% of the capital gain must be reportable in a taxation year.

Generally on the death of a taxpayer, the full value of reserves must be included in the income of the deceased on the terminal return. Paragraph 72(1)(c) provides that no reserve may be claimed under subparagraph 40(1)(a)(iii) in computing a taxpayer's income in the year of death. There are, however, exceptions where the property which gives rise to the reserve is transferred to a surviving spouse or a spousal trust. The following conditions must be present for the rollover of the reserve to be effective:

- the deceased taxpayer must have been a Canadian resident immediately prior to death;

- the property relating to the reserve must be transferred to the spouse or spousal trust, and the property must vest indefeasibly[6] with the spouse or spousal trust; and

---

[6] See generally M.N.R., Interpretation Bulletin IT-449R, "Meaning of 'Vested Indefeasibly'" [Archived] (September 25, 1987), at paragraphs 1 and 2 for CRA's discussion on the meaning of "vest indefeasibly." Also for recent CRA commentary on a qualifying spousal trust, see M.N.R., Technical Interpretation 2003-0008285, "Spousal Trust – Entitlement – Payable" (September 23, 2003) and M.N.R., Technical Interpretation 2002-0126775, "Spousal Trust" (May 3, 2002).

CHAPTER 10 — CALCULATING TOTAL INCOME

- a joint election must be filed between the estate and the spouse or spousal trust in prescribed Form T2069.[7]

In this case, a reserve may be claimed in determining the deceased taxpayer's income for the year of death. Also, you should be aware that property bequeathed to a surviving spouse or to a spousal trust (on which reserves were claimed by the deceased) can continue to be claimed in succeeding years by the trust provided that a joint election under subsection 72(2) is filed.

1.3 Utilizing Capital Losses

If this is the first taxation year of a testamentary trust, the legal representative can make an election[8] to apply a net capital loss against capital gains reported in the terminal return.

This strategy can be very effective where the estate has acquired capital property, which is declining in value after the testator's death. For instance, marketable securities owned by the deceased at the date of death may have given rise to a capital gain reported on the terminal return. However, if the securities have declined in value thereafter, the legal representative could decide to dispose of the investments and create a net capital loss in the estate. The estate's net allowable capital losses can be carried back and applied against the capital gain reported on the terminal return.

Care should be taken to ensure that such capital losses are triggered within the first taxation year of the estate, otherwise the election under subsection 164(6) will not be available. While this strategy works effectively for this type of capital property, the use of a subsection 164(6)

---

[7] Subsection 72(2), election by legal representative and transferee re: reserves. See generally M.N.R., Interpretation Bulletin, IT-236R4, *supra*, note 5 at paragraph 13, "Reserves in Year of Death" and also M.N.R., Interpretation Bulletin IT-305R4, "Testamentary Spouse Trusts" (October 30, 1996).

[8] Subsection 164(6), disposition of property by legal representative of deceased taxpayer. See also Sibson, "Private Companies," 2001 Annual Conference, 5:1; and Rees, "Testamentary Planning to Avoid Double Taxation," 2000 Canadian Tax Journal, No. 1, 155.

PART IV — T3 TRUST INFORMATION & TAX RETURN

election may not be the best choice with respect to the redemption of shares of a privately owned corporation.

This is so because the top effective tax rate of reporting a capital gain is significantly lower than the top tax rate on a deemed dividend, which results from a share redemption strategy. In this scenario, there is less tax paid on a capital gain resulting from a deemed disposition on death, as opposed to a redeem and capital loss strategy, using the provisions of subsection 164(6).

There are, of course, exceptions. Where there is tax-free surplus to distribute using a share redemption strategy (such as a dividend paid out of the corporation's capital dividend account)[9] or where there is refundable dividend tax on hand[10] in the corporation redeeming the shares owned by the estate, filing an election under subsection 164(6) may be a worthwhile strategy.

The legal representative should be aware, however, of various tax traps and pitfalls, which might be encountered by virtue of the affiliated stop-loss rules[11] and the capital dividend stop-loss rules[12] contained within the provisions of the Act.

Subsection 40(3.6) can apply when there is a disposition of shares to a corporation with which the estate is affiliated immediately after the disposition.[13] In such case, the loss on the disposition is deemed to be nil.[14]

---

9 Subsection 83(2), capital Dividend. See also M.N.R., Interpretation Bulletin IT-66R6, "Capital Dividends" (May 31, 1991), at paragraphs 1 and 2.
10 Subsection 129(3), definition of "refundable dividend tax on hand."
11 Subsection 40(3.6), loss on shares.
12 Subsection 112(3.2), loss on shares held by trust.
13 Subsection 251.1(1), definition of "affiliated persons."
14 Subsection 40(3.6). Proposed amendments to the definition of "affiliated persons" which would extend such rules to estates and trusts, were introduced in the 2004 Federal Budget. These proposed amendments create further concerns and complications in this area, in situations where, immediately after the disposition of the shares by the estate, an affiliated person is a "majority interest beneficiary" in the property of the estate. Where this is the case, subsection 40(3.6) will apply to deem the loss realized by the estate on the disposition of the shares to be nil. See the Notice of Ways and Means Motion in section 19(b)

CHAPTER 10 — CALCULATING TOTAL INCOME

An estate would be affiliated with a corporation if the estate controls the corporation. The estate would also be considered to be affiliated with the corporation if (for instance) after the redemption of the estate's shares, the sole trustee of the estate controlled the corporation through the personal ownership of shares in the corporation.[15]

The other big concern in planning to use capital losses is that there is no provision to allocate allowable capital losses to a beneficiary. Consequently, with poor planning there is the potential for capital losses to be wasted.

For instance, capital property, which is transferred to a qualified spousal trust, will ultimately be disposed of at fair market value. If the property diminishes in value, the resulting capital loss will accrue to the trust and may not be able to be utilized. If instead, on the death of the testator, the property is transferred to a tainted spousal trust, the rollout occurs at the adjusted cost base of the property and, on a subsequent disposition of the property, a resulting capital loss may be able to be utilized by the beneficiary.

The legal representative should also be aware of the provisions of subsection 104(13.2), which permit the trustee to make a designation which deems capital gains to be otherwise included in the beneficiary's income under subsection 104(21) not to be payable and, instead, included as income (or as taxable capital gains) of the trust. The effect of this designation is that subsection 104(13.2) permits the trustee to deduct under subsection 104(6) less than the full amount of the taxable capital gains otherwise payable to the beneficiary. The undeducted capital gain

---

of the proposed amendments.

Draft legislation was released on September 16, 2004, which sets out rules for determining when persons are considered to be affiliated with one another. Newly proposed paragraphs 251.1(1)(g) and (h), together with new definitions for "beneficiary", "contributor" "majority interest beneficiary" and "majority interest group of beneficiaries" in subsection 251.1(3) and with new interpretive rules in subparagraphs 251.1(4)(c)(i) to (v), expand the existing "affiliated persons" rules to expressly apply to trusts. See Clause 38 of the Legislative Proposals released on September 16, 2004, detailing examples of the expanded application of the "affiliated persons" rules.

15 See M.N.R., Technical Interpretation 2000-0024775, "Affiliated Rules and Trusts" (February 23, 2001).

PART IV — T3 TRUST INFORMATION & TAX RETURN

can therefore be included in the trust's income for the year and, as a result, creates an amount by which capital losses of the trust realized in prior years might be utilized.[16]

2. Line 02 – Pension Income

Enter on Line 02 all amounts received in respect of the following:

- a registered pension plan (RPP);
- a retirement compensation arrangement (RCA);
- a deferred profit sharing plan (DPSP);
- a superannuation plan; or
- a foreign retirement arrangement.

Amounts received by an estate as superannuation or pension benefits in a year throughout which the trust was resident in Canada can be designated by the estate to a beneficiary so that the pension income retains the nature of its income characterization. In effect, the tax law provides for this treatment where it is reasonable to consider that such amounts would have been paid or payable to such beneficiaries.[17]

If the beneficiary of the trust is a spouse or common-law partner, and the amount received constitutes a life annuity payment, the amount will qualify for designation as eligible pension income to the beneficiary. The trust should complete Schedule 7, "Pension Income Allocations and Designations."

3. Line 03 – Actual Amount of Dividends from Taxable Canadian Corporations

Enter the actual amount of dividends received from taxable Canadian corporations reported on Line 1 of Schedule 8. Attach all applicable T5 and T3 Slips to Schedule 8.

---

16 See also heading 4 of Chapter 4 entitled, "Income Designations under 104(13.1) and 104(13.2)."
17 Subsection 104(27), pension benefits.

CHAPTER 10 — CALCULATING TOTAL INCOME

Also, include "deemed taxable dividends," which can arise from a share redemption or repurchase,[18] a reduction of the paid-up capital of shares owned by the trust,[19] or a distribution of property to the trust from a corporation or a reorganization,[20] which increases the paid-up capital of shares owned by the trust.

If the trust receives a dividend but does not receive a T5 or a T3 Slip, you should determine whether the dividend is a taxable dividend or not. If the dividend paid is less than $50, the payor corporation is not required to issue a slip to the recipient. However, if the dividend is taxable it should still be reported as income on Schedule 8 and included on Line 03 of the return.

Do not include non-taxable dividends such as dividends paid out of a corporation's capital dividend account.[21] Amounts paid on account of a participating insurance policy or as a distribution from a co-operative buying group are also not dividends and should not be included here.

4. Line 04 – Foreign Investment Income

Report the gross amount of investment income from foreign sources, converted to a Canadian dollar equivalent value. Enter the amount here from Line 04 of Schedule 8.

Use the applicable exchange rate in effect on the day foreign income was received by the trust. In general, however, CRA will accept conversions of amounts received in a foreign currency at an average "published" exchange rate for that currency for the taxation year.

Do not reduce the reportable foreign source income by tax withholdings paid to foreign tax authorities.[22]

---

18 Subsection 84(3), redemption.
19 Subsection 84(4), redemption of paid-up capital.
20 Subsection 84(1), deemed dividend.
21 Subsection 83(2).
22 See heading 11 of Chapter 14 entitled, "Schedule 11 – Federal Income Tax" for additional commentary.

PART IV — T3 TRUST INFORMATION & TAX RETURN

5. Line 05 – Other Investment Income

Report the aggregate amount of all interest and other investment income earned from Canadian sources. Enter the amount here from Line 10 of Schedule 8. Attach all slips to Schedule 8.

Interest income, while not defined in the Act, generally is described to include "the return or consideration or compensation for the use or retention of a sum of money owed by another person."

Income to be reported includes bond interest, bank interest, mortgage interest and "interest" implicit in the original issue price of a bond. That is, "below market" discounts are considered interest income, whereas a difference between the face value and purchase price of a bond may be held to be a capital gain or loss, assuming that the investment is held as a capital asset and not as an "adventure in the nature of trade."

Discount gains earned on T Bills are considered interest income.

Applicable to taxation years commencing after 1982, a trust is required to compute and report all interest and other investment income on an accrual basis.[23] Note that interest income accrued from the last date on which interest was payable to the date of death of a taxpayer should be reported as income on the terminal return and not the T3 Estate Return.[24]

Where a trust or estate is party to an enforceable agreement for the sale of property, and the proceeds are not paid or payable until a subsequent taxation year, any payment in excess of the negotiated price received by the vendor from the date of the agreement to the date of payment will be considered to be interest income, and not proceeds of disposition.

---

23 Subsection 12(3), interest income. See also M.N.R., Interpretation Bulletin IT-396R, "Interest Income" (May 29, 1984), at paragraph 15.
24 M.N.R., Interpretation Bulletin IT-210R2, "Income of Deceased Persons – Periodic Payments and Investment Tax Credit" (November 22, 1996), at paragraph 2.

CHAPTER 10 — CALCULATING TOTAL INCOME

Where the trust operates a farming or fishing business and elects to compute income on a "cash basis,"[25] the cash basis of accounting will also be permitted to be used in respect of interest income directly related to that business. However, the rules applicable in subsections 12(3) to (11) would continue to apply in respect of interest income from all other sources.

If the trust has made a loan to a related person, such as a corporation in which it holds shares, the interest paid or payable on the loan must be included in computing the income of the trust. This income would generally be taxed as "property income." However, be aware that technical amendments which were introduced by the Department of Finance on December 20, 2002, have now been further refined on February 27, 2004, to broaden the "tax on split income rule" to include income derived from the provision of "property or services" to a business carried on by a person related to the minor. These recent amendments will result in such interest income being subject to the provisions of section 120.4.[26] Split income of an individual currently is defined to include all amounts (other than certain excluded amounts) required to be included in the individual's income in respect of the provision of "goods or services" by a business, or in support of a business carried on by:

- a person related to the individual;

- a corporation of which a person who is related to the individual is a specified shareholder; or

- a professional corporation of which a person related to the individual is a shareholder.

---

25 Subsection 28(1), farming or fishing business. See also M.N.R., Interpretation Bulletin IT-433R "Farming or Fishing – Use of Cash Method" (June 4, 1993), at paragraphs 1 and 7.

26 Subsection 120.4(1), proposed definition of "split income," clause (c)(ii)(C). The phrase "goods or services" in subparagraph (b)(ii) and clause (c)(ii)(C) in the definition of "split income" under subsection 120.4(1) is replaced, for fiscal periods and taxation years commencing after December 20, 2002, with the phrase "property or services."

PART IV — T3 TRUST INFORMATION & TAX RETURN

The current phrase "goods or services" in the definition of "split income" will be replaced for fiscal periods and taxation years that begin after December 20, 2002, with the phrase "property or services." This change in the definition provides a broader meaning to "split income" and will likely apply to income from property such as interest income and rental income, earned from a business or person related to the minor.

6. Line 06 – Business Income

Enter the trust's gross and net income or loss derived from a business as completed on Form T2124, "Statement of Business Activities." If the trust incurred a loss, enter the amount in brackets. If the trust is a member of a partnership enter the partnership's total gross income and the trust's share of the partnership's net income or loss.

A business is defined by the Act to include a profession, calling, trade, manufacture or undertaking of any kind whatever and includes an adventure or concern in the nature of trade. Rental income earned from real property would generally not be considered to be business income and should not be included in this section (see Line 09 – Rental Income). Income from the sale of real property would be considered to be business income if the principal business involves the trading or development of such properties for re-sale.[27]

If the trust operates a business with a non-calendar year-end, special rules will apply for reporting income based on the alternative method. CRA publishes a guide called "Reconciliation of Business Income for Tax Purposes," which includes prescribed Form T1139. If the business maintains a non-calendar fiscal year, there is a requirement to calculate an "additional business income" amount under the alternative method, which amount must be added to the business income for the year. Consequently the "additional business income" calculated for the prior year can be deducted from the business income reported for the current taxation year.

---

27 See M.N.R., Interpretation Bulletin IT-218R, *supra*, note 2.

CHAPTER 10 — CALCULATING TOTAL INCOME

Form T1139 also provides an election to move to a calendar year basis. In 2004, businesses operating on a non-calendar fiscal year will include into income for tax purposes, 15% of their December 31, 1995, income.[28] No further reserve is provided for after 2004.

7. Line 07 – Farming Income

Enter the trust's gross and net income derived from farming on Line 07.

If the trust incurred a loss, enter the amount in brackets.

See also the following CRA guides:

- Farming Income (Form T2042, Statement of Farming Activities); and

- Farming Income and the CAIS Program (Form T1163, Statement A – CAIS Program Account Information and Statement of Farming Activities for Individuals, or Form T1164, Statement B – CAIS Program Account Information and Statement of Farming Activities for Additional Operations).

8. Line 08 – Fishing Income

Enter the trust's gross and net income derived from fishing on Line 08.

If the trust incurred a loss, enter the amount in brackets.

See also CRA guide "Fishing Income (Form T2121 Statement of Fishing Activities)."

9. Line 09 – Rental Income

Enter the trust's gross and net income derived from the rental of real property, as compiled on Form T776, "Statement of Real Estate Rentals."

---

28 Subsection 34.2(1), definition of "specified percentage."

PART IV — T3 TRUST INFORMATION & TAX RETURN

If the trust incurred a loss, enter the amount in brackets on this line. Note that a loss cannot be created or increased by claiming capital cost allowance on the property. You should complete Form T776 in respect of each such rental property.

Note (Line 06 to Line 09) that if the trust is a member of a partnership, enter the partnership's total gross income and the trust's share of the partnership's net income or loss.

Rental income earned on real property can be either income from a business or income from property. Generally rental income will be considered to be "property income." Rental income will be considered to be "business income" only where the services provided to the tenants go beyond the mere rental of the property. The extent of additional services provided would be the determining factor as to whether the activity constitutes income from a business or property. General services such as the provision of heat, water, parking, laundry, elevator services and the maintenance of the building and property do not constitute the provision of "business services."

Rental income must be accounted for on an accrual basis. The following expenses will generally be deductible from rental income in the year they are incurred:

- property taxes (exceptions for vacant land and property under construction or renovation);

- insurance on the property relating to the period of operation;

- utilities;

- repairs and maintenance (excepting major renovations of a capital nature);

- advertising;

- interest on money borrowed to acquire or to implement capital improvements or renovations;

- salaries, wages, and benefits paid to custodians, superintendents,

CHAPTER 10 — CALCULATING TOTAL INCOME

and maintenance personnel employed in the operation of the rental business;

- accounting and legal fees (other than fees associated with the acquisition of the property);

- commissions paid to agents to collect rents;

- landscaping of grounds around property; and

- office supplies and certain automobile costs.

Be aware that recent provisions introduced by the Department of Finance on October 31, 2003, will apply a test requiring the "reasonable expectation of profit" (REOP)[29] in respect of such property income, particularly with respect to the deductibility of interest paid in connection with the acquisition of a rental property.

Rental income is deemed to be income earned in the province or territory in which the trust is resident for the taxation year, unless the rental income constitutes income from a business. In this case the rental income should be allocated to the province in which it is considered to have been earned.

Rental income, which is considered property income, must be reported on a calendar year basis. Rental income, which is considered to constitute business income, can be reported on a non-calendar fiscal year basis, subject to the post-1995 tax rules relating to the "alternative method" of reporting income.[30]

---

29 See proposed new subsection 3.1(1), wherein losses from a source will not be deductible against other income reported in a taxation year unless the taxpayer can demonstrate that the source of the income giving rise to the loss has a reasonable expectation of profit over the eventual course of the business. The proposal is not targeted to come into force until 2005. See also M.N.R., Interpretation Bulletin IT-533, "Interest Deductibility and Related Issues" (October 31, 2003).

30 See heading 6 of this chapter entitled, "Line 06 – Business Income." See also CRA's Tax Guide "Rental Income (T4036)."

PART IV — T3 TRUST INFORMATION & TAX RETURN

10. Line 10 – NISA Fund 2

Include on this line, the portion of a farm producer's net income stabilization account from a third party source (*i.e.*, interest, bonuses or government contributions).

Calculate all amounts received by the trust out of a NISA Fund 2.

An AGR-1 Slip, "Statement of Farm Support Payments" is required for all farm support programs which the trust received in respect of payment of $100 or more. These include programs administered by federal, provincial and municipal governments and producer associations.

Enter the amount, if any, determined by the following calculation:

$$A - (B - C)$$

Where:

 A = the amount paid in the year out of the fund

 B = the total of all amounts paid out of the fund to the trust, beneficiary spouse/common law partner, or another person's fund

 C = the total of all amounts previously applied to reduce income out of the fund

A separate calculation for each amount is required and either paid or deemed paid.

11. Line 11 – Deemed Realizations

Enter on Line 11, the trust's income and capital gains resulting from "twenty-one year deemed realizations." Attach Form T1055, "Summary of Deemed Realization."

CHAPTER 10 — CALCULATING TOTAL INCOME

The creation of a trust can provide for the deferral of capital gains taxes on trust assets to the extent that they are held for extended periods of time. Unless the capital assets are disposed of by the trust, no capital gains tax would arise.

From a Canadian tax policy perspective, an indefinite tax deferral is not acceptable. Consequently, provisions exist in the Act, which require the recognition of such deferred gains for tax purposes, even though the trust may continue to hold these assets.

These rules are termed the "deemed disposition rules" and such rules apply to deem a disposition to occur for the trust's assets on the twenty-first anniversary of the trust.

This rule applies only to personal trusts and not for an employee benefits plan trust or a trust for a registered education plan. Furthermore, the rule is modified somewhat in the case of a qualifying spousal or common-law partner trust, and alter ego trusts and joint partner trusts.

In effect, a personal trust will be deemed to have disposed of its non-depreciable capital property, resource property and land inventory on certain twenty-one year anniversary dates, and to have reacquired this property immediately thereafter at fair market value.[31] Depreciable property will also be deemed to be disposed of and reacquired by the trust at fair market value[32] on the twenty-first year anniversary date. The relevant dates for the occurrence of this "deemed realization" of assets is as follows:

- for a spousal or common-law partner trust, a deemed realization will occur at the time of death of that person, and every twenty-one years thereafter;

- for a joint spousal or common-law partner trust, a deemed realization occurs on the date of the "last to die;"

- for an alter ego trust, a deemed realization occurs on the date of

---

31 Subsection 104(4), deemed disposition by trust.
32 Subsection 104(5), depreciable property.

death of the settlor, unless the trust filed an election not to be considered an alter ego trust, in which case the deemed realization date would be twenty-one years after the date the trust was created; and

- for all other trusts, a deemed realization will occur every twenty-one years commencing from the later of January 1, 1972, and the date the trust was created.[33]

A deemed disposition of the trust's assets, which occurs on the realization date, will result in the trust realizing all accrued capital gains or losses and recaptured capital cost allowance of assets owned by the trust. For this reason, planning in anticipation of a deemed realization is critical.[34]

12. Line 19 – Other Income

Enter the total income the trust received in the taxation year such as:

- royalties;

- commissions;

- death benefits under the Canada Pension Plan (CPP) or Quebec Pension Plan (QPP);

- retiring allowances,[35] excluding amounts reported by a beneficiary or reported as income for the year of death as a "right or thing;" and

- certain other employment related income.

---

[33] Paragraphs 104(4)(b) and (c), deemed disposition by trust.
[34] See 2.1 of Chapter 6 entitled, "Deemed Realizations at Twenty-One Years" for commentary and planning in anticipation of a twenty-one year deemed realization.
[35] See M.N.R., Interpretation Bulletin IT-337R4, "Retiring Allowances" (October 21, 2003), at paragraph 18.

CHAPTER 10 — CALCULATING TOTAL INCOME

12.1 Death Benefit – Other than CPP or QPP

A death benefit is generally defined to include the aggregate of amounts received by a taxpayer in connection with the deceased's office of employment, in recognition of the deceased person's service of employment.[36] Usually, the death benefit is payable to the surviving spouse or common-law partner. It may, however, be payable to the estate in certain circumstances.

Where this is the case, there are provisions in the Act which permit amounts received in respect of a death benefit[37] by an estate to be considered to be paid or payable to a beneficiary.

The effect of this provision is to treat the death benefit amount received by an estate as a "flow-through" so that the income characterization is maintained in the hands of the beneficiaries.

Where the spouse or common-law partner is the particular beneficiary of the estate for which the amount is payable, the full $10,000 exemption on the receipt of the death benefit can be applied in respect of the spouse or common-law partner. If there are other beneficiaries entitled to the amount, the $10,000 exemption should be pro-rated proportionately among the beneficiaries.

If the amount is to be taxed within the estate or trust according to the provisions of the trust document or will, the first $10,000 of amounts received in respect of the death benefit can be excluded from the trust or estate income.

Amounts reported by the employer, in respect of a death benefit, are generally shown on Box 28 of a T4A Slip, together with a footnote in Box 38. Enter the amount from the T4A Slip on Line 19 of the T3 Return and attach a copy of the T4A Slip to the T3 Return.

---

36 Subsection 248(1), also refer to M.N.R., Interpretation Bulletin IT-508R, "Death Benefits" (February 12, 1996).
37 Subsection 104(28).

PART IV — T3 TRUST INFORMATION & TAX RETURN

12.2 Registered Retirement Savings Plan (RRSP)

As a general rule, all amounts received by a taxpayer from a Registered Retirement Savings Plan (RRSP) on death are included in the taxpayer's income on the terminal return for the year of death. The exception to this situation is where the annuitant's plan is unmatured and the plan qualifies as a refund of premiums.[38] To qualify as a refund of premiums, the unmatured RRSP proceeds must be payable to, or deemed to have been received by, a surviving spouse or common-law partner of the deceased annuitant or, if the deceased annuitant was not survived by a spouse or common-law partner, a financially dependent child or grandchild. In such case, the unmatured RRSP proceeds would be payable to the designated beneficiary and would not be included in the income of the estate.

However, if no person other than the estate of the deceased taxpayer is entitled to receive the unmatured RRSP proceeds, income earned subsequent to the death of the annuitant on the proceeds of the unmatured RRSP will generally accrue and become payable to the estate.[39] Usually this income will be reported on either a T5 or T4RSP Slip. The amount of this income should be reported on Line 19 of the T3 Return and the applicable T5 or T4RSP Slip should also be attached to the T3 Return.

For more information on this area refer to CRA's guide, "RRSPs and other Registered Plans for Retirement."

---

38 Subsection 146(8.9).
39 See also M.N.R., Interpretation Bulletin IT-500R, "Registered Retirement Savings Plans – Death of an Annuitant" (December 18, 1996), at paragraphs 10 and 11. However, there is a provision for the annuitant's spouse to jointly elect with the legal representative of the estate under subsection 146(8.1) to include any such portion of the payment designated as a refund of premiums as income for the spouse, provided that the spouse is a beneficiary of the annuitant's estate. A similar election is available for a financially dependent child or grandchild of the annuitant, if the annuitant had no spouse at death. See applicable CRA Form T2019 "Death of an RRSP Annuitant – Refund of Premiums."

Chapter 11
Calculating Net Income

1. Line 21 – Carrying Charges and Interest Expenses

Enter the total carrying charges and interest expenses of the trust as calculated on Line 15 of Schedule 8.

Schedule 8 lists deductible expenses of the trust related to interest on money borrowed to earn investment income, management, safe custody, accounting fees, investment counsel fees and other carrying charges.

The following guidelines should be considered in determining the deductibility of these items by the trust.

1.1 Interest Expenses

Interest paid in the course of earning income from a "business" or in connection with a "rental property" should not be included on Schedule 8 or reported on Line 21 of the T3 Return.

Instead, interest expense directly related to a business or property should be included as part of the trust's calculation of income or loss and reported on Form T2124, "Statement of Business Activities" or Form T776, "Statement of Real Estate Rentals" respectively.

PART IV — T3 TRUST INFORMATION & TAX RETURN

Interest paid or payable by the trust in respect of other property income should be entered here and the interest would be deductible under the following conditions:

- the interest must have been paid or payable in respect of a legal obligation to pay interest,[1] and

- the borrowed funds must have been used for the purpose of earning income from the property.

Since the trust would generally report income on an accrual basis, interest expense would be deductible in the year to which it relates, whether or not it was actually paid in the year.

1.2 Re-Loaned Funds

To the extent that interest expense exceeds the related investment income of the trust, the net "loss" will be deductible against other income reported by the trust in the year. However, recent legislative amendments introduced by the Department of Finance in the October 31, 2003, Notice of Ways and Means Motion will impose a "reasonable expectation of profit" (REOP) test, in respect of losses occurring for taxation years commencing after 2004.[2]

Interest expense related to a life insurance policy is deductible to the trust, if the policy loan proceeds are used to earn investment income. However if the trust elects to add the policy loan interest to the adjusted cost base of the policy, the interest paid cannot be deducted on Line 21 of the T3 Return. For the interest to be deductible the insurer must complete Form T2210, "Verification of Policy Loan Interest By the Insurer."

---

1 Paragraph 20(1)(c), interest. See also M.N.R., Interpretation Bulletin IT-533, "Interest Deductibility and Related Issues" (October 31, 2003).
2 Proposed new subsection 3.1(1) provides that a taxpayer will be considered to have a loss from a source that is a business or property for a taxation year only if in that year, it is reasonable to assume that the taxpayer will realize a cumulative profit from the business or property.

CHAPTER 11 — CALCULATING NET INCOME

Interest paid on late income tax payments to CRA is not deductible by an estate or trust. Interest expense related to succession duties or estate taxes is also not deductible.

1.3 Other Carrying Charges and Expenses

Amounts paid or payable by the trust in respect of custodial services and the management of investments are deductible and would be included on Schedule 8.

Expenses relating to the safekeeping of investments (safety deposit box charges), accounting and investment counsel fees would also be reported on Schedule 8 and would be reflected on Line 21 of the T3 Return.

If the trust has carrying charges for Canadian and foreign investment income, a separate schedule should be prepared to detail the income and deductions relating to each source.

Commissions paid in connection with the buying or selling of securities should not be reported as a carrying charge. These amounts relate to the capital cost of acquiring or disposing of the security and they should be included as part of the calculation of determining the capital gains or capital losses of the trust as detailed on Schedule 1.

2. Line 24 – Trustee Fees Deductible from Income

The trust is entitled to deduct fees charged by executors and trustees for their services in connection with the administration of the estate or trust, provided that the following conditions are met:

- those fees relate to the earning of income of the estate or trust, including income earned from a rental property, or in respect of amounts paid for the management of a business of the trust; and

- those fees are paid to an executor or trustee whose principal business includes the provision of such services.[3]

Since trustee fees are taxable to the recipient, the trust is required to issue a T4A Supplementary for those amounts. If the trust makes a payment to a non-resident recipient for such services performed in Canada, the trust is required to complete and issue a T4A-NR Supplementary and to make the required withholding tax requirements.

In some situations the executor or trustee may be required to maintain property for the use of a life tenant or beneficiary. Income of the estate or trust applied to maintain the property (such as property taxes, repairs, and maintenance) would generally be considered to be income of the beneficiary.[4]

Fees related to the administration of such property (*i.e.*, real property) for the beneficiary would not be deductible, since the property is not used to earn business or property income.[5]

3. Line 25 – Allowable Business Investment Losses

Enter on Line 25 the trust's allowable business investment loss ("ABIL")[6] for the year. The ABIL is deductible against the trust's other sources of income for the year. If the ABIL reported on Line 25 exceeds all other sources of the trust's income for the year, the excess is deemed to be a non-capital loss and can be applied, subject to certain restrictions against the trust's income for the immediately three preceding taxation years and the seven taxation years thereafter.

---

3 Paragraph 20(1)(bb). See also M.N.R., Interpretation Bulletin IT-238R2, "Fees Paid to Investment Counsel" (October 6, 1983), at paragraph 4.
4 Subsection 105(2), upkeep, etc. See also M.N.R., Interpretation Bulletin IT-342R, "Trusts – Income Payable to Beneficiaries" (March 21, 1990), at paragraph 1.
5 Subsections 105(1) and 104(6).
6 Section 38(c). See also M.N.R., Interpretation Bulletin IT-484R2, "Business Investment Losses" (November 28, 1996), at paragraphs 1-3.

CHAPTER 11 — CALCULATING NET INCOME

If the ABIL cannot be applied as a non-capital loss within this time frame, the unapplied portion becomes a net capital loss in the eighth taxation year and this amount can be used to reduce the trust's taxable capital gains arising in such year or any other following taxation year.

An ABIL can arise only if the trust holds an investment in shares or debt of a small business corporation.[7] Where this is the case, an ABIL can result in any one of the following situations:[8]

- for shares, where there is either a disposition to an arm's length person or where the corporation has become formally bankrupt or insolvent under the Winding-up acts;

- for debt, where there is either a disposition to an arm's length person or where the debt is considered uncollectible and the deemed disposition rules apply.[9]

The issue as to when a debt is "uncollectible" has been addressed in the courts.

As the Act does not define a bad debt, it is necessary to turn to recognized accounting principles of business practice. A debt is recognized to be bad when it has been proved uncollectible in the year. The question of when a debt is to be considered uncollectible is a matter of the taxpayer's own judgement as a prudent businessman.[10]

This issue remains subject to challenge by CRA and review by the courts.

---

7 Subsection 248(1), definition of small business corporation. See also M.N.R., Interpretation Bulletin IT-484R2, *ibid.* at paragraph 4.
8 Paragraph 39(1)(c).
9 Paragraph 50(1)(a). See also M.N.R., Interpretation Bulletin IT-159R3, "Capital Debts Established to be Bad Debts" (May 1, 1989), at paragraph 1; and M.N.R., Interpretation Bulletin IT-484R2, *supra*, note 6 at paragraph 6.
10 *Flexi-Coil Ltd v. R.* (1995), [1996] 1 C.T.C. 2941 at 2950, 1995 CarswellNat 1380 (T.C.C.), affirmed by [1996] 3 C.T.C. 57, 96 D.T.C. 6350, (sub nom. *Flexi Coil Ltd. v. Minister of National Revenue*) 199 N.R. 120, 1996 CarswellNat 1459 (Fed. C.A.).

PART IV — T3 TRUST INFORMATION & TAX RETURN

Case law in 2003 has also highlighted that a debt can be considered to be "bad" or "uncollectible" at the end of a particular fiscal year and that it is the taxpayer who should establish this determination at the end of each fiscal year.[11]

There are, however, certain restrictions in the Act which can apply to limit or deny the access to an ABIL. For instance, where a debt is held with no reasonable expectation of income or profit, a resulting loss therefrom would be deemed to be nil.[12]

Similarly, where a trust has in a prior taxation year, designated a capital gain eligible for the capital gains exemption[13] to one or more beneficiaries of the trust, there will be a reduction in the trust's ABIL equal to the lesser of the actual ABIL for the year and the proportionate amount related to the capital gains designated by the trust in respect of the beneficiaries for any prior taxation years, except to the extent that any other ABIL from a prior year was accordingly reduced by this provision.[14]

4. Line 40 – Other Deductions from Total Income

The trust is generally entitled to deduct other expenses to the extent that they are incurred for the purpose of earning income. Legal and accounting expenses related to the objection or appeal of an assessment of tax, interest or penalties under the federal *Income Tax Act* and/or any provincial income tax act can be claimed on this line.

A deduction for such costs can be made where the trust incurs legal or accounting fees for advice or assistance in making representations, whether or not a formal notice of objection or appeal is subsequently filed with CRA. Such claims for a deduction must be reduced for any

---

11 *MacKay v. R.* (2002), [2003] 1 C.T.C. 2682, 2003 D.T.C 748, 2002 CarswellNat 3507 (T.C.C. [General Procedure]).
12 Paragraph 40(2)(g).
13 Subsection 110.6(1).
14 Subsection 111(8). See also M.N.R., Interpretation Bulletin IT- 484R2, *supra*, note 6 at paragraph 10.

legal costs awarded by a court, in respect of an appeal in relation to the contested assessment of tax, interest or penalties under either the federal or provincial Income Tax acts.

Also, report the trust's eligible resource allowance on Line 40, to the extent that the trust has earned income from resource profits. Such resource profits would include royalties based on oil and gas production. Attach a copy of the T5 Slip from the payor to substantiate the resource allowance.

5. Line 43 – Upkeep, Maintenance and Taxes of a Property Used or Occupied by a Beneficiary

The trust may have incurred expenses relating to the upkeep, maintenance and taxes on a property used by a beneficiary of the trust. To the extent that these expenses are paid out of the income of the trust, the beneficiary is required to include the amounts as income in the year so paid. These "benefits" must be reported as income of the beneficiary on a T3 Supplementary Slip. Such amounts would be included on Line 43 of the T3 Return and would increase the income of the trust before allocations to beneficiaries, for purposes of Line 46 of the T3 Return. To offset this additional inclusion of "trust income," there is an offsetting deduction to the trust as provided for on Line 47, in respect of such "benefits" allocated to beneficiaries.

6. Line 44 – Value of Other Benefits to a Beneficiary

The value of non-cash benefits conferred on a beneficiary or other taxpayer during the trust taxation year may in some circumstances be added to that taxpayer's income and deducted in computing the income of the trust.[15] Exceptions may include the use of personal-use property,

---

15 Subsection 105(1). For a complete discussion on this topic see heading 2 of Chapter 4 entitled, "Income in the Form of Benefits Conferred by the Trust."

including dwellings, scholarships and related vehicles paid for by the trust and settlement payments made by the trust to the beneficiary.

7. Line 47 – Total Income Allocations and Designations to Beneficiaries

Generally, income, which is allocated to the beneficiaries of a trust, as set out in Schedule 9 of the T3 Return should be entered on Line 47 and deducted from the trust's income.

The deduction on Line 47 is consistent with the concept that trust income has been paid or allocated and will be subject to tax in the hands of the beneficiary, and not that of the trust.

However, there are some exceptions to this general rule. For instance, a post-1971 spousal or common-law partner trust, joint spousal or common-law partner trust or alter ego trust cannot deduct any income realized from deemed dispositions of property of the trust, and then distributed to someone other than:

- for a post-1971 spousal or common-law partner trust, the beneficiary spouse or common-law partner;

- for a joint spousal or common-law partner trust, the settlor or the beneficiary spouse or common-law partner, while the settlor or beneficiary spouse or common-law partner is still alive; or

- for an alter ego trust, the settlor.

There is also a restriction in deducting from the trust's income any capital gains realized from deemed dispositions of capital property (other than exempt or excluded property) or income from the sale of land inventory of the trust's business, and Canadian and foreign resource property income arising on the death of:

- for a post-1971 spousal or common-law partner trust, the beneficiary spouse or common-law partner;

CHAPTER 11 — CALCULATING NET INCOME

- for a joint spousal or common-law partner trust, the settlor or the beneficiary spouse or common-law partner, whichever is later;

- for an alter ego trust, the settlor; or

- a deemed payment from NISA Fund 2 that arose on the death of a beneficiary spouse or common-law partner.

A trust cannot deduct income from payments out of NISA Fund 2, unless the trust is a testamentary spousal or common-law partner trust and this income was received while the beneficiary spouse or common-law partner was alive or the trust is a communal organization.

A trust cannot deduct amounts payable in a taxation year to anyone except:

- for a trust that was a post-1971 spousal trust on December 20, 1991, or a spousal or common-law partner trust created after December 20, 1991, the beneficiary spouse or common-law partner, while the beneficiary spouse or common-law partner is alive;

- for a joint spousal or common-law partner trust, the settlor or the beneficiary spouse or common-law partner while either one of them is alive; or

- for an alter ego trust, the settlor while the settlor is alive.

8. Line 49 – Gross-Up Amount of Dividends Retained or Not Designated by the Trust

Normally when a Canadian resident trust receives a taxable dividend on a share of a taxable Canadian corporation, it can designate such part of the amount that is required to be included in computing the beneficiary's income under subsection 104(13) as a taxable dividend to the beneficiary (with all the attributes and the flow-through of the dividend tax credit).[16]

---

16 Subsection 104(19). See also M.N.R., Interpretation Bulletin IT-524, "Trusts –

PART IV — T3 TRUST INFORMATION & TAX RETURN

However, it may sometimes be advantageous, for instance, to retain and tax the dividend income within the trust. This is so when the marginal tax rate of the trust is less than the comparative tax rate for the designated beneficiary. This can apply for a testamentary trust, which is subject to the graduated rates on dividend income from a taxable Canadian corporation, or for an *inter vivos* trust which might be subject to tax in a jurisdiction that is lower than the tax jurisdiction of the designated beneficiary.

To the extent that taxable dividends received by the trust from a taxable Canadian corporation are not designated to beneficiaries under subsection 104(19), the dividend income will be retained within the trust and the gross-up provisions[17] will apply.

The "gross-up" amount to the trust is consistent with the "grossed-up" taxable dividend that would be taxable had the dividend been designated to a resident Canadian individual beneficiary of the trust. Accordingly, income from actual dividends of taxable Canadian corporations, which are retained within the trust, are "grossed-up" by one-quarter and the trust is also afforded the federal and provincial or territorial dividend tax credit on the taxable dividend income retained within the trust.[18]

If dividends from a taxable Canadian corporation are retained by the trust, complete Schedule 8 and then enter on Line 49 of the T3 Return the amount calculated at Line 826 of Schedule 8. The "gross-up" amount of dividends equates to one-quarter of the actual amount of dividends from taxable Canadian corporations, as reported on Line 3 of the T3 Return, that have been retained as income to be taxed within the trust.

Flow-Through of Taxable Dividends to a Beneficiary – After 1987" (March 16, 1990), at paragraphs 1 and 2.
17   Paragraph 82(1)(b).
18   Section 121.

Chapter 12
Calculating Taxable Income

1. Line 51 – Non-Capital Losses of Other Years

Non-capital losses of prior years can be used to reduce the taxable income of the trust for a taxation year. Enter the amount claimed on Line 51 of the T3 Return.

The trust's non-capital losses should be accounted for on a separate schedule in chronological order by taxation year. A non-capital loss can be applied to reduce trust income in the immediately three preceding taxation years and the seven taxation years thereafter.[1] However, if the trust allocated income to beneficiaries in a prior taxation year, the income allocation for that prior year cannot be reduced to utilize a loss arising in the current year. For this reason, care should be taken in determining income allocations where it is conceivable that a non-capital loss may arise in a subsequent taxation year of the trust.

Non-capital losses of a trust can arise from business or property; it can also include the unutilized portion of an allowable business investment loss arising in the eighth taxation year occurring after the recognition of the loss.

---

1 See however, Notice of Ways and Means Motions, Federal Budget of March 23, 2004 at paragraph 9 amending the "Carry-Forward Period for Business Losses" in respect of a non-capital loss for a taxation year that ends after March 22, 2004, from seven to ten years.

PART IV — T3 TRUST INFORMATION & TAX RETURN

If the trust has a non-capital loss arising from a farming or fishing business, the loss can be carried back three years and forward ten years. There are restrictions on the amount of the farm loss that can be deducted in a particular taxation year, depending on whether the farm business constitutes a primary source of income for the trust or whether the loss would be considered a "restricted farm loss."[2]

Where the source of income is not a chief source of income for the trust, the losses resulting from a farm business may be restricted.[3] The farm loss, which can be used to reduce income from other sources for the year, will be limited to the lesser of:

- the farming loss for the year;

- $2,500 plus the lesser of one-half of the amount by which the farming loss for the year exceeds $2,500; and

- $6,250.

The deduction for a "restricted farming loss" is therefore limited to a maximum of $8,750 for any given taxation year. The $8,750 maximum deduction is realized on restricted farming losses of $15,000. The restricted portion of the non-capital loss can be utilized only against farm income of either the three preceding or ten following taxation years. These restricted farm losses should be tracked in a pool separate from other non-capital losses.

2. Line 52 – Net Capital Losses of Other Years

A net capital loss arises where a trust's allowable capital losses exceeds its taxable capital gains in a given taxation year. The excess of these losses over the capital gains represents a net capital loss for that taxation year. Net capital losses can be used to reduce the trust's taxable capital

---

2 See Farming Income and CAIS Program Guide.
3 Section 31. See also M.N.R., Interpretation Bulletin IT-322R, "Farm Losses" (October 25, 1978), at paragraph 1(b).

CHAPTER 12 — CALCULATING TAXABLE INCOME

gains in any of the immediate three preceding taxation years or they can be carried forward indefinitely against future capital gains arising in the trust.

A deduction for a net capital loss should be entered on Line 52 of the T3 Return; the amount entered cannot exceed the taxable capital gains entered on Line 01 for the taxation year.

A net capital loss arising in the first taxation year of a testamentary trust can be applied against income reported on the terminal return of the deceased subject to certain restrictions.[4]

A net capital loss carryback can only be deducted against capital gains retained and taxed within the trust in one of the three preceding taxation years.

The current policy of CRA is that capital gains previously designated to beneficiaries can be amended, so as to accommodate a net capital loss application, provided that the total income allocated to the beneficiaries by the trust for that particular taxation year does not change.[5]

One strategy is to consider applying a net capital loss to a prior taxation year of the trust, where a non-capital loss was previously utilized thereby "restoring" the availability of the non-capital loss.[6]

A net capital loss can also occur on a twenty-one year "deemed realization," when property of the trust is deemed to be disposed of at fair market value. As a planning point, the legal representative should be aware of the provisions which permit a trustee to make a designation which deems capital gains otherwise available for inclusion in a bene-

---

4   Subsection 164(6); see also 1.3 of Chapter 10 entitled, "Utilizing Capital Losses" for additional commentary.
5   M.N.R., Interpretation Bulletin IT-381R3, "Trusts – Capital Gains and Losses and the Flow-Through of Taxable Capital Gains to Beneficiaries" (February 14, 1997), at paragraphs 10 and 11.
6   M.N.R., Interpretation Bulletin IT-232R3, "Losses – Their Deductibility in the Loss Year or in Other Years" (July 4, 1997), at paragraphs 12 and 13.

PART IV — T3 TRUST INFORMATION & TAX RETURN

ficiary's income not to be payable, and instead included as taxable capital gains of the trust.[7]

The effect of this designation is that the trustee is permitted to deduct less than the full amount of the taxable capital gains, otherwise payable to the beneficiary. The "undeducted" capital gains are therefore included in the trust's income for the year and, as a result, creates an amount by which net capital losses of the trust realized in a prior taxation year might be utilized.

3. Form T3A – Request for Loss Carryback by a Trust

Complete this form to apply an unused loss to a prior taxation year. To be valid, the trust must file this form on or before the due date for the T3 Return for the taxation year in which the trust incurred the loss.

You can file the T3A separately or with the current year's T3 Return.

A non-capital loss can be used to reduce the taxable income of a trust for any of the three immediately preceding taxation years. However, if the trust allocated income to beneficiaries in any of those preceding taxation years, the income so allocated cannot be subsequently reduced to facilitate the use of a loss carryback.[8]

A net capital loss carryback is deductible only to the extent that taxable capital gains are retained in the trust. If taxable capital gains were payable to beneficiaries in a prior taxation year, it is possible to reduce the net taxable capital gains payable to beneficiaries in that year, insofar as the total income allocated to beneficiaries for the year does not change.

---

[7] Subsection 104(13.2). See also M.N.R., Interpretation Bulletin IT-342R, "Trusts – Income Payable to Beneficiaries" (March 21, 1990), at paragraph 4. See also heading 4 of Chapter 4 entitled, "Income Designations under 104(13.1) and 104(13.2)" for additional commentary.

[8] See also heading 1 of this chapter entitled, "Line 51 – Non-Capital Losses of Other Years" for a discussion on this point. Also refer to M.N.R., Interpretation Bulletin IT-232R3, *supra*, note 6.

CHAPTER 12 — CALCULATING TAXABLE INCOME

The effect of reducing the net taxable capital gains payable to beneficiaries would increase the taxable capital gains retained in the trust, thereby permitting the application of a carryback from a loss year.[9]

4. Line 53 – Capital Gains Deduction for Resident Spousal or Common-Law Partner Trust Only

A Canadian resident spousal or common-law partner trust, which meets the definition as provided for in subsection 70(6), can claim the unused portion of the beneficiary's capital gains deduction in the year in which the beneficiary spouse or common-law partner dies.[10]

To claim an eligible deduction, complete Schedule 5 and file with the T3 Return. Enter on Line 53, the amount computed on Line 10 of Schedule 5.

The deduction is not available to a pre-1972 spousal trust which filed Form T1015, "Election by a Trust to Defer the Deemed Realization Day," or to joint spousal or common-law partner trust or to an alter ego trust.

The unused capital gains deduction is $250,000 less amounts claimed by the spouse or common-law partner in prior taxation years, adjusted for the applicable capital gains inclusion rate for the particular taxation year.

This deduction is available only with respect to net taxable capital gains from the disposition of qualified farm property[11] and shares of a qualified small business corporation[12] for the year.

---

9 See also heading 2 of this chapter entitled, "Line 52 – Net Capital Losses of Other Years" for commentary on this point.
10 Subsection 110.6(12). See also M.N.R., Interpretation Bulletin IT-381R3, *supra*, note 5 at paragraphs 14 to 17.
11 Subsection 110.6(2), defined in subsection 110.6(1).
12 Subsection 110.6(2.1), defined in subsection 110.6(1).

PART IV — T3 TRUST INFORMATION & TAX RETURN

Note that in the case of a share of a small business corporation, generally 90% or more of the value of the corporation's assets must be used in an active business carried on primarily in Canada, in order for the share to qualify. This provision is somewhat modified however, in the case of death.[13] In particular, if the 90% test is not met immediately before death, the share is still considered to qualify as long as it was a share of a qualified small business corporation at any time in the twelve month period immediately prior to the date of death.

5. Line 54 – Other Deductions to Arrive at a Taxable Income

Enter on Line 54 other deductions available to the trust, including:

- the amount of foreign income reported that is exempt from tax in Canada because of a tax treaty or convention;

- limited partnership losses from a prior year attributing to the estate or trust; and

- farming or fishing losses arising from a prior taxation year.[14]

---

13 Paragraphs 110.6(14)(c) and 110.6(14)(g).
14 See heading 1 of this chapter entitled, "Line 51 – Non-Capital Losses of Other Years" outlining certain restrictions for the application of farming or fishing losses. Also refer to heading 3 of this chapter entitled, "Form T3A – Request for Loss Carryback by a Trust."

Chapter 13
Summary of Tax and Credits

1. Line 81 – Total Federal Tax Payable

Enter on Line 81, the total federal tax payable as computed on Line 37 of Schedule 11. You may have to complete Schedule 12 to calculate the trust's minimum tax payable. If the federal minimum tax as computed on Line 55 of Schedule 12 exceeds the regular federal tax as calculated on Schedule 11, enter the minimum federal tax payable on Line 81 of the T3 Return.

Minimum tax might apply where a trust:

- reports taxable dividends;

- reports taxable capital gains;

- reports a capital gains deduction;

- claims a loss resulting from or increased by resource expenditures, including a claim for resource and depletion allowance on resource properties; and

- reports losses resulting from capital cost allowance on rental or leasing properties, or certified films or videotapes.

PART IV — T3 TRUST INFORMATION & TAX RETURN

If minimum federal tax applies and the trust is tax resident in Ontario, complete Chart 1 – Ontario Minimum Tax Carryout. Otherwise complete Chart 2 – Calculation of Provincial and Territorial Minimum Tax.[1]

2. Line 82 – Provincial or Territorial Tax Payable

A trust is generally liable for provincial or territorial tax at the rate that applies for the jurisdiction in which the trust has a tax residence.[2]

Use the applicable provincial or territorial tax form to calculate the provincial or territorial tax and enter the tax on Line 82 of the T3 Return.

Where federal minimum tax is applicable, complete Schedule 12 (Chart 1 or Chart 2 as appropriate) to determine the provincial or territorial minimum tax payable.

A trust, which is tax resident in a particular province or territory, may carry on a business with a permanent establishment in another province or territory. In such case, you should calculate the trust's income pertaining to the particular province or territory and determine the provincial or territorial tax liability on the income allocated to each province or territory.

In general practice, you may wish to prepare a schedule allocating the trust's taxable income to each permanent establishment and determine the provincial and territorial tax thereon.

3. Line 83 – Part XII.2 Tax Payable

Complete Schedule 10 if the trust is allocating income to non-resident or other designated beneficiaries. Enter the total Part XII.2 taxes due on Line 83 of the T3 Return from Line 12 of Schedule 10.

---

1 Refer to heading 2 of Chapter 3 entitled, "Minimum Tax" for additional commentary on this topic.
2 See heading 1 of Chapter 3 entitled, "Tax Residency of a Trust."

CHAPTER 13 — SUMMARY OF TAX AND CREDITS

Part XII.2 tax applies when a trust:

- has designated income (described at 3.1);
- has a designated beneficiary (described at 3.2); and
- allocates or designates any of its income.

Part XII.2 tax does not apply to a trust that was one of the following throughout the year:

- a testamentary trust;
- a mutual fund trust;
- certain types of trusts generally exempted from the "twenty-one year rule;"
- a trust that was exempt from Part I tax under subsection 149(1);
- a non-resident trust; and
- for taxation years ending after 2002, a deemed resident trust.

3.1 Designated Income

Designated income of a trust generally means its taxable capital gains or allowable capital losses from the disposition of taxable Canadian property, certain property transferred to a trust in contemplation of a person beneficially interested in the trust ceasing to reside in Canada and the total income (or loss) from the following sources:[3]

- businesses carried on in Canada;
- real properties located in Canada, such as land or buildings;
- timber resource properties; and

---

3 Subsection 210.2(2).

PART IV — T3 TRUST INFORMATION & TAX RETURN

- Canadian resource properties the trust acquired after 1971.

3.2 Designated Beneficiary[4]

A designated beneficiary for the purpose of Part XII.2 tax includes a beneficiary who is:

- a non-resident person;

- a non-resident-owned investment corporation;

- a trust whose beneficiaries include a person or partnership that is a designated beneficiary or a trust, other than:

    - a testamentary trust;

    - a mutual fund trust;

    - a trust exempt from Part I tax under subsection 149(1); or

    - a trust whose interest in the first trust was owned at all times by persons who were exempt from Part I tax under subsection 149(1) and has no designated beneficiary;

- a partnership whose members include another partnership or a designated beneficiary, unless the interest in the trust was owned at all times by the partnership or persons who were exempt from Part I tax under subsection 149(1) and there is no designated beneficiary; or

- a person exempt from Part I tax under subsection 149(1), if that person acquired an interest in the trust, directly or indirectly, from a beneficiary of the trust after October 1, 1987.

A person exempt from Part I tax is not a designated beneficiary if:

- after either October 1, 1987, or the date the interest was created,

---

4 Section 210.

CHAPTER 13 — SUMMARY OF TAX AND CREDITS

whichever is later, any person exempt from Part I tax continuously held the interest; or

- the person exempt from tax is a trust governed by a registered retirement savings plan or registered retirement income fund, and the trust acquired its interest directly or indirectly from its beneficiary, the beneficiary's spouse or common-law partner, or former spouse or common-law partner.

A designated beneficiary is usually not entitled to the refundable tax credit for Part XII.2 tax that the trust paid. This means that the trust will not complete Box 38 on the T3 Slip for a designated beneficiary who is a Canadian resident. Also, before the trust calculates the applicable Part XIII non-resident withholding tax, it should reduce the income payable to a non-resident beneficiary by the non-resident beneficiary's share of the Part XII.2 tax.

4. Line 85 – Tax Paid by Installments

Enter on Line 85 the total installment payments made by the trust in respect of the taxation year. You may wish to attach a schedule detailing the payment date and amount, aggregating the installment payments made for the year.

5. Line 86 – Total Tax Deducted

Enter on Line 86 the aggregate of all tax withholdings relating to income earned and reported by the trust in the taxation year. Typically this information will be reported on the information slips issued to the trust by the payor. Where an information slip is not available, you should attempt to obtain a duplicate or replacement copy from the issuer. Otherwise, prepare a statement indicating the name of the payor, the income reported and the taxes withheld.

PART IV — T3 TRUST INFORMATION & TAX RETURN

6. Line 88 – Refundable Investment Tax Credit

For a trust, where each beneficiary is an individual or a Canadian-controlled private corporation eligible to claim the small business deduction, the refund available is 40% of the unused investment tax credit generated in the year. For other trusts, the refund is 20% of the unused investment tax credit.[5]

The refundable portion of the credit should be calculated on Form T2038(IND) and entered on Line 88 of the T3 Return.

The refund is available only in respect of qualifying expenditures made in the year, which are eligible for the investment tax credit.

7. Line 90 – Part XII.2 Tax Credit

If the trust is a beneficiary of another trust and received a T3 Slip from that trust with an amount in Box 38, enter that amount on Line 90 of the T3 Return.[6]

8. Line 91 – Other Credits

The trust may be eligible to claim tax credits in respect of the items described at 8.1 through 8.4.

8.1 Newfoundland and Labrador Research and Development Tax Credit

To be eligible the trust must:

---

[5] Subsections 127.1(1) and 127.1(2). See also M.N.R., Interpretation Bulletin IT-151R5, "Scientific Research and Experimental Development Expenditures" [Consolidated] (July 23, 2003), at paragraphs 51-55.

[6] See commentary in heading 3 of this chapter entitled, "Line 83 – Part XII.2 Tax Payable."

CHAPTER 13 — SUMMARY OF TAX AND CREDITS

- operate a business with a permanent establishment in Newfoundland and Labrador; and

- have made eligible expenditures for scientific research and experimental development carried out in Newfoundland and Labrador.

Complete Form T1129, "Newfoundland and Labrador Research and Development Tax Credit (Individuals)." You can designate some or all of this credit to beneficiaries of the trust. Do this by reducing the total credit by the amount designated to the beneficiaries. On Line 91, enter the credit from Form T1129 minus the amount of credit designated to the beneficiaries on Schedule 9. Attach Form T1129 to the T3 Return.

8.2 Yukon Mineral Exploration Tax Credit

To be eligible the trust must:

- be a tax resident in the Yukon at the end of the year; and

- have incurred qualified mineral exploration expenses in connection with determining the existence, location, extent or quality of a mineral resource in the Yukon.

Complete Form T1199, "Yukon Mineral Exploration Tax Credit" and enter the amount of the tax credit on Line 91 of the T3 Return. Also attach Form T1199 to the T3 Return.

8.3 Yukon Research and Development Tax Credit

To be eligible the trust must:

- be tax resident in the Yukon at the end of the year; and

- have incurred eligible expenditures for Scientific Research and Experimental Development (SR&ED) in the Yukon.

PART IV — T3 TRUST INFORMATION & TAX RETURN

Complete Form T1232, "Yukon Research and Development Tax Credit (Individuals)." The trust can designate all or a portion of this credit to its beneficiaries. Do this by reducing the total credit by the amount designated to the beneficiaries. On Line 91, enter the amount from Form T1232, less the amount of any credits designated to beneficiaries on Schedule 9. Attach Form T1232 to the T3 Return.

8.4 British Columbia Mining Exploration Tax Credit

To be eligible the trust must:

- be a tax resident of British Columbia at the end of the year; and

- have incurred qualifying mineral exploration expenses in connection with determining the existence, location, extent or quality of a mineral resource in British Columbia.

Complete Form T88, "British Columbia Mining Exploration Tax Credit (Individuals)" and enter the amount on Line 91 of the T3 Return. Also attach Form T88 to the T3 Return.

9. Line 94 – Refund or Balance Owing

Compute the refund or balance owing by subtracting Total Credits (Line 93) from Total Taxes (Line 84). CRA policy is to neither charge nor refund a difference that is $2 or less. Indicate the balance on Line 94 of the T3 Return. If the balance is an amount refundable, indicate the amount in brackets.

Payment for a balance owing should be made payable to the Receiver General of Canada. The trust's account number should be indicated on the back of the cheque with a reference to the applicable taxation year for which payment should be applied.[7]

---

[7] See also heading 5 of Chapter 7 entitled, "Interest and Penalties" for additional commentary.

CHAPTER 13 — SUMMARY OF TAX AND CREDITS

If the trust is filing for a refund, CRA will pay interest on the balance refundable, on a compounded daily basis, commencing from the latest of:

- the thirty-first day after the date the return is due;

- the thirty-first day after the T3 Return is filed; or

- the day after the overpayment arises.

10. Line 95 – Amount Enclosed

Indicate on Line 95 of the T3 Return the amount of payment being enclosed with the return.

Payment should be made by cheque or money order payable to the Receiver General of Canada. Attach the cheque or money order to the front of the T3 Return. The trust's account number should be indicated on the back of the cheque to ensure that payment is properly credited to the trust's account.

If payment is made through a bank account at a financial institution outside Canada, the preferred method of negotiating payment is one of the following:

- an International Money Order drawn in Canadian dollars; or

- a bank draft in Canadian funds drawn on a Canadian bank (available at most foreign financial institutions).

Indicate the amount of payment being enclosed on Line 95 of the T3 Return. A dishonoured payment will be subject to a fee charged by CRA. Generally this fee is $15 for each "NSF item," plus interest charges, where applicable.

PART IV — T3 TRUST INFORMATION & TAX RETURN

11. Line 100 – Refund Code

If the trust is filing for a refund, enter one of the following codes in Line 100.

0 – refund the overpayment;

1 – apply the credit to the trust's installment account for the subsequent taxation year; or

2 – apply the credit to an expected assessment of an additional amount to be paid. If you choose this option, you should attach a letter to CRA explaining the details of the situation.

If no code is indicated, CRA will automatically refund the credit to the trust.

12. Name and Address of Person or Company (Other than Trustee, Executor, Liquidator or Administrator)

Complete this box if a person other than the trustee, executor, liquidator or administrator of the trust prepared the T3 Return.

The preparer should be aware of penalties which can apply in circumstances where they knowingly, or in circumstances amounting to culpable conduct, are involved in the filing of an income tax or information return containing false statements or omissions.

13. Certification

Enter the legal name of the trustee, executor, liquidator or administrator of the trust who has the authority to sign and file the T3 Return. Indicate the position or title of the authorized person.

CHAPTER 13 — SUMMARY OF TAX AND CREDITS

The authorized person should sign the T3 Return in the Certification section indicating their approval and consent in filing the T3 Return and all attached documents.

The authorized person signing and filing the T3 Return and attached documents should be aware of the potential penalty provisions, which can apply in respect of income tax or information returns containing false statements or omissions.[8]

---

[8] Refer to heading 6 of Chapter 7 entitled, "Liability of Trustees and Personal Representatives" for additional commentary.

Chapter 14
Trust Schedules and Forms

1. Schedule 1 – Dispositions of Capital Property

Complete Schedule 1 (see Figure 14.1) if the trust realized dispositions or deemed dispositions of capital property in the taxation year. If the amount computed at Line 21 (total taxable capital gains) is positive, transfer that amount to Line 01 of the T3 Return. If the amount computed on Line 21 is negative, do not report the amount on Line 01 of the T3 Return, as net capital losses realized by a trust cannot be deducted against other trust income reportable in the year.[1]

Where the trust realizes a capital gain on the gift of certain property to a "qualified donee,"[2] report the gain on Schedule 1A (see Figure 14.2). A qualified donee generally includes:

- a registered charity;
- a registered Canadian amateur athletic association;
- certain housing corporations resident in Canada;
- a municipality in Canada;
- the United Nations or an agency thereof;

---
[1] See also 1.3 of Chapter 10 entitled, "Utilizing Capital Losses" for commentary on capital losses realized by a trust. See also Chapter 12, heading 2 entitled, "Line 52 - Net Capital Losses of Other Years," and heading 3 entitled, "Form T3A – Request for Loss Carryback by a Trust."
[2] Subsection 149.1(1), definition of qualified donee.

PART IV — T3 TRUST INFORMATION & TAX RETURN

- a prescribed university outside Canada;
- a listed charitable organization outside Canada; and
- the federal or provincial government.

Note that a qualified donee does not include a private foundation.

A capital gain to a qualified donee can arise on the disposition of property that includes a share or debt obligation, rights listed on a prescribed stock exchange, shares of a mutual fund corporation, units of a mutual fund trust or other capital property.

Note that for gifts made applicable to the 2000 and subsequent taxation years, a trust may be eligible to include the resulting capital gain in its income at the reduced 25% inclusion rate.[3]

For this reason, where the trust intends on making such a gift, a disposition of capital property to a qualified donee will result in a more favourable tax treatment than disposing of the property and making a gift of the cash proceeds.

If the trust has deemed realizations resulting from the twenty-one year deemed realization rule, complete Form T1055 "Summary of Deemed Realizations." Do not report twenty-one year deemed realizations on Schedule 1.[4]

Note also that a Canadian resident trust which distributes property, including certain taxable Canadian property, to a non-resident beneficiary in satisfaction of all or part of the beneficiary's capital interest in

---

3 Section 38(a.1). Note that s. 38(a.1) includes provisions for adjustments to the inclusion rate where a taxation year commences after February 28, 2000, and ends before October 17, 2000, or includes February 28, 2000, or October 17, 2000.

4 For more information about twenty-one year deemed realizations, refer to heading 2 of Chapter 6 entitled, "Deemed Realizations."

Figure 14.1
Schedule 1

T3 – [ ]

DISPOSITIONS OF CAPITAL PROPERTY — **SCHEDULE 1**

- Enter the applicable taxation year in the box above.
- For information on completing this schedule, see Chapter 3 in the *T3 Trust Guide*.
- Attach a separate sheet of paper if you need more space. **Attach a completed copy of this schedule to the trust's return.**

Note: Do not use this schedule to claim an allowable business investment loss from disposing of shares or debts of a small business corporation (see Line 25 in the *T3 Trust Guide*).	(1) Year of acquisition	(2) Proceeds of disposition	(3) Adjusted cost base	(4) Outlays and expenses (from dispositions)	(5) Gain (or loss) (column 2 minus columns 3 and 4)	
Qualified small business corporation shares — No. of shares / Name of corporation and class of shares						
Total		1011		Gain (or loss)	1012	1
Qualified farm property — Address or legal description						
Total		1021		Gain (or loss)	1022 +	2
Mutual fund units and other shares (report capital gains or losses shown on an information slip on line 10) — No. of shares / Name of fund or corporation and class of shares						
Total		1031		Gain (or loss)	1032 +	3
Bonds, debentures, promissory notes, and other similar properties — Face value / Maturity date / Name of issuer						
Total		1041		Gain (or loss)	1042 +	4
Real estate and depreciable property (do not include losses on depreciable property) — Address or legal description						
Total		1051		Gain (or loss)	1052 +	5
Personal-use property (full description)						
		1061		(If negative, enter "0")	1062 +	6
Listed personal property (LPP) (full description)						
Note: You can only apply LPP losses against LPP gains.		1071			1072	7
Enter LPP losses from line 7 of Form T1055, and unapplied LPP losses from other years (provide details).					1080 –	8
Net gain (line 7 minus line 8)					+	9

Information slips – Capital gains (or losses) (attach T3, T5, T4PS, and T5013 slips)		1100 +	10
Capital losses from a reduction in business investment loss		1130 –	11
Capital gains reduction on flow-through entities		1142 –	12
Total of amounts in column 5 before reserves (add lines 1 to 6, 9, and 10, then subtract lines 11 and 12)		=	13
Capital gains (losses) from reserves (line 5, column 3 of Schedule 2) (if it is a capital loss, do **not** put in brackets)		1170 +	14
Subtotal (line 13 plus line 14)		=	15
Adjusted capital gains on gifts of certain capital property (line 6 of Schedule 1A)		+	16
Capital gains from gifts of other capital property (see Schedule 1, Line 16 in the guide)	1191 — 17		
Total capital losses transferred under 164(6) (do **not** put this amount in brackets)		1646 +	18
Subtotal (add lines 15, 16, and 18)		=	19
		x 1/2	
Total taxable capital gains (or net capital losses) (line 19 multiplied by 1/2)		1220 =	21

If line 21 is positive, enter it on line 01 of the return. If it is negative, see Line 01 in the *T3 Trust Guide*.

T3 SCH 1 (03)
Printed in Canada

(Français au verso)

Canada

PART IV — T3 TRUST INFORMATION & TAX RETURN

Figure 14.2
Schedule 1A

CHAPTER 14 — TRUST SCHEDULES AND FORMS

the trust is deemed to have disposed of such property for proceeds equal to its fair market value at the time. Accordingly, the trust should report capital gains resulting from such distributions.[5]

1.1 Meaning of "Disposition"

A "disposition" of capital property generally occurs for tax purposes when the "vendor" is entitled to receive proceeds of disposition,[6] with the result that title to property passes from the vendor to the purchaser.

For publicly traded securities, such as stocks and bonds, the disposition date is the "settlement date" of the transaction. The "settlement date" is the date the transaction is settled or cleared through the exchange, and it is usually one to three days after the "trade date" (the date the broker actually executed the buy or sell order).

The timing of the date of disposition is relevant as to when the disposition is recognized for tax purposes. For instance, if the trade order is settled in the subsequent taxation year of the trust (even though the order is placed within the last few days of the taxation year), the gain or loss on the disposition will be deferred and recognized in the subsequent taxation year.

In this way the taxation of capital gains can be deferred for an entire taxation year; conversely, where the objective is to trigger and realize capital losses in a particular taxation year to offset capital gains recognized earlier in the current year, it is essential to consider the timing of the transaction to ensure that the disposition for tax purposes occurs as planned.

---

5 See also M.N.R., Interpretation Bulletin IT-130, "Capital Property Owned on December 31, 1971 – Actual Cost of Property Owned by a Testamentary Trust" (November 20, 1973), for commentary on capital property subject to V-Day considerations.
6 Paragraph 54(c)(i), proceeds of disposition. See also M.N.R., Interpretation Bulletin IT-133, "Stock Exchange Transactions — Date of Disposition of Shares" (November 30, 1973), at paragraph 11.

PART IV — T3 TRUST INFORMATION & TAX RETURN

There can also be circumstances where a disposition has occurred under the general meaning of the term, but where there are no actual or deemed proceeds resulting from the disposition. In such case, the deemed proceeds would be considered to be nil for purposes of computing a loss from the disposition.[7] This situation can arise in the following circumstances:

- where capital property is stolen or destroyed and there is no entitlement or right to compensation;

- where capital property is lost or abandoned and there is no reasonable expectation of recovery;

- where a taxpayer holds shares in a corporation, or an interest in a partnership which is dissolved or liquidated, and no proceeds are payable on the liquidation; or

- where a taxpayer holds a debt obligation which is determined to be uncollectible by the taxpayer.

The provisions contained in subsection 50(1) of the Act, describe when a debt is deemed to be uncollectible, with a resulting deemed disposition and reacquisition at a nil cost base.[8]

Certain transactions are not considered to result in a disposition for tax purposes, even though there may appear to be a conveyance of the property. For instance, a transfer to a "bare" trust, where there is no change in beneficial ownership,[9] does not result in a disposition for tax

---

7 M.N.R., Interpretation Bulletin IT-460, "Dispositions – Absence of Consideration" (October 6, 1980), at paragraph 3.
8 See also M.N.R., Interpretation Bulletin IT-159R3, "Capital Debts Established to be Bad Debts" (May 1, 1989), at paragraphs 1-4. See also heading 3 of Chapter 11 entitled, "Line 25 – Allowable Business Investment Losses" for additional commentary.
9 See Department of Finance Technical Notes released June 15, 2000, and re-released March 16, 2001, "transfer to bare trusts, protective trusts and other vehicles," where there is no change in beneficial ownership. The 2001 amendments preserve CRA's administrative position with respect to bare trusts, which effectively treat such trusts as agents for their beneficiaries. However, where a Canadian resident transfers property to a non-resident bare trust after December

CHAPTER 14 — TRUST SCHEDULES AND FORMS

purposes. A transfer of ownership of the property for the purposes only of securing a debt or a loan, or for the purposes only of re-registering ownership of the property previously used as security for the debt or loan cannot be regarded as a disposition for tax purposes either.

1.2 Qualified Small Business Corporation Shares (QSBCS)

Capital gains from the disposition of QSBC shares may qualify for the capital gains deduction[10] provided certain tests are met.

- The shares must be shares of a Canadian controlled private corporation that are considered to be shares of a small business corporation, as defined in subsection 248(1).

- At the time of disposition, the corporation must have "all or substantially all" (generally taken to be 90%) of the fair market value of its assets employed or used in an active business carried on primarily (more than 50%) in Canada.

- Throughout the twenty-four months preceding the date of disposition at least 50% of the fair market value of the corporation's assets must have been used principally in an active business carried on in Canada or to finance an active business of a "connected"[11] corporation. Where the subject property involves the shares of a holding company ("stacked corporations"), the 50% test is effectively replaced with a more onerous 90% test for the twenty-four months preceding the date of disposition.

- The shares must also meet an "ownership test," in that they must be owned by either the taxpayer or a related person during the twenty-

---

23, 1998, the transfer will be considered to result in a disposition of the property and the bare trust will be treated as an ordinary trust. Where a bare trust is not utilized, a transfer of property not resulting in a change of beneficial ownership will, for transactions occurring after December 23, 1998, be treated as a "disposition" for tax purposes.
10 Subsection 110.6(2.1).
11 Subsection 186(2).

PART IV — T3 TRUST INFORMATION & TAX RETURN

four months preceding the disposition. The death of a taxpayer does not shorten the twenty-four month holding period requirement. Consequently, care must be exercised to ensure that shares transferred to a trust as a consequence of the death of a taxpayer, do indeed meet all of the required criteria to qualify for QSBCS status.

A person or partnership is considered to be "related" to a personal trust for purposes of meeting that test as contemplated for a QSBCS in the following circumstances:

- where the person or partnership is a beneficiary of the trust;

- where the trust is a member of the partnership;

- where the person is a member of a partnership, which in turn is a member of another partnership, and therefore is deemed to be "related" to the second partnership; or

- where the trust disposes of shares, all the beneficiaries of which are related to the person from whom the trust acquired the shares.

CRA provides extensive commentary on their administrative policies and filing positions, including a definition of "qualified small business corporation share."[12]

If the trust is a spousal or common-law partner trust, it may be entitled to claim the capital gains deduction in respect of a gain resulting from a deemed disposition of the shares, arising from the death of the spouse or common-law partner. Use Schedules 3, 4 and 5 to calculate the available deduction. If the trust is allocating and designating the eligible capital gains to one or more beneficiaries, complete Schedules 3 and 4 and allocate the relevant amounts on Schedule 9.[13]

---

12 M.N.R., Publication T4037, "Capital Gains 2003."
13 Also, refer to headings 2 and 3 of Chapter 15 entitled "Completing the T3 Summary" and "Completing the T3 Slips," respectively.

CHAPTER 14 — TRUST SCHEDULES AND FORMS

1.3 Qualified Farm Property

The provisions of the Act are designed to encourage the intergenerational transfer of farm property, including shares of a qualified family farm corporation to the children or grandchildren in order to encourage the continuing operation of the family farm business after the death of the farming parent or grandparent.

Qualifying farm property can be transferred on a tax-deferred rollover basis directly from the deceased taxpayer to a child or grandchild.[14]

Note however, that the ability to do so does not extend to a sale of property by the estate, unless the transfer or distribution of property resulting from the sale to the child occurs as a consequence of the taxpayer's death.

Qualifying farm property can also be transferred on death to a spouse or spousal trust[15] on a rollover basis or indirectly to a child or grandchild through a qualifying spousal trust.[16] Where this situation is the case, subsections 70(9.1) and 70(9.3) do not require that the spouse, spousal trust or the child actually use the property in a farming business immediately prior to the death of the spouse. Consequently a rollover under subsection 70(9.1) or 70(9.3) is permitted as long as the farm property was rented or leased to any other person who used it in a farming business during the time the spousal trust held the property.

Where qualified farm property is transferred on death to a "tainted spousal trust" the rollover provisions to a child or grandchild under subsections 70(9.1) and 70(9.3) will not be permitted, as these provisions are allowed only in respect of a transfer from a "qualifying spousal trust." However, a "tainted spousal trust" can be untainted by means of a certain election,[17] thereby permitting the rollover provisions to apply.

---

14 Subsection 70(9).
15 Subsection 70(7).
16 Subsections 70(9.1) and 70(9.3).
17 Subsection 70(7). See also M.N.R., Interpretation Bulletin IT-305R4, "Testamentary Spouse Trusts" (October 30, 1996), at paragraph 18.

PART IV — T3 TRUST INFORMATION & TAX RETURN

The definition of a qualified farm property is outlined in subsection 110.6(1) and generally includes the following:

- real property that was used in the farming business by an individual or a beneficiary of a personal trust including a spouse, child or parent of the individual;

- a share of a corporation which meets the criteria of a share of a stock of a family farm corporation owned by the individual, spouse, child or parent of the individual; or

- an interest in a partnership which meets the criteria of an interest in a family farm partnership of the individual, or a spouse, child or parent of the individual.

The property must be used in the course of carrying on the business of farming in Canada for any particular twenty-four month period that the property is held by the individual or trust beneficiary, including a spouse, child, or parent of the individual. To qualify, the property need not actually be used in carrying on a farming business at the date of disposition. Property is considered to have been used in a farming business in Canada if two tests are met.

> 1. The property must have been held or have represented substituted property held for a period of twenty-four months prior to the disposition date by one of the qualified persons as noted above.

> 2. In any two years of ownership by a family member (or a personal trust), which includes a qualified person as described above, the gross revenue of the qualified individual from the farming business, in which the property was principally used, must have exceeded income from all other sources, or where the property consists of shares of a family farm corporation, or an interest in a family farm partnership, the qualified individual must have been actively engaged on a regular and continuous basis in the farming business for at least a twenty-four month period.

CHAPTER 14 — TRUST SCHEDULES AND FORMS

For property acquired prior to June 18, 1987, or after that date pursuant to an agreement entered into before that date, property can still be considered to be "qualified farm property" provided that it was used principally in a farming business in Canada in the year of disposition or in at least five years during which time it was owned by any of the related, qualified persons described above.

Whether a person is "actively engaged on a regular and continuous basis" is a question of fact. Generally this condition will be considered to be met where a person is actively engaged in the day-to-day management and operations of the farming business. Factors to consider include the time and effort contributed to the business.[18]

Capital gains realized by a trust from the disposition of qualified farm property may qualify for the $500,000 capital gains deduction. If the trust is a spousal or common-law partner trust, it may be entitled to claim the capital gains deduction in respect of a gain resulting from a deemed disposition of the qualified farm property, which can arise from the death of the spouse or common-law partner. Use Schedules 3, 4, and 5 to calculate the available deduction. If the trust is allocating and designating the eligible capital gains to one or more beneficiaries, complete Schedules 3 and 4 and allocate the relevant amounts on Schedule 9.[19]

1.4 Mutual Fund Units and Other Shares

Report on Schedule 1 the trust's capital gains or losses resulting from the disposition of mutual fund units and other shares. Indicate the number of shares or units disposed of, the name of the security or mutual fund and the year acquired.

---

18 M.N.R., Interpretation Bulletin IT-349R3, "Intergenerational Transfers of Farm Property on Death" (November 7, 1996), at paragraph 16.
19 Also refer to headings 2 and 3 of Chapter 15 entitled "Completing the T3 Summary" and "Completing the T3 Slips," respectively. The T3 Summary and T3 slip(s) must be completed if the estate or trust allocates or designates amounts on Schedule 9.

PART IV — T3 TRUST INFORMATION & TAX RETURN

Calculate the capital gain or loss[20] for each security by subtracting the adjusted cost base of the security, plus any costs of disposition, from the proceeds of disposition of the security.

Be aware that such securities are subject to the identical property rules, for purposes of determining the adjusted cost base of the property.

The cost of identical properties is determined at any time by taking the aggregate adjusted cost base (ACB) of all "identical properties" owned by the trust, divided by the aggregate number owned.[21] A new average ACB results each time another identical property is acquired and added to the pool.

The cost of identical properties (other than depreciable property or an interest in a partnership) owned by the trust on December 31, 1971, is also the average cost of all such properties. However, there is a requirement to maintain two separate pools. One pool should be maintained for identical properties acquired before 1972 and another pool for identical properties acquired after December 31, 1971.

1.5 Bonds, Debentures, Promissory Notes and Other Similar Properties

Bonds and other debt obligations are considered to be identical properties if they are identical in respect of their legal entitlement, including the rights and conditions to the debt holder. Accordingly, the disposition of such securities should be computed as though they are "identical properties," for purposes of computing a capital gain or loss.

A capital loss from the disposition of a debt is deemed to be nil, unless the debt was acquired for the purpose of gaining or producing income from a business or property (excluding exempt income), or as consideration for the disposition of capital property in an arm's length situation.[22]

---

20 See 1.1 of Chapter 10 entitled, "General Rules" for commentary on the calculation of capital gains or losses.
21 Section 47.
22 Subparagraph 40(2)(g)(ii).

CHAPTER 14 — TRUST SCHEDULES AND FORMS

If the trust disposes of an interest bearing debt obligation between interest payment dates, the accrued interest to the date of sale should be reported as interest income and not proceeds of disposition.[23]

Note that accrued interest paid on the acquisition of an interest-bearing debt obligation should not increase the ACB of the obligation. Instead the accrued interest paid on acquisition should be deducted as an expense on Schedule 8, with the effect of reducing the overall interest income to be reported on the debt obligation.[24]

The trust may receive Form T5008, "Statement of Securities Transactions." If so, attach the form and ensure that proceeds reported on Schedule 1 reconcile with the amount reported on Form T5008.

1.6 Real Estate and Depreciable Property

(a) General Comments

Provide details on the proceeds of disposition, ACB, and outlays and costs relating to the sale of each property disposed of in the taxation year by the trust, including an allocation between non-depreciable land and depreciable real estate for each such property.

For depreciable property, ACB is defined as the "capital cost" of the depreciable property and such amount is not subject to the ACB adjustments provided for under subsections 53(1) and 53(2). Be aware

---

[23] Subsection 20(14) applies with respect to the transfer (after November 12, 1981) of most debt obligations, and requires the transferor to include the interest accrued on the obligation, prior to the date of transfer or sale, as income for the taxation year in which the debt obligation was disposed. See commentary in M.N.R., Interpretation Bulletin IT-410R, "Debt Obligations – Accrued Interest on Transfer" [Archived] (September 4, 1984), at paragraph 3. For additional commentary, see M.N.R., Technical Interpretation 2002-014675A, "Computation Interest on Bonds/Estate" (June 3, 2003) and also M.N.R., Technical Interpretation 9228680, "Treatment of Interest Accrued on Transferred Debt" (November 25, 1992).

[24] Paragraphs 20(14)(b) and 53(2)(i). See also M.N.R., Interpretation Bulletin IT-410R, *ibid.*, at paragraph 6. See also M.N.R., Technical Interpretation 9228680, *ibid.* at Answer 1.

that there can be a difference in the "capital cost" for capital cost allowance and recapture purposes, particularly in respect of elections, which might have been made in respect of property owned on February 23, 1994.[25]

A capital loss resulting from the disposition of depreciable capital property is deemed to be nil.[26]

(b) Non-Arm's Length Transfers

Special rules apply in respect of depreciable capital property acquired in a non-arm's length transaction.

For instance, the deemed capital cost of depreciable property to an estate will be equal to the deemed proceeds of disposition of the property to the deceased, except where the deceased's capital cost exceeds the deemed capital cost of the property to the estate as determined under paragraph 70(5)(b). For the purposes of sections 13 and 20 of the Act dealing with depreciable property and capital cost allowance, the capital cost (for purposes of future capital cost allowance) to the estate is deemed to be the same as the deceased's cost. In effect, the difference between this cost and the deemed proceeds of disposition is deemed to be capital cost allowance claimed by the estate.

On a subsequent disposition of the property, the estate would be required to include recaptured capital cost allowance as income up to the amount of the deemed capital cost, where actual proceeds on the disposition exceed the undepreciated capital cost "flowed-through" to the estate.

Certain rules apply where there is a transfer of property, including non-depreciable land and depreciable capital property, to which paragraph 70(5)(d) applies. For instance, special rules provide for the reallocation of the proceeds of disposition between land and building where a normal computation would otherwise result in a capital gain on the land and a terminal loss on the building. In such case, the terminal loss

---

25 Subsection 110.6 (24).
26 Subparagraph 39(1)(b)(i).

CHAPTER 14 — TRUST SCHEDULES AND FORMS

otherwise calculated is applied to reduce the proceeds of disposition of the land, thereby reducing the capital gain realizable on the land. The proceeds of disposition on the building would be increased by the amount of the adjustment on the land, thereby eliminating the terminal loss calculated on the building.[27]

(c) *Valuation Day (V-Day) Considerations*

A tax on capital gains was introduced into the Canadian tax system effective for capital properties disposed of after December 31, 1971. However, the introduction of this new taxing system also provided for various transitional rules, which ensured that unrealized capital gains accruing on capital properties owned prior to 1972 would not be subject to taxation. To facilitate this new system, the concept of a Valuation Day (V-Day) was introduced. The fair market value of capital properties owned or held on V-Day is December 22, 1971, for publicly traded securities or shares and December 31, 1971, for all other capital property.[28]

The transitional rules generally provide for the deemed cost or deemed proceeds of disposition of capital property owned on December 31, 1971, so that any gain or loss on a subsequent disposition is computed from the V-Day value. However, these transitional rules do not apply to the property of a taxpayer who became resident in Canada after 1971.[29]

There are two methods for determining the deemed cost of capital property. The first is the "median rule" or "tax-free-zone" method, while the second is termed the "Valuation Day" election. The tax-free-zone method designates the adjusted cost base of the property based on the median or middle of the three amounts. These amounts are the original cost of the property, its fair market value on V-Day or the proceeds of disposition of the property. The median rule or tax-free-zone method ensures that the V-Day value is designated as the adjusted cost base for tax purposes, when a taxpayer disposes of a consistently appreciating capital property. However, where a property is disposed of for proceeds

---

27 Subsection 13(21.1).
28 ITAR 24
29 ITAR 26(10).

less than the historical cost amount, no capital loss will be recognized, as the cost for tax purposes will be deemed to be the same as the proceeds received on disposition. The first method applies automatically to capital property owned on December 31, 1971, unless the trust makes an election for the V-Day method to apply. The two methods cannot be mixed or matched among capital properties owned on December 31, 1971. Once one method is chosen, that method must be applied to all capital properties owned on V-Day.

Where depreciable property acquired by a trust was owned by a deceased individual on December 31, 1971 (V-Day), and the capital cost of the property to the deceased was less than its corresponding fair market value on V-Day and less than the deemed proceeds of disposition, the estate's capital cost for tax purposes will be the fair market value on V-Day, with the effect that any portion of the capital gain accrued prior to January 1, 1972, will not be subject to capital gains tax.[30]

If instead, the V-Day value is less than the original cost, the Income Tax Application Rules (ITAR) would not apply and the ordinary rules in subsection 40(1) will apply to determine any subsequent capital gain realized by the estate.

(d) Land

The disposition of undeveloped land may be subject to tax as ordinary income. However, where vacant land is held with the intention of using or developing the property into a business or for lease in connection with the earning of property income, a subsequent disposition would generally be viewed as a sale of capital property and, accordingly, should be reported on Schedule 1. Interest paid on a debt obligation relating to the acquisition of vacant land is not deductible unless there is income from the vacant land in excess of interest paid on the debt. The non-deductible interest paid would be added to the adjusted cost base of the land.[31]

---

30 ITAR 20(1)(a). See also M.N.R., Interpretation Bulletin IT-217R, "Depreciable Property Owned on December 31, 1971" [Archived] (August 16, 1996), at paragraph 2, for commentary where this might be applicable.
31 Subparagraph 53(1)(h)(i).

CHAPTER 14 — TRUST SCHEDULES AND FORMS

(e) Principal Residence

If a personal trust acquires a principal residence, it will generally be exempt from tax on any capital gain realized on the disposition or deemed disposition of the property. For example, where a spousal trust acquires a principal residence where subsection 70(6) applies, the trust will be deemed to have owned the property as a principal residence throughout the period that the deceased owned the property, and the property is deemed to be the principal residence for any taxation year for which it would have qualified as a principal residence of the deceased.[32] To claim the principal residence exemption, the residence must be designated by the trust as its principal residence.[33] A residence can be designated only if a "specified beneficiary," such as the particular beneficiary, the beneficiary's spouse or common-law partner, former spouse or former common-law partner, or child ordinarily inhabits and lives in the residence.

The trust can designate only one property as a principal residence; also the "specified beneficiary" cannot designate any other property as a principal residence.

Although subsection 40(4) deems the principal residence of the deceased to be a principal residence of the trust during the entire period for which that property was the principal residence of the deceased, this provision does not restrict the spouse from designating another property owned at December 31, 1981 (a cottage, for instance), as a principal residence for years of ownership prior to 1982.

When a personal trust distributes a principal residence to a beneficiary (to the spouse or common-law partner beneficiary for post-1971 spousal or common-law partner trusts; to the settlor, spouse or common-law partner beneficiary for joint spousal or common-law partner trusts; or to the settlor of an alter ego trust), the trust can elect for the deemed disposition to occur at the fair market value of the principal residence.

---

32 Subsection 40(4).
33 Prescribed Form T1079, "Designation of a Property as a Principal Residence by a Personal Trust."

PART IV — T3 TRUST INFORMATION & TAX RETURN

The trust can then apply the principal residence exemption to any resulting capital gain resulting from the deemed disposition.

1.7 Personal-Use Property

Losses arising from the disposition of personal-use property are not included for purposes of determining the net taxable capital gains or allowable capital losses of a trust.[34] This is so, even against gains from the disposition of other personal-use property.

However, a capital gain from the disposition of personal-use property is able to be included for tax purposes whether the asset constitutes listed personal property or any other type of personal-use property. There is, however, a special rule, which provides a floor of $1,000 for the disposition of such property. This rule deems both the adjusted cost base and the proceeds of disposition of personal-use property to be no less than $1,000 in each case, with the result that a taxable capital gain will occur only when proceeds of disposition exceed $1,000 on the sale of such property.[35]

1.8 Listed Personal Property (LPP)

Listed personal property is defined to include personal-use property that is any of the following:

- a print, drawing, painting, sculpture or other similar work of art;
- jewellery;
- a rare manuscript or book;
- a stamp or stamp collection; or

---

34 Subparagraph 40(2)(g)(iii). See also M.N.R., Interpretation Bulletin IT-332R, "Personal-Use Property" [Archived] (November 28, 1984), at paragraph 4.

35 Subsection 46(1). See also M.N.R., Interpretation Bulletin IT-332R, *ibid.* at paragraph 11 for general commentary on the personal-use property rules. For recent commentary see also M.N.R., Technical Interpretation 2003-0019555 "Personal-use Property" (July 3, 2003) and M.N.R., Technical Interpretation 9632335, "Personal-Use Property" (October 17, 1996), citing the loss arising from the disposition of rights to Hockey Seats, to be nil as those rights would be considered to be personal-use property.

CHAPTER 14 — TRUST SCHEDULES AND FORMS

- a coin or coin collection.

Assets not specifically described above, which are acquired for personal use and enjoyment, would be considered to be personal-use property.

A capital gain from LPP arises only where proceeds for a particular property exceeds $1,000, since each individual LPP asset is always deemed to have an adjusted cost base of at least $1,000.

Capital losses from the disposition of LPP are claimable, but only against capital gains from the disposition of LPP. If an item of LPP has an actual cost of less than $1,000, a capital loss resulting from its disposition will result only if it is disposed of for less than its actual cost; this capital loss can only be applied against capital gains from the disposition of LPP assets.

1.9 Information Slips

Enter on Line 10 of Schedule 1, the aggregate of all amounts reported as capital gains or capital losses, realized by the trust, from all reporting slips.

Note that the applicable slip reports the full amount of the capital gain or capital loss and that amount should be entered on Schedule 1.

The following amounts apply:

- capital gains from Box 21 of a T3 Slip;
- insurance segregated fund capital losses from Box 37 of a T3 Slip;
- capital gains dividends from Box 18 of a T5 Slip;
- capital gains (or losses) from Box 34 of a T4PS Slip; and
- capital gains (or losses) from Box 23 of a T5013 Slip.

1.10 Capital Gains (or Losses) from Reserves

If the trust is claiming, or has in a prior taxation year claimed, a reserve in respect of a disposition of capital property, the trust should complete

PART IV — T3 TRUST INFORMATION & TAX RETURN

Schedule 2.[36] The amount of the capital gains from reserves for the current taxation year should be included and entered on Line 14 of Schedule 1.

1.11 Capital Gains from Gifts of Other Capital Properties

Enter on Line 17 of Schedule 1, capital gains resulting from the deemed disposition of capital property from a gift or bequest made by the trust.

A gift or bequest of capital property is deemed to be a disposition of the property for tax purposes, with the result that either a capital gain or a capital loss may arise. This section discusses a "gift" as distinct from a distribution of capital to a beneficiary of a trust.

Generally, where a gift is made, the proceeds of disposition are deemed to be the fair market value of the property at the time of the gift.

Notably, there is an exception where a gift of capital property is made to a registered charity. In such case, an election can be filed to value the donated property for purposes of calculating the capital gain, at any amount between the adjusted cost base of the property and its fair market value at the time of the gift.[37]

Also, donated property (for gifts made after February 18, 1997), consisting of certain publicly traded securities, is subject to inclusion at one-half the normal amount. In effect, for 2001 and subsequent taxation years, only 25% of the capital gain need be included as taxable income rather than the normal 50% inclusion rate.[38]

---

36 See also commentary at 1.2 of Chapter 10 entitled, "Reserve for Proceeds Not Due." See also M.N.R., Interpretation Bulletin IT-236R4, "Reserves – Disposition of Capital Property" [Archived] (July 30, 1999). See also M.N.R., Technical Interpretation 2000-0051115, "Capital Gains Reserve" (April 19, 2001). A reserve claimed in a prior taxation year is included in income for the current year pursuant to subparagraph 40(1)(a)(ii) of the Act and a new reserve, if applicable, is determined pursuant to subparagraph 40(1)(a)(iii) of the Act.
37 Subsection 118.1(6).
38 For information on dispositions of Canadian cultural property refer to the "Gifts

CHAPTER 14 — TRUST SCHEDULES AND FORMS

1.12 Total Losses Transferred under 164(6)

Enter on Line 18 of Schedule 1, the total amount of capital losses transferred under subsection 164(6) to the deceased person's T1 Terminal Return.[39]

For the subsection 164(6) election to be valid, only capital losses realized in the first taxation year of the estate, following the date of death of the testator, can be included for purposes of this amount. Amounts transferred to the deceased's T1 Terminal Return cannot be claimed as a capital loss by the estate.

CRA will not reassess the T1 Terminal Return until the T3 Return is filed and assessed. However, if the loss to be applied to the T1 Terminal Return can be quantified with certainty before the T3 Return is due to be filed, the personal representative can submit a written request to apply the subsection 164(6) losses to the T1 Terminal Return. Although the claim will not be allowed on the initial assessment of the T1 final, CRA will hold the request for the subsection 164(6) application and duly process a Notice of Reassessment for the T1 Terminal Return, once the losses are verified on the assessment of the T3 Return.

2. Schedule 2 – Reserve on Disposition of Capital Property

Complete and attach Schedule 2 (see Figure 14.3) to the T3 Return in connection with a reserve claimed on the disposition of capital property by the trust in respect of any amounts reported at the end of the trust's prior taxation year or reported at the end of the trust's current taxation year.

---

and Income Tax" pamphlet published by CRA and also see "Selling or Donating Certified Canadian Cultural Property," in the Capital Gains Guide. Additional commentary is contained in M.N.R., Interpretation Bulletin IT-407R4, "Dispositions of Cultural Property to Designated Canadian Institutions" [Consolidated] (October 12, 2001).

39 See 1.3 of Chapter 10 entitled, "Utilizing Capital Losses" for a discussion of the tax issues and strategies pertaining to a subsection 164(6) election.

PART IV — T3 TRUST INFORMATION & TAX RETURN

Figure 14.3
Schedule 2

T3 – ☐☐☐☐ **RESERVES ON DISPOSITIONS OF CAPITAL PROPERTY** SCHEDULE 2

- Enter the applicable taxation year in the box above. **Attach a completed copy of this schedule to the trust's return.**
- Complete this schedule if you claimed a reserve on the disposition of the trust's capital property at the end of the previous year, or are claiming a reserve on the disposition of the trust's capital property at the end of the current taxation year.
- Use the information from this schedule to complete Schedule 1, *Dispositions of Capital Property*, Schedule 3, *Eligible Taxable Capital Gains*, and Schedule 12, *Minimum Tax*.
- A trust cannot claim a reserve if, at the end of the year, or at any time in the immediately following year, it was not a resident of Canada or was exempt from tax. This restriction does not apply to a charitable gift of a non-qualifying security.
- In most cases, you can only claim a reserve for four years. However, if the disposition occurred before November 13, 1981, there is an exception. There is also a maximum amount you can claim as a reserve. For more details, see Interpretation Bulletin IT-236, *Reserves – Disposition of Capital Property*.

Reserves on dispositions of capital property	(1) Previous-year reserve	(2) Current-year reserve	(3) Column 1 minus column 2 (see note below) Include the total in current-year capital gains	
For dispositions after November 12, 1981 from:				
• Qualified farm property	2311 ●	2312 ●		1
• Qualified small business corporation shares	2321 ●	2322 ●		2
• Other property	2341 ●	2342 ●		3
For dispositions before November 13, 1981	2151 ●	2152 ●		4
Total (add lines 1 to 4)		2363 ●		5

Notes

- Transfer the total from column 3 (line 5) to line 14 of Schedule 1.
- If the amount in column 2 is more than the amount in column 1, use brackets in column 3 to show the negative amount.
- If the trust is claiming reserves for dispositions before November 13, 1981, contact us.
- A trust that makes a gift of a non-qualifying security after December 20, 2002, may claim a reserve not exceeding the **eligible amount** of the gift. Include the reserve on line 3. For more information and an explanation of eligible amount, see the *Capital Gains* guide.

T3 SCH 2 (03)
Printed in Canada   (Français au verso)   Canadä

CHAPTER 14 — TRUST SCHEDULES AND FORMS

Reserves deducted in the prior taxation year must be included in Column 1 of Schedule 2 and included as income for the current taxation year.[40] The reserve calculated for the current taxation year should be entered in Column 2,[41] with the difference between Columns 1 and 2 entered in Column 3. The total amount computed on Line 5 of Column 3 represents the net inclusion or exclusion of capital gains determined in respect of the reserved amounts, and this sum should be entered on Line 14 of Schedule 1 and included as part of the trust's taxable capital gains for the taxation year.

Where a trust is reporting a capital gain and claiming a reserve for proceeds not due, minimum tax might apply.[42] Also, capital gains included in the current taxation year, in respect of amounts reserved in a prior year, may be eligible for the capital gains deduction. (Refer to Schedule 3, "Eligible Taxable Capital Gains.")

3. Schedule 3 – Eligible Taxable Capital Gains

Eligible taxable capital gains include only gains from the disposition or deemed dispositions of qualified farm property (QFP) or qualified small business corporation shares (QSBCS).

Complete and attach this schedule to the T3 Return in respect of "eligible" net taxable capital gains reported by the trust, which have been allocated to a beneficiary who is either an individual or another trust, in order to determine the eligible portion of the capital gain for the beneficiary.[43]

Also complete Schedule 3 (see Figure 14.4) where the trust is a spousal or common-law partner trust and the trust is claiming a capital

---

40 Refer to 1.10 of this chapter entitled, "Capital Gains (or Losses) from Reserves."
41 Refer to 1.2 of Chapter 10 entitled, "Reserve for Proceeds Not Due."
42 Refer to heading 12 of this chapter entitled, "Schedule 12 – Minimum Tax" for further commentary.
43 See heading 9 of this chapter entitled, "Schedule 9 – Income Allocations and Designations to Beneficiaries." Where eligible taxable capital gains are "designated" to beneficiaries, Schedule 9 must be completed.

PART IV — T3 TRUST INFORMATION & TAX RETURN

gains deduction in respect of an "eligible" gain from a disposition or deemed disposition occurring in the taxation year of the trust, which includes the date of death of the beneficiary spouse or common-law partner.[44] The amount calculated on Line 34 of Schedule 3 should be reported on Line 1 of Schedule 5 to determine the spousal or common-law partner trust's capital gains deduction which can be claimed in the trust's taxation year.

4. Schedule 4 – Cumulative Net Investment Loss

Complete this schedule (see Figure 14.4) in respect of the trust's total investment expenses deducted for taxation years ending after 1987, in excess of the trust's total investment income reported for taxation years ending after 1987.

Schedule 4 is designed to track the trust's cumulative net investment loss (CNIL) for purposes of computing the eligible amount of taxable capital gains on the disposition of qualified farm property, a share in the capital stock of a family farm corporation, or a qualified small business corporation share that is:

- designated as an eligible taxable capital gain to an individual beneficiary; or

- claimed as a capital gains deduction by a spousal or common-law partner trust in the year the beneficiary spouse or common-law partner dies.

The CNIL, as calculated on Line 27 of Schedule 4, will reduce the trust's cumulative capital gains limit for purposes of the amount claimable on Schedule 3. Accordingly, a balance in the trust's CNIL account will reduce the trust's eligible taxable capital gains that qualify for the capital gains deduction.

---

44 See heading 4 of Chapter 12 entitled, "Line 53 – Capital Gains Deduction for Resident Spousal or Common-Law Partner Trust Only."

CHAPTER 14 — TRUST SCHEDULES AND FORMS

Figure 14.4
Schedule 3
(page 1 of 2)

PART IV — T3 TRUST INFORMATION & TAX RETURN

Figure 14.4 (continued)
Schedule 3
(page 2 of 2)

- **Line 22 – Adjusted cumulative loss amount reported after 1984 and before the current year**
  You have to make an adjustment if the trust claimed net capital losses of other years in a taxation year after 1984 and before 1992 if, in the same taxation year, the trust reported a pre-1985 reserve. You have to reduce the net capital losses of other years claimed in a year by the taxable portion of the pre-1985 reserve reported in the year. The following chart will help you calculate this adjustment for line 21. If you have never made this calculation, you have to make it in the current year for all the years from 1985 to 1991.

Calculation for line 21

Year	(1) Net capital losses of other years claimed in the year	(2) Reserves related to capital dispositions before 1985	(3)	(4) Taxable portion of reserve (column 2 × column 3)	(5) Lesser of amounts in column 1 and column 4 (if negative, enter "0")
1985	$	$	x 1/2	$	$
1986	$	$	x 1/2	$	$
1987	$	$	x 1/2	$	$
1988	$	$	x 2/3	$	$
1989	$	$	x 2/3	$	$
1990	$	$	x 3/4	$	$
1991	$	$	x 3/4	$	$
Total					$

Enter the total of column 5 on line 21 of this schedule.

1. Net capital losses of other years claimed in the year – for 1985 and 1986, line 6 of Part I of Form T672; for 1987, line 523 of Schedule 5B; for 1988 to 1991, line 52 of the T3 return. Also include any capital loss carrybacks claimed in each year.

2. Reserves related to capital disposition before 1985 – for 1985, previous-year reserve from Schedule 2; for 1986, line 511 of Schedule 5; for 1987, 1985 and prior net reserve (line 513 **minus** line 514) from Schedule 5A; for 1988 and 1989, line 575 of Schedule 5C; and for 1990 and 1991, line 215 of Schedule 2.

Related Schedules

If you complete Schedule 3, you also have to complete and submit Schedule 4, *Cumulative Net Investment Loss*. You will need the amount you calculated on line 34 on Schedule 3 when you complete Schedule 5, *Beneficiary Spouse or Common-Law Partner Information and Spousal or Common-Law Partner Trust's Capital Gains Deduction*, and Schedule 9, *Income Allocations and Designations to Beneficiaries*. This is the amount of the trust's taxable capital gain that qualifies for a capital gains deduction for a spousal or common-law partner trust (line 1 of Schedule 5) or an individual beneficiary (line 930 of Schedule 9).

Printed in Canada

CHAPTER 14 — TRUST SCHEDULES AND FORMS

Figure 14.5
Schedule 4
(page 1 of 2)

T3 – [ ][ ][ ][ ]   **CUMULATIVE NET INVESTMENT LOSS**   **SCHEDULE 4**

- Enter the applicable taxation year in the box above.
- Complete this schedule if the trust is a personal trust that has qualified farm property or qualified small business corporation shares, is reporting any investment income or claiming any investment expenses, and is:
  - designating taxable capital gains from qualified farm property, qualified small business corporation shares, or reserves on these properties to an individual beneficiary; or
  - a spousal or common-law partner trust claiming a capital gains deduction on Schedule 5, *Beneficiary Spouse or Common-Law Partner Information and Spousal or Common-Law Partner Trust's Capital Gains Deduction*, in the year the beneficiary spouse or common-law partner dies.
- The cumulative net investment loss (CNIL) is the trust's total investment expenses for years ending after 1987, minus the trust's total investment income for years ending after 1987. For purposes of the CNIL, investment income and expenses generally refer to income and expenses related to property including dividends, interest, rental income, and royalties.
- Trusts with qualified farm property or qualified small business corporation shares should complete this schedule each year and keep it with the trust's records. Do this even for years when the trust is not reporting capital gains or losses, and is not designating eligible taxable capital gains to its beneficiaries. The balance in the trust's CNIL account is a cumulative total. You need the total of the trust's investment income and expenses for 1988 and following years to calculate eligible taxable capital gains on Schedule 3, *Eligible Taxable Capital Gains*.
- The CNIL calculated on line 27 on this schedule will reduce the trust's cumulative gains limit calculated on Schedule 3. This may reduce the trust's eligible taxable capital gains that qualify for the capital gains deduction.

Investment expenses

Investment expenses claimed in the year

Carrying charges and interest expenses (line 21 of the T3 return)			1
Accounting fees (do not include amounts included above as a carrying charge)	4020 • +		2
Trustee fees against any property income	4030 • +		3
Foreign taxes relating to property (deducted under subsection 20(11) or 20(12))	4040 • +		4
Debt obligations under subsection 20(21)	4050 • +		5
Net rental losses (line 09 of the T3 return)		+	6
Share of partnership's net loss other than allowable capital losses (see Note 1), plus loss from a limited partnership deducted by the trust	4070 • +		7
Other property expenses not included above (see Note 2)	4060 • +		8
Net capital losses of other years deducted in the year (line 52 of the T3 return)		9	
Amount from line 13 of Schedule 3	–	10	
Subtotal (line 9 minus line 10; if negative, enter "0")	=	▶	11
Total investment expenses claimed in the year (add lines 1 to 8 and line 11)		=	12
Total investment expenses claimed in previous years (line 14 of previous year's Schedule 4)	4130 • +		13
Cumulative investment expenses (line 12 plus line 13)		= ▶	14

Note 1
- Only a specified member should report a share of a partnership's net loss excluding allowable capital losses. A specified member is generally a limited partner or a partner who is not actively engaged in a partnership business (other than financing that business), or in a similar business outside of the partnership.

Note 2
- Other property expenses can include:
  - 50% of resource and exploration expenses renounced by a corporation, or incurred by a partnership, while the trust was a specified member;
  - expenses to buy or sell units, interests, or shares, or to borrow money;
  - repayments of inducements;
  - repayments of refund interest;
  - the uncollectible portion of proceeds from dispositions of depreciable property (except passenger vehicles that cost more than $30,000);
  - sale or agreement for sale or mortgage included in proceeds of disposition in a previous year under subsection 20(5);
  - life insurance premiums deducted from property income; and
  - capital cost allowance claimed on certified films and videotapes.

T3 SCH 4 E (03)   (Vous pouvez obtenir ce formulaire en français à www.adrc.gc.ca ou au 1 800 959-3376.)   Canadä

PART IV — T3 TRUST INFORMATION & TAX RETURN

Figure 14.5 (continued)
Schedule 4
(page 2 of 2)

Investment income

Enter the cumulative investment expenses from line 14		14

Investment income reported in the year

Taxable dividend income (line 03 of the T3 return)	X 1.25) =		15
Foreign investment income (line 04 of the T3 return)		+	16
Other investment income (line 05 of the T3 return)		+	17
Net rental income (line 09 of the T3 return)		+	18
Specified member's share of partnership's net income other than taxable capital gains (see Note 3)		4250 ● +	19
Other property income (see Note 4)		4260 ● +	20
Taxable capital gains (losses) for the year (total of amounts from line 21 of Schedule 1, line 25 of Form T1055, and line 5 of Schedule 3, if applicable)	21		
Amount from line 10 of Schedule 3, if applicable	− 22		
Subtotal (line 21 minus line 22; if negative, enter "0")	=	▶ +	23
Total investment income reported in the year (add lines 15 to 20 and 23)		=	24
Total investment income reported in previous years (line 26 of previous year's Schedule 4)		4310 ● +	25
Cumulative investment income (line 24 plus line 25)		=	▶ − 26
Cumulative net investment loss (line 14 minus line 26; if negative, enter "0") Enter this amount on line 25 of Schedule 3.		=	27

Note 3
- A specified member is generally a limited partner or a partner who is not actively engaged in a partnership business (other than financing that business), or in a similar business outside of the partnership.

Note 4
- Other property income can include:
  - capital gains from ineligible property (line 9 of Schedule 3 minus line 6 of Schedule 3);
  - recaptured capital cost allowance related to property income, including insurance proceeds (other than amounts included on line 18);
  - amounts paid out of Net Income Stabilization Account (NISA) Fund 2, reported on line 10 of the T3 return;
  - home insulation or energy conversion grants under paragraph 12(1)(u);
  - payments received as an inducement or reimbursement; and
  - income from the appropriation of property to a shareholder.

CHAPTER 14 — TRUST SCHEDULES AND FORMS

5. Schedule 5 – Beneficiary Spouse or Common-Law Partner Information and Spousal or Common-Law Partner Trust's Capital Gains Deduction

The general rule that applies when capital property has been transferred to a spousal or common-law partner trust is that the property is deemed to be disposed of at fair market value on the death of the beneficiary spouse or common-law partner.[45] Consequently, any tax-deferred gains inherent in the property will be realized on the death of the beneficiary spouse or common-law partner.

However, subsection 110.6(12) provides some relief in respect of "eligible" capital property in that the spousal or common-law partner trust is entitled to claim any unused capital gains deduction that the deceased beneficiary spouse or common-law partner had not utilized at the date of death. (See Figure 14.6.)

This relieving provision accords the trust a similar tax treatment, as would have been realized, had the trust disposed of the property immediately prior to the death of the beneficiary spouse or common-law partner and designated the capital gain to be taxed in the hands of the spouse or common-law partner.[46]

The ability for the trust to utilize this provision is restricted to only "eligible" taxable capital gains as determined on Schedule 3 (Line 34). If the spousal or common-law partner trust is subject to the deemed realization rule, see heading 11 in Chapter 10, entitled "Deemed Realizations"[47] and Form T1055.

Note also, that the capital gains deduction is available only to a spousal or common-law partner trust, to the extent of the unused lifetime portion of the deceased beneficiary spouse or common-law partner's capital gains deduction.

---

45 Paragraph 104(4)(a).
46 Subsections 104(21), 104(21.1), 104(21.2) and 104(21.3).
47 Refer to heading 2 of Chapter 6 entitled, "Deemed Realizations."

PART IV — T3 TRUST INFORMATION & TAX RETURN

Figure 14.6
Schedule 5

T3 – ☐☐☐☐   BENEFICIARY SPOUSE OR COMMON-LAW PARTNER INFORMATION   SCHEDULE 5
                 AND SPOUSAL OR COMMON-LAW PARTNER TRUST'S
                 CAPITAL GAINS DEDUCTION

- Enter the applicable taxation year in the box above.
- Use this schedule to calculate a spousal or common-law partner trust's capital gains deduction for the taxation year in which the beneficiary spouse or common-law partner died.
  Note: A joint spousal or common-law partner trust, an alter ego trust, or a trust that elected to defer the deemed realization day, **cannot** claim a capital gains deduction.
- Before completing this schedule, you have to calculate:
  - the trust's eligible taxable capital gains (line 34 of Schedule 3, *Eligible Taxable Capital Gains*); and
  - the spouse's or common-law partner's unused lifetime capital gains deduction limit for the year the spouse or common-law partner died (Form T657, *Calculation of Capital Gains Deduction*, for the year of death).
- If the spousal or common-law partner trust is subject to the deemed realization rule, see the section, "Form T1055, *Summary of Deemed Realizations*" in the *T3 Trust Guide*.
- A **post-1971 spousal or common-law partner trust** can claim a capital gains deduction on qualified farm property or qualified small business corporation shares in the taxation year the beneficiary spouse or common-law partner dies. The trust can claim the deduction to the extent that the beneficiary spouse or common-law partner could have claimed a deduction for the eligible taxable capital gains if the gains had belonged to that spouse or common-law partner and not to the trust.
- A **pre-1972 spousal trust** can claim a capital gains deduction on qualified farm property or qualified small business corporation shares when reporting a deemed realization on the day the beneficiary spouse dies. The trust can claim this deduction if the trustee has never elected to defer the deemed realization day.
- For definitions of **post-1971 spousal or common-law partner trust** and **pre-1972 spousal trust**, see the *T3 Trust Guide*.

Part A – Deceased beneficiary spouse or common-law partner information

Name of deceased beneficiary spouse or common-law partner	Address	Social insurance number	Date of death Year Month Day

Part B – Calculating the spousal or common-law partner trust's capital gains deduction on all property

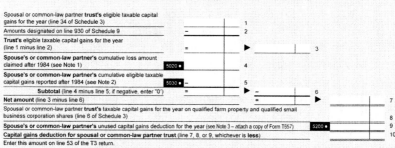

Note 1
The cumulative loss amount claimed after 1984 is the amount on line 30 of Form T657.

Note 2
The cumulative eligible taxable capital gains reported after 1984 is the amount on line 23 of Form T657.

Note 3
The unused capital gains deduction is the **lesser** of lines 52 and 55 of Form T657, **minus** the amount entered on line 56 of Form T657.

T3 SCH 5 (03)
Printed in Canada   (Français au verso)   Canada

CHAPTER 14 — TRUST SCHEDULES AND FORMS

A joint spousal or common-law partner trust or an alter ego trust is not eligible to claim this deduction.

6. Schedule 6 – Trusts' Agreement to Allocate the Basic Exemption from Minimum Tax

Schedule 6 (see Figure 14.7) need only be completed when the trust is one of two or more trusts established by the same settlor, and the trusts are entitled to take advantage of the $40,000 basic exemption from minimum tax. This might be the case where, for example, minimum tax applies to any one of the trusts. In such case, the $40,000 exemption must be allocated among all of the trusts by completing and attaching Schedule 6 to each of the trust returns.

Minimum tax does not apply to some types of trusts in certain circumstances.[48] Note that the "Agreement Section" of Schedule 6 must be signed by the trustee or legal representative of each trust in the group.

7. Schedule 7 – Pension Income Allocations and Designations

This schedule (see Figure 14.8) applies only to testamentary trusts.

An amount received by an estate as a superannuation or pension benefit in a taxation year, throughout which it was resident in Canada, can be designated by the estate as pension income to the beneficiary, thereby retaining the nature and character of the pension income for tax purposes in the hands of the beneficiary.[49]

If the beneficiary is a spouse or common-law partner of the deceased, the amount designated will qualify as pension income for purposes of the pension income credit[50] claimable on the beneficiary's personal income tax return.

---

48 See heading 2 of Chapter 3 entitled, "Minimum Tax" for additional commentary.
49 Subsection 104(27).
50 Subsection 118(3) and section 118.8; see also M.N.R., Interpretation Bulletin

PART IV — T3 TRUST INFORMATION & TAX RETURN

Figure 14.7
Schedule 6

T3 – ☐☐☐☐ **TRUSTS' AGREEMENT TO ALLOCATE THE BASIC EXEMPTION FROM MINIMUM TAX** **SCHEDULE 6**

- Enter the applicable taxation year in the box above.
- We allow a $40,000 basic exemption from minimum tax to testamentary or grandfathered inter vivos trusts. For a definition of testamentary and grandfathered inter vivos trusts, see the *T3 Trust Guide*.
- Use this schedule when more than one qualifying trust is formed from contributions by the same individual and you have to allocate the $40,000 basic exemption among the trusts (see the example below).
- If we request this schedule in writing, and you do not send us the completed schedule within 30 days, we may allocate the $40,000 exemption among the qualifying trusts ourselves.
- The "Agreement" section of this schedule has to be signed by the trustee or legal representative of each trust in the group.
- If you need more space, attach a separate sheet.

Names and addresses of all trusts contributed to by the same individual	Trust account number	Allocated amount
	T ☐☐ – ☐☐☐☐ – ☐☐	
	T ☐☐ – ☐☐☐☐ – ☐☐	
	T ☐☐ – ☐☐☐☐ – ☐☐	
	T ☐☐ – ☐☐☐☐ – ☐☐	

Enter the allocated amount on line 28 of Schedule 12, *Minimum Tax*.

Agreement

It is hereby agreed that the $40,000 exemption from minimum tax is allocated as shown above.

Trust's name	Authorized officer's signature	Position or office	Date
			Year Month Day
			Year Month Day
			Year Month Day
			Year Month Day

Example
Kate is an individual who created five trusts. Kate was divorced twice before 1970, and when she divorced she set up two trusts – one for each of her former spouses. In her will, Kate created three new separate trusts – one for her grandchildren, one for her children, and one for her current spouse. If minimum tax applies to any of the trusts, you have to allocate the $40,000 basic exemption among the trusts. Attach this schedule to each of the trust returns.

T3 SCH 6 (02)
Printed in Canada   (Français au verso)   Canadä

IT-517R, "Pension Tax Credit" [Archived] (July 5, 1996), at paragraph 11. See also M.N.R., Technical Interpretation 2003-0011587, "Pension Tax Credit RRIF Payments" (April 16, 2003).

CHAPTER 14 — TRUST SCHEDULES AND FORMS

Figure 14.8
Schedule 7

T3 – ☐☐☐☐ **PENSION INCOME ALLOCATIONS AND DESIGNATIONS** **SCHEDULE 7**

- Enter the applicable taxation year in the box above.
- Complete this schedule only if you are designating pension income to the beneficiaries of a testamentary trust in a year throughout which it was a resident of Canada. How this income is designated will affect its tax treatment for the beneficiaries. You need the amounts from this schedule to complete lines 922, 926, 931, and 936-1 of Schedule 9, *Income Allocations and Designations to Beneficiaries*. You also have to complete the applicable box on the beneficiary's T3 slip.
- You can allocate all pension income as "Other Income." If you do, include the amount on line 926 of Schedule 9 and in box 26 of the T3 slip, and **do not** complete this schedule. However, the beneficiary will not be able to:
  - transfer the qualifying income to a registered retirement savings plan (RRSP) or a registered pension plan (RPP);
  - claim the pension income amount; or
  - transfer the qualifying income to acquire an eligible annuity for a minor beneficiary.
- **Do not write in the shaded areas.**
- Enter the pension income in one of the following columns:

  Column A: Lump-sum pension income designated to a beneficiary spouse or common-law partner. These amounts qualify for a transfer to the beneficiary spouse's or common-law partner's RRSP or RPP.

  Column B: Other pension income.

  Column C: Pension income designated to a beneficiary spouse or common-law partner that qualifies for the pension income non-refundable tax credit.

  Column D: Pension income that qualifies for a transfer to acquire an eligible annuity for a minor beneficiary.

- For more information on pension income or transfers, see the *RRSPs and Other Registered Plans for Retirement* guide.

Pension income received by the trust, that is being allocated and designated	Column A Lump-sum pension income	Column B Other pension income	Column C Qualifying pension income	Column D Qualifies for an eligible annuity for a minor
1. **Lump-sum payment from an RPP** (box 18 of a T4A slip) that was:				
a) designated to the beneficiary spouse or common-law partner				
b) designated to a minor beneficiary who was under 18 when the person died and was a child or grandchild of the deceased (enter the same amount in columns B and D)				
c) allocated to a beneficiary who is not a person described in a) or b) above				
2. **Life annuity out of a superannuation or pension plan** (box 16 of a T4A slip) that was:				
a) designated to the beneficiary spouse or common-law partner (enter the same amount in columns B and C)				
b) allocated to a beneficiary who is not the beneficiary spouse or common-law partner				
3. **Life annuity out of a pension plan for the deceased person's services while not a resident of Canada** that was:				
a) designated to the beneficiary spouse or common-law partner (enter the same amount in columns B and C)				
b) allocated to a beneficiary who is not the beneficiary spouse or common-law partner				
4. **Lump-sum payment out of a pension plan for the deceased person's services while not a resident of Canada** that was:				
a) designated to the beneficiary spouse or common-law partner or former spouse or common-law partner				
b) allocated to a beneficiary who is not the beneficiary spouse or common-law partner or former spouse or common-law partner				
5. **Lump-sum payment out of a foreign retirement arrangement received for the deceased person's, or the deceased person's spouse or common-law partner, or former spouse or common-law partner's contributions to the plan** that was:				
a) designated to the beneficiary spouse or common-law partner				
b) allocated to a beneficiary who is not the beneficiary spouse or common-law partner				
6. **Lump-sum payment from a deferred profit-sharing plan** (box 18 of a T4A slip) that was:				
a) designated to the beneficiary spouse or common-law partner				
b) allocated to a beneficiary who is not the beneficiary spouse or common-law partner				
7. **Periodic payments from an annuity of a minor** (see 1b) for a definition of a minor)				

Pension income being allocated and designated ▶

| Total pension income cannot be more than the lesser of:
 • the amount on line 02 of the T3 return; and
 • the amount on line 46 of the T3 return. | Column A total _____
 Column B total + _____
 Total pension = _____ | Enter this amount on line 922 of Schedule 9. | Include this amount on line 928 of Schedule 9. | Enter this amount on line 931 of Schedule 9. | Enter this amount on line 936-1 of Schedule 9. |

T3 SCH 7 (03)
Printed in Canada

(Français au verso)

Canada

PART IV — T3 TRUST INFORMATION & TAX RETURN

If the trust is designating pension income to a beneficiary, complete this schedule. Also, you should transfer the amounts computed on this schedule to the applicable lines on Schedule 9, "Income Allocations and Designations to Beneficiaries."

8. Schedule 8 – Investment Income, Carrying Charges, and Gross-Up Amount of Dividends Retained by the Trust

Complete and attach Part A of Schedule 8 (see Figure 14.9) to the T3 Trust Information and Income Tax Return in respect of interest, dividends and other investment income reported by the trust in the taxation year as detailed below.

8.1 Line 1 – Actual Amount of Dividends from Taxable Canadian Corporations

Attach a statement listing the actual amount of dividends received from taxable Canadian corporations. The actual amount of dividends will be reported in Box 23 of T3 Slips and in Box 10 of T5 Slips issued to the trust. Enter the total on Line 03 of the T3 Return.[51]

8.2 Lines 2 to 4 – Foreign Investment Income

Report the gross amount of foreign source investment income earned by the trust (in Canadian dollars). The amounts to be reported here include foreign source interest income and foreign source dividends. Enter the total on Line 04 of the T3 Return.[52]

---

51 See heading 3 of Chapter 10 entitled, "Line 03 – Actual Amount of Dividends from Taxable Canadian Corporations" for additional commentary.
52 See heading 4 of Chapter 10 entitled, "Line 04 – Foreign Investment Income."

CHAPTER 14 — TRUST SCHEDULES AND FORMS

Figure 14.9
Schedule 8

T3 – ☐☐☐☐   **INVESTMENT INCOME, CARRYING CHARGES, AND GROSS-UP AMOUNT OF DIVIDENDS RETAINED BY THE TRUST**   **SCHEDULE 8**

- Enter the applicable taxation year in the box above.

Part A – Calculating investment income and carrying charges
- Attach any information slips received.
- Enter the names of the payers at the appropriate lines below. If there is not enough space, attach a separate sheet.
- Include amounts credited through banks, trust companies, brokers, etc.

Actual amount of dividends from taxable Canadian corporations
(box 23 of T3 slip or box 10 of T5 slip) _____ 1
Enter the amount from line 1 on line 03 of the T3 return, and line 16 below.

Foreign investment income

Interest from foreign sources _____ 2
Other foreign investment income _____ + 3
Total foreign investment income (line 2 plus line 3) _____ = 4
Enter the amount from line 4 on line 04 of the T3 return.

Other investment income

Interest	Bonds, trust companies, banks		5
	Other deposits (specify)	+	6
	Mortgages, notes, and other securities	+	7

Other dividends (including dividends received under a dividend rental arrangement) _____ + 8
Other (specify) _____ + 9
Total other investment income (add lines 5 to 9) _____ = 10
Enter the amount from line 10 on line 05 of the T3 return.

Carrying charges and interest expenses

Interest on money borrowed to earn investment income (attach a statement – see the *T3 Trust Guide* for details)	8160 ●		11
Management, safe custody, or accounting fees (specify)	8170 ●	+	12
Investment counsel fees	8180 ●	+	13
Other (specify)	8190 ●	+	14
Total carrying charges (add lines 11 to 14)		=	15

Enter the amount from line 15 on line 21 of the T3 return.

Part B – Calculating the gross-up amount of dividends retained or not designated by the trust

Total dividends reported before applying expenses (line 1 above) _____ 16
Dividends designated to beneficiaries (line 923, Part A of Schedule 9) _____ – 17
Total dividends **not** designated by the trust (line 16 minus line 17) _____ = 18
Dividends allocated, but **not** designated, to non-resident beneficiaries
(dividends from line 926, Column 2 of Schedule 9)   8240 ● – 19
Total dividends retained (resident beneficiaries only) or **not** designated by the trust (line 18 minus line 19) = 20
Line 20 multiplied by 25%   x 25%
Gross-up amount of dividends retained or not designated by the trust = 21
Enter the amount from line 21 on line 24 of Schedule 11, *Federal Income Tax*, or on
line 19 of Schedule 12, *Minimum Tax*, if applicable, and on line 49 of the T3 return.

T3 SCH 8 (03)
Printed in Canada   (Français au verso)   Canada

PART IV — T3 TRUST INFORMATION & TAX RETURN

8.3 Lines 5 to 10 – Other Investment Income

Report amounts received in respect of bond interest, bank interest, mortgage interest and interest earned on all other debt obligations. Also include refund interest received from CRA on tax assessments and reassessments.

Interest income should be reported by the trust on an accrual basis. If necessary, attach a schedule detailing other investment income from all sources. Enter the total on Line 05 of the T3 Return.[53]

8.4 Lines 11 to 15 – Carrying Charges and Interest Expenses

Include amounts paid or payable by the trust in respect of expenses incurred in connection with the earning of investment income. Such expenses can include:

- interest on money borrowed to earn investment income;
- management fees paid in connection with the trust's investments;
- custodial fees paid in respect of investments held by the trust;
- safety deposit box charges;
- accounting fees[54] incurred in connection with the trust's investments; and
- investment counsel fees.

Interest paid to CRA on unpaid income taxes and late or deficient installments is not deductible by the trust for taxation purposes. Compute the total of all amounts deductible and enter that sum on Line 21 of the T3 Return.[55]

---

53 See heading 5 of Chapter 10 entitled, "Line 05 – Other Investment Income" for additional commentary.
54 See also M.N.R., Interpretation Bulletin IT-99R5, "Legal and Accounting Fees" [Consolidated] (December 14, 2000), at paragraphs 1 and 2.
55 See heading 1 of Chapter 11 entitled, "Line 21 – Carrying Charges and Interest Expenses" for additional information.

CHAPTER 14 — TRUST SCHEDULES AND FORMS

8.5 Lines 16 to 21 – Calculating the Gross-Up Amount of Dividends Retained or Not Designated by the Trust

Part B of Schedule 8 (see Figure 14.9) should be completed where a trust reports actual dividends from taxable Canadian corporations, which are to be retained by the trust and not paid or allocated as income to its beneficiaries in the taxation year. The amount of dividends not paid or allocated by the trust then becomes subject to tax at the applicable tax rates of the trust.

CRA's T3 Trust Guide refers to certain amounts in completing Schedule 9 as "Income Allocations and Designations to Beneficiaries." Be advised, however, that CRA considers the term "designation" (for purposes of their T3 Trust Guide) to mean an amount of income allocated and "to keep the identity of certain types of allocated income or credits (so that) the beneficiaries can take advantage of deductions or credits that relate directly to the type of income, such as the dividend tax credit."

CRA does not intend that the meaning of "designation," as used within the T3 Trust Guide, should mean amounts designated by a trust under subsections 104(13.1) and 104(13.2). In fact, designations made under subsections 104(13.1) and 104(13.2) by a trust result in exactly the opposite. That is, the trust's actual income distributions can be so designated to provide that such "designated amounts" are deemed not to have been paid or payable in the year by the trust, with the result that such "designated amounts" will neither be deductible to the trust nor taxable in the hands of the beneficiaries. Consequently, amounts designated under subsections 104(13.1) and 104(13.2) are, in effect, retained as income within the trust.

In completing Part B of Schedule 8, include on Line 16 the actual amount of dividends from taxable Canadian corporations, reported on Line 01 of the Schedule. From this amount, subtract the actual amount of dividends "paid or payable" to beneficiaries in the taxation year as appearing from Line 923 (Part A of Schedule 9).

PART IV — T3 TRUST INFORMATION & TAX RETURN

Note that if the trust designated (for tax purposes) "dividend income" under subsection 104(13.1), it should not appear on Schedule 9 and would then not be entered on Line 17 of Schedule 8.

Line 19 of Schedule 8 provides that the actual dividends of the trust, which are allocated to non-resident beneficiaries, do not enjoy the "gross-up" and corresponding dividend tax credit. Accordingly, dividends allocated to a non-resident beneficiary (from Schedule 9) should be entered here.

The net difference, which is reflected on Line 20, is the amount of the actual dividends of the trust (retained as income) which become subject to the gross-up amount and dividend tax credit. This amount is then multiplied by 25% to calculate the gross-up amount on Line 21 of Schedule 8. Enter the amount from Line 21 of Schedule 8 on Line 49 of the T3 Return and also on Line 24 of Schedule 11 (Federal Income Tax) or on Line 19 of Schedule 12 (Minimum Tax) as is applicable.

9. Schedule 9 – Income Allocations and Designations to Beneficiaries

The general concept under Canadian tax law is that income, including taxable capital gains, will be taxable in the estate or trust unless certain conditions are met, which provide for the allocation or "payment" of income and taxable capital gains to its beneficiaries.

There are, in essence, four situations where income and capital gains can be deducted from the income of the estate or trust and included in the beneficiaries' income. These situations are as follows:

    1. where income is payable to the beneficiary by virtue of the provisions of the will or trust document;[56]

    2. where income is deemed payable to a minor beneficiary;[57]

---

56 Subsections 104(6) and 104(13).
57 Subsection 104(18).

CHAPTER 14 — TRUST SCHEDULES AND FORMS

3. where the trust and the beneficiary jointly elect, in respect of the accumulating income of the trust, that the beneficiary will include such amounts as income ("preferred beneficiary election"); and

4. where the trustee makes a payment in respect of the maintenance of property for the use and enjoyment of the beneficiary.[58]

Where any one of these four situations is present, trust income can either be (in whole or in part) allocated as income to the beneficiaries or taxed (in whole or in part) in the trust, according to the provisions of the will or trust document.

If the trust income is paid or payable to beneficiaries, a designation under subsection 104(13.1) can be made to report the income on the trust's return, insofar as the trust is a resident of Canada throughout the year and not otherwise exempt from tax.

Such "income designations" under subsection 104(13.1) may be useful where a trust has taxable income for the year and a non-capital loss carryforward. By making a subsection 104(13.1) designation, the trust can retain and be subject to tax on such income, thereby providing the means to apply a non-capital loss from a prior taxation year.[59]

If the trust makes an income designation under subsection 104(13.1), the designation will proportionately reduce each beneficiary's share of trust income to be allocated for the taxation year.

A trust can make a similar designation under subsection 104(13.2) if taxable capital gains are included as income reported on the trust's T3 Income Tax Return for the taxation year. A designation under subsection 104(13.2) will proportionately reduce each beneficiary's taxable capital gains allocated from the trust. This strategy is worth employing when the trust has a non-capital or a net capital loss carryforward, which can

---

58 Subsection 105(2).
59 See commentary and planning considerations outlined in heading 4 of Chapter 4 entitled, "Income Designations under 104(13.1) and 104(13.2)."

PART IV — T3 TRUST INFORMATION & TAX RETURN

be applied for the taxation year against taxable capital gains retained in the trust.

Income, including interest, dividends and capital gains designated by the trust to its beneficiaries, retains its character for tax purposes in the hands of the beneficiaries. Consequently, this "flow-through" attribute permits beneficiaries to make use of the dividend tax credit on the designation of dividend income from taxable Canadian corporations, the use of the capital gains exemption on eligible capital gains, and access to tax credits in respect of the designation of eligible pension income. Basically, the following type of trust income can be designated as income to beneficiaries:

- net taxable capital gains;
- certain lump-sum pension income amounts;
- dividends from taxable Canadian corporations;
- foreign business income;
- foreign non-business income;
- interest and other investment income;
- eligible pension income;
- pension income that qualifies for an eligible annuity for a minor beneficiary; and
- retiring allowances which qualify for a transfer to a registered pension plan (RPP) or a registered retirement savings plan (RRSP).

There are certain exceptions and restrictions relating to the designation of income and capital gains to beneficiaries. These are detailed below.

- Income realized from a deemed disposition of trust property can only be deducted from the trust's income if it is paid and designated to:

CHAPTER 14 — TRUST SCHEDULES AND FORMS

- o the spouse or common-law partner of a post-1971 spousal or common-law partner trust;

- o the settlor or beneficiary spouse or common-law partner of a joint spousal or common-law partner trust, insofar as one of the settlor or the beneficiary spouse or common-law partner is living at the time of the designation; and

- o the settlor in respect of an alter ego trust.

- Capital gains realized from a deemed disposition of trust property or income arising from the disposition of land inventory relating to the trust's business, and any Canadian and foreign resource profits, can only be deducted from the trust's income if paid and designated on the death of:

    - o the spouse or common-law partner of a post-1971 spousal or common-law partner trust;

    - o the settlor or beneficiary spouse or common-law partner of a joint spousal or common-law partner trust, whoever is the last to die; and

    - o the settlor, in respect of an alter ego trust.

- Income "payable" to a beneficiary in a taxation year can only be deducted from the trust's income if it is designated to:

    - o in the case of a post-1971 spousal trust in existence on December 20, 1991, or a spousal or common-law partner trust created after December 20, 1991, the beneficiary spouse or common-law partner, insofar as the beneficiary spouse or common-law partner is alive;

    - o in the case of a joint spousal or common-law partner trust, either the settlor or the beneficiary spouse or common-law partner, insofar as either beneficiary is alive; or

    - o in the case of an alter ego trust, the settlor insofar as that individual is alive.

PART IV — T3 TRUST INFORMATION & TAX RETURN

Enter the "designated income amounts" on Part B of Schedule 9 (see Figure 14.10), including foreign income taxes paid, Part XII.2 taxes and other credits, which would "flow through" to the beneficiary. If the trust designates income amounts to beneficiaries on Schedule 9, it should also complete a T3 Summary and the applicable T3 Supplementary Slip in respect of each such beneficiary. If the trust designates income to non-resident beneficiaries, the trust must complete an NR4 Summary together with the applicable NR4 Slip in respect of each non-resident beneficiary receiving an income designation.

CRA has published a number of Interpretation Bulletins which are directly relevant to the tax treatment of trusts and their beneficiaries, in respect of income allocations and designations made for a taxation year. These materials provide comprehensive commentary on the subject matter.[60]

10. Schedule 10 – Part XII.2 Tax and Part XIII Non-Resident Withholding Tax

Part XII.2 tax does not apply to testamentary trusts. Part XII.2 tax applies where an *inter vivos* trust has one or more non-resident beneficiaries and earns income that includes taxable capital gains from dispositions of taxable Canadian properties, income from real property or business carried on in Canada or Canadian resource or timber resource property income. Income of the trust from such sources is taxed at a flat federal rate of 36%.[61] (See Figure 14.11.)

---

60 M.N.R., Interpretation Bulletin IT-342R, "Trusts – Income Payable to Beneficiaries" (March 21, 1990), at paragraph 4; M.N.R., Interpretation Bulletin IT-381R3, "Trusts – Capital Gains and Losses and the Flow-Through of Taxable Capital Gains to Beneficiaries" (February 14, 1997), at paragraphs 3-5; and M.N.R., Interpretation Bulletin IT-524, "Trusts – Flow-Through of Taxable Dividends to a Beneficiary – After 1987" (March 16, 1990), at paragraphs 1 and 2.

61 Section 210.2.

CHAPTER 14 — TRUST SCHEDULES AND FORMS

Figure 14.10
Schedule 9

T3 – ☐☐☐☐   **INCOME ALLOCATIONS AND DESIGNATIONS TO BENEFICIARIES**   **SCHEDULE 9**

- Enter the applicable taxation year in the box above. For information on completing this schedule, see Chapter 3 in the *T3 Trust Guide*.
- Do not complete this schedule if line 46 of the return is zero, or negative, unless the trust is an insurance segregated fund that is allocating capital losses.
- Do not write in the shaded areas.

Part A – Total income allocations and designations to beneficiaries
1. Number of beneficiaries (including beneficiaries being allocated less than $100 for whom no T3 slip is being prepared) to whom income on line 928 is being allocated. ....
2. Total income allocated without T3 slips. ....
3. Do the T3 slips include income attributed to the transferor?. .... Yes ☐ No ☐
   If *yes*, submit a statement showing the name of the beneficiary, the name of the transferor, and the amount.
4. Was each beneficiary allocated an equal share of the income? .... Yes ☐ No ☐
   If *no*, submit a statement showing the breakdown.

Box no.	Type of income	Column 1 Resident	Column 2 Non-resident	Column 3 By preferred beneficiary election	Column 4 Total	
21	Taxable capital gains	*1		*1		921
22	Lump-sum pension income					922
23	Actual amount of dividends					923
24	Foreign business income					924
25	Foreign non-business income					925
26	Other income					926
	Totals		*2		*3	928

Part B – Summary of other amounts designated to beneficiaries

Box no.	Description	Column 1 Resident	Column 2 Non-resident	Column 3 By preferred beneficiary election	Column 4 Total	
30	Taxable capital gains eligible for deduction	*1		*1		930
31	Qualifying pension income					931
32	Taxable amount of dividends (see Line 932 in the *T3 Trust Guide*)					932
33	Foreign business income tax paid					933
34	Foreign non-business income tax paid					934
35	Eligible death benefits					935
36	Miscellaneous: Pension income qualifying for an eligible annuity for a minor					936-1
	Retiring allowance qualifying for transfer to RPP and RRSP					936-2
	Eligible amount of charitable donations	*4				936-3
37	Insurance segregated fund capital losses	*1				937
38	Part XII.2 tax credit					938
39	Federal dividend tax credit (line 932 × 13.3333%) =					939
40	Investment costs or expenditure for investment tax credit (ITC)					940
41	Investment tax credit (ITC)					941
45	Other credits					945

Footnote amounts (included in boxes 21, 26, and 30 of T3 slips)

Box no.	Footnote	Column 1 Resident	Column 2 Non-resident	Column 3 By preferred beneficiary election	Column 4 Total	
21	Non-business income for foreign tax credit					921-3
26	Eligible capital property – qualified farm property					926-1
26	Self-employment earnings	*4				926-3
30	Qualified farm property	*1		*1		930-1
30	Qualified small business corporation shares	*1		*1		930-2

* 1 When completing T3 slips and the T3 Summary, multiply these amounts by 2.
* 2 Enter this amount on line 15 of Schedule 10, *Part XII.2 Tax and Part XIII Non-Resident Withholding Tax*.
* 3 Total on line 928 cannot be more than the amount on line 46 of the return.
* 4 Only communal organizations can designate these amounts. See the *T3 Trust Guide* for more information.

T3 SCH 9 (03)
Printed in Canada   (Français au verso)   **Canada**

PART IV — T3 TRUST INFORMATION & TAX RETURN

Figure 14.11
Schedule 10

T3 – ☐☐☐☐ **PART XII.2 TAX AND PART XIII NON-RESIDENT WITHHOLDING TAX** **SCHEDULE 10**

- Enter the applicable taxation year in the box above.
- All references to "the guide" are to the *T3 Trust Guide*.

Part A – Calculating Part XII.2 tax and the refundable Part XII.2 tax credit

- Part XII.2 tax does not apply to testamentary trusts, mutual fund trusts, or most trusts exempt from tax under Part I. For a complete list of trusts to which Part XII.2 tax does not apply, and for more information on completing this schedule, refer to Chapter 3 in the guide.
- Part XII.2 tax is calculated on income allocated by trusts to designated beneficiaries where the trust has specified income.
- We define **designated beneficiary** and **specified income** in the guide, under "Schedule 10 – *Part XII.2 Tax and Part XIII Non-Resident Withholding Tax*."
- Part XII.2 tax is due no later than 90 days after the trust's taxation year end. Trustees are personally liable for any Part XII.2 tax not paid by the due date.
- Eligible beneficiaries will receive a refundable tax credit for Part XII.2 tax that the trust paid.

Specified income

Net business income (loss) from businesses carried on in Canada (lines 06 to 08 of the return)	10010 ●	1
Net income (loss) from real properties (land and buildings) located in Canada (line 09 of the return)	10020 ● +	2
Net income (loss) from timber resource properties	10030 ● +	3
Net income (loss) from Canadian resource properties the trust acquired after 1971	10040 ● +	4
Taxable capital gains and allowable capital losses from the disposition of certain properties	10050 ● +	5
Total specified income (add lines 1 to 5)	=	6

Calculating Part XII.2 tax
Amount allocated and designated to beneficiaries other than by preferred beneficiary elections

Resident beneficiaries (line 928, column 1 of Schedule 9)	7	
Non-resident beneficiaries (line 928, column 2 of Schedule 9) +	8	
Subtotal (line 7 plus line 8) =	▶	9
Taxable benefits (line 44 of the return) –	10	
Adjusted amount allocated and designated to beneficiaries (line 9 minus line 10) =	▶	11
Part XII.2 tax payable (Line 6 or line 11, whichever is **less**, × 36%) =		12

Enter the amount from line 12 on line 83 of the return.

Calculating Part XII.2 refundable tax credit for eligible beneficiaries

Income allocated to designated beneficiaries _____ × Amount from line 12 _____ = _____ 13
Divide by amount from line 11 _____

Enter the amount from line 13 on line 21 of Part B below.
Part XII.2 refundable tax credit for eligible beneficiaries (line 12 minus line 13) = _____ 14

Enter the amount from line 14 on line 938 of Schedule 9, *Income Allocations and Designations to Beneficiaries*. If there is only one eligible beneficiary, enter the amount from line 14 in box 38 of that beneficiary's T3 slip (Part XII.2 tax credit). If there is more than one eligible beneficiary, see Schedule 10, Line 14 of the guide for instructions on how to calculate the box 38 amount for each eligible beneficiary.

Part B – Calculating Part XIII non-resident withholding tax   Payer's remittance no. **N R** ☐☐☐☐☐☐

- For more information on completing this part, refer to Chapter 3 in the guide.

Total income paid or payable to non-resident beneficiaries (line 928, column 2 of Schedule 9)	15	
Adjustment for non-cash items included above (provide reconciliation) (if negative, enter in brackets)	10210 ● +	16
Amounts paid or payable (line 15 plus line 16)	= ▶	17
Amounts not subject to Part XIII tax:		
Capital gains distributions of mutual fund trusts	10230 ●	18
Distributions by certain trusts established before 1949	10240 ● +	19
Other (specify) _____	10250 ● +	20
Amount from line 13	+	21
Subtotal (add lines 18 to 21)	= ▶ –	22
Amount subject to non-resident tax (line 17 minus line 22)	=	23
Non-resident tax payable (Multiply the amount on line 23 by the appropriate rate of tax. This amount has to be the same as the amount reported on the NR4 Summary and the related NR4 slip(s).)		24
Amounts previously remitted on Form NR-76, *Non-Resident Tax Statement of Account*	–	25
Part XIII tax due (line 24 minus line 25)	=	26

Remit the Part XIII tax with Form NR-76, NR4 Summary, and NR4 slip(s).

T3 SCH 10 (03)
Printed in Canada   (Français au verso)   Canadä

CHAPTER 14 — TRUST SCHEDULES AND FORMS

A withholding tax of 25%, unless reduced by an applicable Tax Treaty, also applies on the net amount distributed to non-resident beneficiaries.[62]

The total of the Part XII.2 (the flat 36%) and the Part XIII non-resident withholding taxes will generally equate to the Part I tax, plus the provincial or territorial taxes that would otherwise apply to the income if the beneficiaries were resident in Canada.

The trust should also complete a NR4 Summary together with the appropriate NR4 Slips and remit the Part XIII withholding taxes with Form NR-76 no later than ninety days after the trust's taxation year.

Part XIII withholding taxes cannot be avoided by retaining such income in the trust. In this circumstance, the income is deemed to be paid to the non-resident beneficiary on the day that is ninety days after the end of the trust's taxation year.[63]

However, the amount deemed to be payable for purposes of Part XIII taxes is generally limited to the amounts which would be included in the income of the beneficiary, to the extent that the beneficiary is resident in Canada. Consequently, Part XIII withholding taxes would be calculated taking into account, deductible expenses of the trust and losses arising from a prior taxation year.

Note, however, that amounts payable to a non-resident beneficiary, which would otherwise be exempt from tax if paid to a Canadian resident beneficiary (such as a capital dividend), are subject to Part XIII withholding taxes.

A Canadian resident beneficiary is entitled to a Part XII.2 tax credit in respect of the proportionate share of such "specified income" allocated or designated to the beneficiary. The Part XII.2 tax credit calculated for a Canadian resident beneficiary is also included in the income allocated to such beneficiaries. In effect, the Part XII.2 tax credit replaces the income that the beneficiary would have received if the trust had not paid the Part XII.2 tax.

---

62 Paragraph 212(1)(b).
63 Paragraph 214(3)(f).

PART IV — T3 TRUST INFORMATION & TAX RETURN

Note that the Part XII.2 refundable tax credit for eligible Canadian beneficiaries should also be entered on Line 938 of Schedule 9, "Income Allocations and Designations to Beneficiaries."

11. Schedule 11 – Federal Income Tax

Schedule 11 (see Figure 14.12) should be used to calculate the federal income tax payable by the trust. The trust might be subject to minimum tax[64] (see Schedule 12). If the minimum tax calculated on Schedule 12 exceeds the federal income tax determined on Schedule 11, the trust will be subject to the greater amount. If federal minimum tax applies, provincial minimum tax will also apply.

Note that the progressive rates of federal tax apply in respect of all testamentary trusts and to grandfathered *inter vivos* trusts established prior to June 18, 1971. Otherwise, *inter vivos* trusts are subject to tax at the top federal tax rate (29% for the 2004 taxation year).

Testamentary and *inter vivos* trusts are entitled to claim the federal dividend tax credit in respect of taxable dividends retained as income within the trust. The federal dividend tax credit is two-thirds of the "gross-up" amount calculated on Line 21 of Schedule 8.[65]

A federal foreign tax credit is available to a resident Canadian trust in respect of foreign income or profit taxes paid on foreign source income. All amounts claimed as a credit should be converted to a Canadian currency equivalent.

The federal foreign tax credit can be claimed for each foreign country equal to the lesser of the foreign taxes paid by the trust to a foreign country or the tax payable to Canada, that is attributable to that portion of foreign source income earned in the foreign country.

---

64 See heading 2 of Chapter 3 entitled, "Minimum Tax."
65 See 8.5 of this chapter entitled, "Lines 16 to 21 - Calculating the Gross-Up Amount of Dividends Retained or Not Designated by the Trust."

CHAPTER 14 — TRUST SCHEDULES AND FORMS

Figure 14.12
Schedule 11
(page 1 of 2)

T3 – 2003 **FEDERAL INCOME TAX** **SCHEDULE 11**

- For information on completing this schedule, see Chapter 3 in the *T3 Trust Guide*.

Enter your **taxable income** from line 56 of the T3 return .... _____ 1

Step 1 – Tax on taxable income

Testamentary trusts or grandfathered inter vivos trusts –
Use the amount from line 1 to determine which **one** of the
following columns you have to complete.

If the amount from line 1 is:		$32,183 or less	more than $32,183, but not more than $64,368	more than $64,368, but not more than $104,648	more than $104,648	
Enter the amount from line 1 above	2					2
Income base	3	– 0 00	– 32,183 00	– 64,368 00	– 104,648 00	3
Line 2 minus line 3	4	=	=	=	=	4
Tax rate	5	× 16%	× 22%	× 26%	× 29%	5
Multiply line 4 by line 5	6	=	=	=	=	6
Tax on income base	7	+ 0 00	+ 5,149 00	+ 12,230 00	+ 22,703 00	7
Federal tax on taxable income (line 6 plus line 7)	8	=	=	=	=	8

Inter vivos trusts (other than grandfathered)
Federal tax on taxable income   Line 1 _____ × 29% = _____ 9

Step 2 – Donations and gifts tax credit

Donations plus government gifts made after February 18, 1997. Include the **eligible amount** only – see the *T3 Trust Guide*. .... 11121 _____ 10
25% of taxable capital gains from gifts of capital property
(see Schedule 11, line 25 in the *T3 Trust Guide*) .... 11123 _____ 11
25% of recapture of CCA on donated depreciable property .... 11124 + _____ 12
75% of net income (line 50 of the return) .... + _____ 13
Total charitable donations limit (add lines 11 to 13) .... = _____ 14

Line 10 or line 14, whichever is less .... _____ 15
Cultural and ecological gifts plus government gifts made or agreed to before
February 19, 1997 .... 11122 + _____ 16
Total donations and gifts (line 15 plus line 16) .... = _____ 17

	On the first $200 or less	× 16% =	18
	On the balance of	× 29% = +	19

Donations and gifts tax credit (line 18 plus line 19) .... = ▶ 11120 _____ 20

Step 3 – Federal tax

Federal tax on taxable income (line 8 or 9 above)	11080	_____	21
Tax adjustments – Lump-sum payments under ITAR 40 (see Schedule 11, line 22 in the *T3 Trust Guide*)	11090	+ _____	22
Adjusted federal tax (line 21 plus line 22)		= _____	23
Federal dividend tax credit (line 21 of Schedule 8) × 2/3 = 11110		_____	24
Donations and gifts tax credit (line 20 above)		+ _____	25
Minimum tax carryover from previous years (line 72 of Schedule 12)	11130	+ _____	26
Total credits (add lines 24 to 26)		= ▶ – _____	27
Basic federal tax (line 23 minus line 27 – if negative, enter "0")	11150	= _____	28

Continue Step 3 on the other side.

T3 SCH 11 E (03)   (Vous pouvez obtenir ce formulaire en français à www.adrc.gc.ca ou au 1 800 959-3376.)   **Canadä**

PART IV — T3 TRUST INFORMATION & TAX RETURN

Figure 14.12 (continued)
Schedule 11
(page 2 of 2)

Step 3 continued

Basic federal tax from line 28 on page 1		28
Surtax on income not subject to provincial or territorial tax (portion of line 28 not subject to these taxes) × 48%) = 11160 +		29
Subtotal (line 28 plus line 29) =		30
Federal foreign tax credit (available to resident trusts only, attach Form T2209, *Federal Foreign Tax Credits*) 11180	31	
Total federal political contributions 11191	32	
Allowable federal political contribution tax credit (from the calculation for Schedule 11, line 33 in the *T3 Trust Guide*) 11190 +	33	
Investment tax credit (from Form T2038(IND)) 11200 +	34	
Other credits (see Schedule 11, line 35 in the *T3 Trust Guide*) 1121X +	35	
Total credits (add lines 31, 33, 34, and 35) = ▶ −		36
Federal tax payable (line 30 minus line 36; if negative, enter "0") =		37

If minimum tax applies to the trust, continue the calculations on Schedule 12.
If not, enter the amount from line 37 on line 81 of the return.

Refundable Quebec abatement (see Schedule 11, line 38 in the *T3 Trust Guide*)
Enter this amount on line 87 of the return.   (Line 28   × 16.5%) =   38

Printed in Canada

CHAPTER 14 — TRUST SCHEDULES AND FORMS

The trust should complete Form T2209, "Federal Foreign Tax Credits" to calculate the trust's claim for a federal foreign tax credit. The amount of the federal foreign tax credit which can be claimed by the trust should relate only to income retained within the trust. Enter the amount calculated on Form T2209 on Line 31 of Schedule 11.

If the taxes paid to a foreign country exceed the federal foreign tax credit as calculated on Form T2209, the excess tax paid, which relates to foreign business income, can be claimed as a tax credit for either the three preceding or seven subsequent taxation years. Unused federal foreign non-business taxes paid are not subject to these carryover provisions; however, the trust may be able to claim some or all of the unused amount as a provincial or territorial tax credit on Form T2036, "Provincial or Territorial Foreign Tax Credit" or a deduction on Line 40 of the T3 Return.[66]

Testamentary and *inter vivos* trusts are entitled to claim a federal tax credit in respect of charitable donations made by the trust in the taxation year. There are generally four types of donations or gifts which qualify for the federal tax credit.

> 1. *Donations to a Qualified Donee* – A qualified donee will generally be a registered charitable organization, including a public or private foundation, that has a registered charity number and will issue an official receipt upon acceptance of the donation or gift.
>
> 2. *Gifts to Canada* – These gifts can be made to the country as well as a province, or a territory.
>
> 3. *Gifts of Cultural Property* – For this type of gift, the trust should attach Form T871, "Cultural Property Income Tax Certificate," which must be completed by the Canadian Cultural

---

[66] See M.N.R., Interpretation Bulletin IT-506, "Foreign Income Taxes as a Deduction from Income" (January 5, 1987). Also refer to M.N.R., Interpretation Bulletin IT-270R2, "Foreign Tax Credit" (February 11, 1991) and M.N.R., Interpretation Bulletin IT-201R2, "Foreign Tax Credit – Trust and Beneficiaries" (February 12, 1996).

PART IV — T3 TRUST INFORMATION & TAX RETURN

Property Export Review Board and the official tax receipt from the institution).

4. *Gifts of Ecological Property* – For this type of gift, the trust should attach a "Certificate for Donation of Ecologically Sensitive Land," issued by the Minister of the Environment, as well as the official receipt from the institution.

The maximum federal donation tax credit for a trust is limited to the aggregate of the following amounts:

- Seventy-five per cent of the trust's net income for the taxation year (Line 50 of the T3 Return);

- Twenty-five per cent of the taxable capital gains arising from the donation of capital property, minus any capital gains deduction claimed in respect of the donated property; and

- Twenty-five per cent of the recaptured capital cost allowance arising from the donation of depreciable capital property.

For more information, see also CRA's "Gifts and Income Tax" (P113) pamphlet.

Note that where a gift is made by virtue of an individual's will, it is deemed to have been made by the individual immediately before the individual died.[67] In this instance, the gift is not considered to be made by the estate and there would be no entitlement by the estate for any claim.

A trust can claim any portion of its donations as a federal tax credit, up to the maximum amount detailed above. Any unused portion of the trust's donations can be carried forward for five taxation years.

---

67 Subsection 118.1(5), gift by will.

CHAPTER 14 — TRUST SCHEDULES AND FORMS

12. Schedule 12 – Minimum Tax

Minimum tax may apply to a personal trust in a taxation year where income is reported from the following sources:

- taxable dividends;

- taxable capital gains;

- losses claimed in respect of resource expenditures, or resource and depletion allowances on resource properties;

- elections made on certain pension benefits under ITAR 40; or

- losses resulting from, or increased by, capital cost allowance on rental or leasing property or certified films or videotapes.

If the trust is reporting income from or claiming losses or deductions in any one of the above items, Schedule 12 (see Figure 14.13) should be completed to determine whether minimum tax might apply.

Note that a spousal or common-law partner trust, a joint spousal or common-law partner trust or an alter ego trust is not subject to minimum tax on amounts resulting from the first deemed realization under the twenty-one year rule.

Also, in calculating minimum tax for a trust, special adjustments apply in respect of capital gains allocated to beneficiaries. The $40,000 basic exemption from minimum tax is available only to testamentary trusts and certain qualified pre-1972 *inter vivos* trusts. Where trusts, which qualify for the $40,000 exemption, have arisen from contributions by the same contributor, the $40,000 exemption must be allocated between them on an annual basis.[68]

---

68 See heading 2 of Chapter 3 entitled, "Minimum Tax" and also heading 6 of this chapter entitled, "Schedule 6 – Trusts' Agreement to Allocate the Basic Exemption from Minimum Tax."

PART IV — T3 TRUST INFORMATION & TAX RETURN

Figure 14.13
Schedule 12
(page 1 of 6)

T3 – 2003   **MINIMUM TAX**   **SCHEDULE 12**
Page 1 of 6

- Use this schedule to calculate a trust's minimum tax.
- See page 4 for trusts not subject to minimum tax in the taxation year.
- For information on how to complete this schedule, see the instructions on pages 4 and 5.
- To calculate provincial or territorial minimum tax, or the Ontario minimum tax carryover, see pages 5 and 6.

Part 1 – Calculating net adjusted taxable income for minimum tax
Complete sections C, D, and E only if the trust is claiming losses from these sources.

A. Calculating the non-taxable portion of capital gains reported in the year and retained in the trust
Do **not** include taxable capital gains from mortgage foreclosures, conditional sales repossessions, or a reserve from a disposition before November 13, 1981. If the trust is reporting reserves for dispositions before November 13, 1981, deemed realization of capital property on Form T1055, or capital gains from donated property, contact us before completing Part A.

Taxable capital gains (line 21 of Schedule 1) _____ 1
Taxable capital gains allocated and designated to beneficiaries (line 921 of Schedule 9) _____ – 2
Capital gains retained in the trust (line 1 minus line 2) _____ = 2A
Capital gains conversion rate × 3/5 2B
Non-taxable portion of capital gains retained in the trust (line 2A multiplied by line 2B) 12030 ● = ▶ _____ 3

B. The elected portion of pension benefits under ITAR 40 12040 ● + _____ 4

C. Rental and leasing property
Capital cost allowance (CCA) and carrying charges claimed on rental and leasing property 12050 ● 5
Net income from rental and leasing property before CCA and related carrying charges
(if a loss, enter "0"). See the Note on page 4. 12060 ● – 6
Loss, if any, created or increased by CCA and related carrying charges (line 5 minus line 6) = ▶ + _____ 7

D. Film property
CCA and carrying charges claimed on certified film property acquired after 1987 and before March 1996 12080 ● 8
Net income reported from certified film property before CCA and related carrying charges (if a loss,
enter "0"). See the Note on page 4. 12090 ● 9
Loss, if any, created or increased by CCA and related carrying charges (line 8 minus line 9) = ▶ + _____ 10

E. Resource property and royalties and flow-through shares
Total of all resource deductions and allowances and depletion allowances and carrying charges related
to resource property and flow-through shares 12110 ● 11

  a) Income from production of petroleum, gas, and minerals, including
royalties before resource deductions and allowances and depletion
allowances and related carrying charges (if a loss, enter "0") 12120 ● 12

  b) Income from dispositions of foreign resource properties and
recovery of exploration and development expenses
(if a loss, enter "0") 12130 ● + 13

Total resource income (line 12 plus line 13) = ▶ – _____ 14
Loss, if any, created or increased by resource deductions and allowances and depletion allowances
and related carrying charges (line 11 minus line 14) = ▶ + _____ 15

F. Limited partnership and tax shelter losses – Include the trust's total share of the partnership loss. 12160 ● + _____ 16

G. Limited and specified member partnership interest – Amount, if any, by which carrying charges related to acquiring
a partnership interest are more than the trust's income from the partnership interest. 12170 ● + _____ 17

Total additions to taxable income for minimum tax purposes
(add lines 3, 4, 7, 10, 15, 16, and 17) = _____ 18

T3 SCH 12 E (03)   (Vous pouvez obtenir ce formulaire en français à www.adrc.gc.ca ou au 1 800 959-3376.)   **Canadä**

CHAPTER 14 — TRUST SCHEDULES AND FORMS

Figure 14.13 (continued)
Schedule 12
(page 2 of 6)

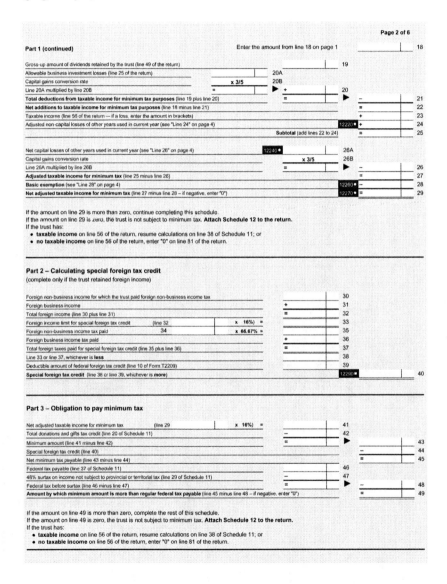

PART IV — T3 TRUST INFORMATION & TAX RETURN

Figure 14.13 (continued)
Schedule 12
(page 3 of 6)

Page 3 of 6

Part 4 – Basic federal tax for the year

Basic federal tax (line 28 of Schedule 11)		50
Minimum amount (from line 43)		51
Basic federal tax for the year (line 50 or line 51, whichever is more)	12420●	52

To calculate provincial or territorial minimum tax, use Chart 2 on page 6.

Part 5 – Calculating federal tax payable (minimum tax)

Net minimum tax payable from line 45		53
Surtax on income not subject to provincial or territorial tax (portion of line 52 not subject to provincial or territorial tax) × 48%) = +		54
Federal tax payable (line 53 plus line 54). Enter this amount on line 81 of the return. = ▶		55

Refundable Quebec abatement	(line 52)	× 16.5%) =	56

Enter the amount from line 56 on line 87 of the return.

Part 6 – Calculating this year's additional taxes paid for minimum tax carryover

Minimum amount from line 43		57
Basic federal tax (line 28 of Schedule 11)	58	
Special foreign tax credit (line 40)		
Deductible amount of federal foreign tax credit from line 39	−	59
Subtotal (line 59 minus line 60) =		60
		61
Amount from line 34		62
Amount from line 36	+	63
Total (line 62 plus line 63) =		64

line 61	×	line 37 / line 64	= +	65

Total (line 58 plus line 65) = ▶ −		66
Additional taxes available to carry over to subsequent years (line 57 minus line 66)	12670● =	67

Part 7 – Calculating the total minimum tax carryover

Minimum tax carryover from previous years (1996 to 2002)	12680●	68
Tax payable before carryover (line 52)	69	
Minimum amount (from line 43) −	70	
Maximum carryover that can be applied this year (line 69 minus line 70 – if negative, enter "0") =	71	

Minimum tax carryover applied this year:

Claim an amount that is not more than line 68 or line 71, whichever is **less**, and enter it on line 26 of Schedule 11	−	72
Balance of minimum tax carryover (line 68 minus line 72)	=	73
Additional taxes available from this year (line 67)	+	74
Line 73 plus line 74	=	75
Additional 1996 taxes not applied	−	76
Minimum tax carryover available for next year (line 75 minus line 76)	12690● =	77

CHAPTER 14 — TRUST SCHEDULES AND FORMS

Figure 14.13 (continued)
Schedule 12
(page 4 of 6)

Is the trust subject to minimum tax?
The following trusts are not subject to minimum tax:
- a mutual fund trust;
- a related segregated fund trust;
- a spousal or common-law partner trust, or a joint spousal or common-law partner trust, or an alter ego trust, if it reports in the year its first deemed realization under the 21-year rule; and
- a master trust.

Any other trust is liable to pay minimum tax if the net minimum tax payable on line 45 is more than the regular tax payable on line 48. A trust may have to pay minimum tax for the year if it:

- reports taxable capital gains (line 01 of the return)
- reports taxable dividends (line 03 of the return)
- claims a loss resulting from, or increased by, resource expenditures, or claims resource and depletion allowances on resource properties (line 06 or line 19 of the return)
- makes an election on pension benefits under ITAR 40 (line 02 of the return and line 22 of Schedule 11)
- claims a loss resulting from, or increased by, capital cost allowance or carrying charges claimed on:
  – rental or leasing property (line 09 of the return); or
  – certified films or videotapes (line 06 of the return)

Part 1 – Calculating adjusted taxable income

Use Part 1 to calculate the net adjusted taxable income for minimum tax.

Net adjusted taxable income for minimum tax purposes applies to:
- certain losses that limited partners, specified members of a partnership, or partners of a tax shelter deduct for their partnership interest (for this purpose, losses allocated from a partnership are applied against gains from the same partnership source);
- losses from tax shelters; and
- carrying charges for interests in limited partnerships, tax shelters, rental and leasing, film and resource properties, which increase or create a loss from these sources.

Note
Net income from rental and leasing property, and film property includes income from these investments (before CCA and related carrying charges) **plus** any net taxable capital gains from the disposition of these investments **minus** any losses from these investments (before CCA and related carrying charges). You also have to subtract allocated partnership losses from gains from the same partnership source.

Line 24 – Adjusted non-capital losses of other years used in the current year
If the trust claimed non-capital losses of other years, you may have to reduce the non-capital losses for minimum tax purposes. This reduction is any portion of the non-capital losses attributable to:
- capital cost allowance or carrying charges claimed on:
  – rental or leasing property; or
  – films certified by the Canadian Film and Videotape Certification office;
- resource expenditures; or
- resource and depletion allowances.

Enter the reduction on line 24.

For taxation years beginning after 1994, for minimum tax purposes, a non-capital loss which is carried forward is calculated according to the minimum tax rules in effect for the year in which the loss was incurred.

Line 26 – Net capital losses of other years used in the current year
You may have claimed a capital loss from prior years on line 52 of the return. If this is the case, you will have to adjust the trust's income for minimum tax purposes. On line 26A, enter the net capital losses of other taxation years that you claimed in the current year on line 52 of the return. Do not include capital losses on mortgage foreclosures and conditional sales repossessions.

If the amount on line 52 of the return is less than the capital gains remaining in the trust after allocation to beneficiaries, **and** the trust has additional unapplied losses of other years, you may be able to increase the amount on line 26A. Call us for details.

Line 28 – Basic exemption
We allow a basic exemption of $40,000 to testamentary and grandfathered inter vivos trusts. Allocate the $40,000 basic exemption among the trusts if more than one qualifying trust is formed from contributions by the same individual. To allocate the basic exemption, complete Schedule 6, *Trusts' Agreement to Allocate the Basic Exemption From Minimum Tax*. On line 28, enter the basic exemption, or the trust's allocated amount of the exemption from Schedule 6.

PART IV — T3 TRUST INFORMATION & TAX RETURN

Figure 14.13 (continued)
Schedule 12
(page 5 of 6)

Page 5 of 6

Part 5 – Calculating federal tax payable (minimum tax)
Line 56 – Refundable Quebec abatement
For information, see Schedule 11, line 38 in the *T3 Trust Guide*.

Part 6 – Calculating this year's additional taxes paid for minimum tax carryover
Lines 57 to 67
Use Part 6 to calculate the amount of any additional minimum tax payable by the trust for this year that you can carry over to a future year. You may be able to deduct this amount from the trust's regular tax liability on line 26 of Schedule 11 in future years. You can claim a carryforward for a period of seven years.

Part 7 – Calculating the total minimum tax carryover
Lines 68 to 77
Use Part 7 to calculate the minimum tax carryover from previous years that you can claim on Schedule 11 in this year. You can carry over minimum tax from the seven previous taxation years. In the trust's best interests, apply the oldest available carryover first. For example, apply any carryover from 1997 before any carryover from 1998.

You also use Part 7 to calculate the total minimum tax carryover, if any, that may be carried forward to later years.

Provincial and territorial minimum tax payable
Use *Chart 2 – Calculation of Provincial and Territorial Minimum Tax*, on the next page, to calculate the trust's provincial and territorial tax payable.

Ontario minimum tax carryover
Use Chart 1 below to calculate your Ontario minimum tax carryover. If one of the following situations applies to the trust, call us for information on how to calculate the Ontario minimum tax carryover:
- The trust is **resident in Ontario** in 2003, and:
  – it is subject to tax in multiple jurisdictions (with taxable income in Ontario); or
  – in a year after 1999, it was **not** resident in Ontario, and minimum tax was applied in one of these years.
- The trust is **not resident in Ontario** in 2003, but has business income in Ontario.
- The trust was subject to tax in multiple jurisdictions in a year after 1999, **and** it was subject to Ontario minimum tax.

Chart 1 - Ontario Minimum Tax Carryover

Ontario minimum tax carryover available for 2003		
Line F from the 2002 Schedule 12, Ontario minimum tax carryover chart	_____	1
Amount from line 72 _____ × 37.5%	+ _____	2
Ontario minimum tax carryover available for 2003 (line 1 plus line 2)	= _____	3

Applying a minimum tax carryover against 2003 Ontario tax payable
Note: You cannot claim a minimum tax carryover if the trust has to pay minimum tax.

Line 13 of Form T3ON	_____	4
Total of lines 14 and 15 of Form T3ON	− _____	5
Carryover that can be applied this year (line 4 minus line 5)	= _____	6
Enter the amount from line 3 or line 6, whichever is less	_____	7

Ontario carryover applied this year (enter on line 8 below and line 16 of Form T3ON an amount not more than line 7)

Ontario minimum tax carryover available for future years		
Ontario carryover applied this year	− _____	8
Line 3 minus line 8 – if negative, enter "0"	= _____	9
Ontario additional minimum tax from line E on page 6	+ _____	10
Line 9 plus line 10	= _____	11
Additional 1996 taxes not applied .... line 76 _____ × 37.5% =	− _____	12
Ontario minimum tax carryover available for future years (line 11 minus line 12)	= _____	F

294

CHAPTER 14 — TRUST SCHEDULES AND FORMS

Figure 14.13 (continued)
Schedule 12
(page 6 of 6)

Chart 2 – Calculation of Provincial and Territorial Minimum Tax

Page 6 of 6

Newfoundland and Labrador
Line 67 _____ 1
Newfoundland and Labrador rate × 62.2% 2
Newfoundland and Labrador additional minimum tax (line 1 multiplied by line 2). Enter amount A on line 19 of Form T3NL. = _____ A

Nova Scotia
Line 67 _____ 1
Nova Scotia rate × 57.5% 2
Nova Scotia additional minimum tax (line 1 multiplied by line 2). Enter amount B on line 19 of Form T3NS. = _____ B

New Brunswick
Line 57 _____ minus line 58 _____ = _____ 1
New Brunswick rate × 57% 2
New Brunswick additional minimum tax (line 1 multiplied by line 2). Enter amount C on line 19 of Form T3NB. = _____ C

Prince Edward Island
Line 67 _____ 1
Prince Edward Island rate × 57.5% 2
Prince Edward Island additional minimum tax (line 1 multiplied by line 2). Enter amount D on line 19 of Form T3PE. = _____ D

Ontario
Line 49 _____ 1
Ontario rate × 37.81% 2
Ontario additional minimum tax (line 1 multiplied by line 2). Enter amount E on line 19 of Form T3ON. = _____ E

Manitoba
Line 57 _____ minus line 58 _____ = _____ 1
Manitoba rate × 50% 2
Manitoba additional minimum tax (line 1 multiplied by line 2). Enter amount G on line 20 of Form T3MB. = _____ G

Saskatchewan
Line 57 _____ minus line 58 _____ = _____ 1
Saskatchewan rate × 50% 2
Saskatchewan additional minimum tax (line 1 multiplied by line 2). Enter amount H on line 21 of Form T3SK. = _____ H

Alberta
Line 57 _____ minus line 58 _____ = _____ 1
Alberta rate × 35% 2
Alberta additional minimum tax (line 1 multiplied by line 2). Enter amount I on line 12 of Form T3AB. = _____ I

British Columbia
Line 57 _____ minus line 58 _____ = _____ 1
British Columbia rate × 37.8% 2
British Columbia additional minimum tax (line 1 multiplied by line 2). Enter amount J on line 19 of Form T3BC. = _____ J

Nunavut
Line 67 _____ 1
Nunavut rate × 45% 2
Nunavut additional minimum tax (line 1 multiplied by line 2). Enter amount K on line 19 of Form T3NU. = _____ K

Northwest Territories
Line 67 _____ 1
Northwest Territories rate × 45% 2
Northwest Territories additional minimum tax (line 1 multiplied by line 2). Enter amount L on line 19 of Form T3NT. = _____ L

Yukon
Line 67 _____ 1
Yukon rate × 44% 2
Yukon additional minimum tax (line 1 multiplied by line 2). Enter amount M on line 19 of Form T3YT. = _____ M

Printed in Canada

Part V
Completing the T3 Summary and T3 Slips

Chapter 15
Filing Requirements

1. General

The trustee, executor, liquidator or administrator must compile a statement of trust income allocations and designations in respect of trust income allocated to one or more beneficiaries in the year. This compilation should be reported on Schedule 9 "Income Allocations and Designations to Beneficiaries."[1]

The trust income allocations and designations reported on Schedule 9 will form the basis of reporting for the T3 Summary and the individual T3 slips. The trust must complete a T3 Summary even if there is only one T3 Slip. The T3 Summary serves to record the total of all amounts reported on the related T3 Supplementaries. CRA requires that only one T3 Summary be filed for a personal trust.

While there is no technical requirement to complete a T3 Slip for a beneficiary with less than $100 of income allocated, there is still a requirement to notify the beneficiary of the allocated amount, since it still has to be reported as income on the beneficiary's tax return. For this reason, the practical solution is for the trust to prepare and file T3 Slips for all beneficiaries, no matter the extent of income, so that income allocated or designated on the T3 Slips will reconcile in total to the amounts reported on the T3 Summary for the year.

---

[1] See heading 9 of Chapter 14 entitled, "Schedule 9 – Income Allocations and Designations to Beneficiaries," for a discussion on the completion of Schedule 9.

PART V — COMPLETING THE T3 SUMMARY AND T3 SLIPS

2. Completing the T3 Summary

There are many general items to complete on the T3 Summary (see Figure 15.1).

- *Identification* – Complete this area using the same information entered in the identification area on the T3 Trust Income Tax and Information Return.

- *Total Number of T3 Slips Filed* – Enter the total number of T3 Slips included with the T3 Summary.

- *Account Number* – Enter the account number for the trust assigned by CRA. If this is the first year of the trust, and an account number has not been assigned, enter "nil." Do not leave the space blank.

- *Taxation Year* – Indicate the taxation year of the trust for which the T3 Summary relates.

- *Testamentary Trust* – If the trust is a testamentary trust, enter the Social Insurance Number (SIN) of the deceased individual.

- *First Return* – Check the Box "YES," if this is the first return for the trust, otherwise check the Box "NO."

- *T3 Slip Totals* – The line numbers appearing on the T3 Summary correspond with the same box numbers appearing on each of the T3 Slips. Ensure that the totals of each box number appearing on the T3 Slips, arithmetically correspond to the total amounts entered on the corresponding line numbers of the T3 Summary.

    A computerized T3 tax preparation software program should do this addition automatically. If you are preparing the T3 Return and T3 Summary and Slips manually, you should check that amounts entered on the T3 Slips do agree to the totals reported on the T3 Summary.

- *Summary of Footnote Amounts* – Boxes 21, 26 or 30 on a T3 Slip may contain amounts identified with an asterisk (*). These amounts

CHAPTER 15 — FILING REQUIREMENTS

Figure 15.1
T3 Summary

Canada Customs and Revenue Agency / Agence des douanes et du revenu du Canada

SUMMARY OF TRUST INCOME ALLOCATIONS AND DESIGNATIONS

- Complete this summary if the trust allocated income to a resident beneficiary, including a preferred beneficiary, in the year.
- If you are filing your T3 slips on magnetic media (tape, CD-ROM, or diskette), see "Filing on magnetic media," in Chapter 1 of the *T3 Trust Guide*.
- File this summary with copy 1 of the related T3 slips, and the *T3 Trust Income Tax and Information Return*, no later than 90 days after the end of the trust's taxation year. Do **not** attach the summary and slips to the return.
- See the back of this summary for instructions.

Identification

Name of trust

Account number: T | | | – | | | | – | | |

Complete this area if you do not have an account number and you are submitting a paper return.

Name of trustee, executor, liquidator, or administrator

Mailing address of trustee, executor, liquidator, or administrator (or name and mailing address of the person to contact, if different)

If this is a testamentary trust, enter the social insurance number of the **deceased**

Postal code | Telephone number ( )

Summary for taxation year: From Year Month Day To: Year Month Day

Total number of T3 slips filed: 10

Is this the first return for the trust? Yes ☐ No ☐

T3 slip totals
Summary of income allocated and designated to resident beneficiaries (including preferred beneficiaries)

Box	Item
21	Capital gains
22	Lump-sum pension benefits
23	Actual amount of dividends
24	Foreign business income
25	Foreign non-business income
26	Other income

Summary of amounts designated to resident beneficiaries (including preferred beneficiaries)

Box	Item
30	Capital gains eligible for deduction
31	Qualifying pension income
32	Taxable amount of dividends
33	Foreign business income tax paid
34	Foreign non-business income tax paid
35	Eligible death benefits

Miscellaneous — footnotes to box 36

Box	Item
36-1	Pension income eligible for transfer
36-2	Retiring allowance eligible for transfer
36-3	Eligible charitable donations
37	Insurance segregated fund capital losses
38	Part XII.2 tax credit
39	Federal dividend tax credit

Investment tax credit

Box	Item
40	Investment cost or expenditures
41	Tax credit
45	Other credits

(Do not use this area)

Summary of footnote amounts

- Box 21 – Non-business income for foreign tax credit
- Box 26 – Eligible capital property - qualified farm property
- Box 26 – Self-employment earnings
- Box 30 – Qualified farm property
- Box 30 – Qualified small business corporation shares

Certification

I, _____ (Please print) certify that the information given on the T3 Summary and the related T3 slips, is, to the best of my knowledge, correct and complete.

Date | Authorized person's signature | Position or title

T3 Summary E (03)

(Vous pouvez obtenir ce formulaire en français à www.adrc.gc.ca ou au 1 800 959-3376.)

Canada

PART V — COMPLETING THE T3 SUMMARY AND T3 SLIPS

should be explained in the footnote area of each slip. For each footnote type, enter the sum total of amounts appearing on the T3 Slips filed with the T3 Summary and enter this total on the corresponding line of the T3 Summary.

- *Certification* – Ensure that the trustee, executor, liquidator or administrator dates and signs the T3 Summary before filing with CRA.

3. Completing the T3 Slips

The following information must be reported on each T3 Slip (see Figure 15.2) prepared and filed with the T3 Summary.

- *Year* – Use a four-digit number to indicate the applicable taxation year of the recipient for reporting purposes.

- *Trust Year Ending* – Use a four-digit number to indicate the year and a two-digit number to indicate the month in which the trust's taxation year ends.

- *Name and Address of Trust* – Enter the full legal name and address of the trust, as it would appear on the T3 Information and Income Tax Return.

- *Account Number* – Enter the trust's account number assigned by CRA. If the trust does not have an account number, enter "nil." Do not leave the box blank.

- *Recipient's Name and Address* – If the recipient is an individual, enter the beneficiary's name and address. If there are joint beneficiaries, enter both names. If the recipient is another trust, enter the name of the trust and not the names of individual beneficiaries. If the recipient is an association, organization or other institution, enter that name accordingly. Include the recipient's full address, including the street address, city, province and postal code.

- *Recipient Identification Number – Box 12* – Enter in Box 12, the recipient's identification number. The recipient identification number is one of the following:

CHAPTER 15 — FILING REQUIREMENTS

Figure 15.2
T3 Slip

IMPORTANT
For completion instructions of this form, please see reverse.
Voir les instructions à l'endos sur la façon de remplir ce formulaire.

PART V — COMPLETING THE T3 SUMMARY AND T3 SLIPS

  - o the social insurance number (SIN), if the beneficiary is an individual (other than a trust);

  - o the business number (BN), if the beneficiary is a corporation or partnership; or

  - o the trust account number, if the beneficiary is a trust.

    If you have attempted to obtain the applicable number and have been unsuccessful in doing so, do not delay in completing the information slip beyond the filing deadline; otherwise serious penalties can apply.[2] Instead, file the T3 Slip and enter "nil" in Box 12.

- *Beneficiary Code – Box 18 –* Enter one of the following codes to identify the type of beneficiary (do not leave this box blank):

Code	Type of Beneficiary
1	an individual
2	a joint beneficiary
3	a corporation
4	an association, a trust (fiduciary, trustee, nominee, or estate), a club, or a partnership
5	a government, a government enterprise, an international organization, a charity, a non-profit organization or other tax-exempt entity, or a deferred income plan that is exempt from tax.

- *Report Code – Box 16 –* Enter one of the following codes:

---

[2] Refer to heading 5 of Chapter 7 entitled, "Interest and Penalties" for commentary on this point. For more information see M.N.R., Information Circular 82-2R2, "Social Insurance Number Legislation that Relates to the Preparation of Information Slips" (November 20, 1992).

CHAPTER 15 — FILING REQUIREMENTS

Code	Type of Slip
0	original slip
1	amended or cancelled slip[3]

Once the basic information is reported on the T3 Slip, the remaining task is to enter the beneficiary's share of all relevant income allocations and designations, as summarized on Schedule 9 of the T3 Information and Income Tax Return. This is set out below.

3.1 Dividends

Box 23	Actual Amount of Dividends

Enter the beneficiary's share of the amount on Line 923 of Schedule 9.

If the beneficiary is an individual or a trust, complete Box 32 and Box 39.

Box 32	Taxable Amount of Dividends

If the beneficiary is an individual or a trust enter the amount of dividends from taxable Canadian corporations reported in Box 23, multiplied by 1.25.

Box 39	Federal Dividend Tax Credit

If the beneficiary is an individual or a trust, enter 13.3333% of the amount in Box 32.

---

[3] If you use code 1, refer to heading 6 of this chapter entitled, "Amending the T3 Summary," as there will also be a requirement to prepare and file an amended T3 Summary.

PART V — COMPLETING THE T3 SUMMARY AND T3 SLIPS

3.2 Capital Gains

| Box 21 | Capital Gains |

Enter the beneficiary's share of the amount on Line 921 of Schedule 9, multiplied by 2.

Note: If Box 21 includes capital gains from foreign property, enter an asterisk (*) beside the amount in Box 21. In the footnote area, for each country, enter "non-business income for foreign tax credit" and the taxable portion of the amount included in Box 21 that relates to the disposition of foreign property.

| Box 30 | Capital Gains Eligible for Deduction |

Enter the beneficiary's share of the amount on Line 930 of Schedule 9, multiplied by 2.

Do not include farming income from the disposition of eligible capital property identified in the footnote to Box 26.

Note: Enter an asterisk (*) beside the amount in Box 30, and, in the footnote area, enter either "qualified farm property" or "qualified small business corporation shares," whichever applies, and the amount eligible for the capital gains deduction.

3.3 Other Income Allocations and Designations

| Box 26 | Other Income |

Enter the beneficiary's share of the amount on Line 926 of Schedule 9.

Include amounts such as the following in this box:

CHAPTER 15 — FILING REQUIREMENTS

- death benefits;

- retiring allowances;

- pension income other than lump-sum pension benefits already included in Box 22;

- net rental income;

- net business, farming and fishing income; and

- interest income.

Notes: Enter an asterisk (*) beside the amount in Box 26 if it includes any farming income from the disposition of eligible capital property, which is qualified farm property. In the footnote area, enter "eligible capital property – qualified farm property" and the amount of the beneficiary's share from Line 926-1 of Schedule 9.

Enter an asterisk (*) beside the amount in Box 26 if it includes business, farming or fishing income from a communal organization. In the footnote area, enter "self-employment earnings for CPP purposes," and indicate the type of income – business, farming or fishing – and the amount of the beneficiary's share from Line 926-3 of Schedule 9.

No other footnotes are required for Box 26.

Box 24	Foreign Business Income

Enter the beneficiary's share of the amount on Line 924 of Schedule 9 (before withholding taxes).

Notes: Enter an asterisk (*) beside the amount in Box 24. In the footnote area, identify each foreign country and the amount of business income from each country.

Report all amounts in Boxes 24, 25, 33 and 34 in Canadian dollars.

PART V — COMPLETING THE T3 SUMMARY AND T3 SLIPS

| Box 33 | Foreign Business Income Tax Paid |

Enter the beneficiary's share of the amount on Line 933 of Schedule 9.

Note: Enter an asterisk (*) beside the amount in Box 33. In the footnote area, identify each foreign country and the amount of foreign tax paid on business income from each country.

| Box 25 | Foreign Non-Business Income |

Enter the beneficiary's share of the amount on Line 925 of Schedule 9 (before withholding taxes).

Note: Enter an asterisk (*) beside the amount in Box 25. In the footnote area, identify each foreign country and the amount of non-business income from each country.

| Box 34 | Foreign Non-Business Income Tax Paid |

Enter the beneficiary's share of the amount on Line 934 of Schedule 9.

Note: Enter an asterisk (*) beside the amount in Box 34. In the footnote area, identify each foreign country and the amount of foreign tax paid on non-business income from each country.

| Box 22 | Lump-Sum Pension Benefits |

Enter the beneficiary spouse's or common-law partner's share of the amount on Line 922 of Schedule 9.

CHAPTER 15 — FILING REQUIREMENTS

Box 31	Qualifying Pension Income

Enter the beneficiary spouse or common-law partner's share of the amount on Line 931 of Schedule 9. This amount is included in Box 26.

Box 35	Eligible Death Benefits

Enter the beneficiary's share of the amount on Line 935 of Schedule 9. This amount is included in Box 26.

Box 36	Miscellaneous

Enter the beneficiary's share of the following amounts:

- pension income that is eligible for a transfer to an eligible annuity for certain minors, from Line 936-1 of Schedule 9 (also included in Box 26);

- a retiring allowance, which qualifies for a transfer to a registered pension plan or registered retirement savings plan, from Line 936-2 of Schedule 9 (also included in Box 26); and

- charitable donations or gifts of a communal organization, from Line 936-3 of Schedule 9.[4]

Note: Enter an asterisk (*) beside the amount in Box 36. In the footnote area, enter the details of this amount. If you are designating more than one type of these amounts to one beneficiary, prepare a separate T3 Slip for each type.

---

4 See M.N.R., Information Circular 78-5R3, "Communal Organizations" (September 11, 1998).

PART V — COMPLETING THE T3 SUMMARY AND T3 SLIPS

3.4 Tax and Other Credits

Part XII.2	Tax Credit

Enter the beneficiary's share of the amount on Line 938 of Schedule 9.[5]

Boxes 40 and 41	Investment Tax Credit

Only a testamentary trust is eligible to allocate this credit. Include amounts here from Form T2038 (IND). The investment code should be identified as a footnote on the T3 Slip.[6]

If the trust made eligible expenditures in different permanent establishments and the investment tax credit rates differ, prepare a separate T3 Slip for each designation to each such beneficiary. Also, enter the beneficiary's share of the amount on Line 940 of Schedule 9 (Investment Cost or Expenditure) in Box 40 of the T3 Slip.

Box 45	Newfoundland and Labrador Research and Development Tax Credit

Enter the beneficiary's share of the amount on Line 945 of Schedule 9.

---

5 See heading 3 of Chapter 13 entitled, "Line 83 – Part XII.2 Tax Payable" for commentary on this point.
6 See also heading 6 of Chapter 13 entitled, "Line 88 – Refundable Investment Tax Credit" for commentary on this point.

CHAPTER 15 — FILING REQUIREMENTS

Box 45	Yukon Research and Development Tax Credit

Enter the beneficiary's share of the amount on Line 945 of Schedule 9.

Note: Enter an asterisk (*) beside the amount in Box 45. In the footnote area, enter "Newfoundland and Labrador R&D" or "Yukon R&D," whichever applies, and the amount of this credit from Box 45.

4. Filing the T3 Summary and T3 Slips

4.1 Filing

For trusts resident in Canada, the T3 Summary and the related T3 Supplementaries should be filed separate and apart from the T3 Trust Information and Income Tax Return.

(a) *Paper Filing*

File one paper copy of the T3 Summary and copy 1 of the T3 Supplementaries to:

> OTTAWA TECHNOLOGY CENTRE
> Canada Revenue Agency
> Ottawa ON K1A 1A2

(b) *Magnetic Media*

Send a tape, CD-ROM or diskette (do not send CRA a paper copy of the T3 Summary or T3 Slips) to:

> MAGNETIC MEDIA PROCESSING TEAM
> Ottawa Technology Centre
> Canada Revenue Agency
> Ottawa ON K1A 1A2

PART V — COMPLETING THE T3 SUMMARY AND T3 SLIPS

4.2 Distributing the T3 Slip

(a) Paper Filing

Forward copies 2 and 3 of the T3 Slip to the recipient's address shown on the T3 Slip no later than ninety days after the end of the trust's taxation year.

Retain copy 4 of the T3 Slips with the trust's copy of the T3 Summary.

(b) Magnetic Media

You can provide recipients with an electronic version of their T3 Slips in this format.

5. Amending, Cancelling or Issuing Duplicate T3 Slips

5.1 Amended Slips

If you detect that a T3 Slip includes an error before the slip is filed, simply prepare a new slip, destroy any incorrect copies and include the corrected T3 Slip with the T3 Summary for filing. The report code (Box 16) should still be entered as "0," as this represents the correct original T3 Slip.

If you detect that a T3 Slip includes an error after the original slip is filed, you should correct the entries and prepare an amended slip. Print the word "AMENDED" at the top of the revised T3 Slip and enter "1" in the report code (Box 16). Also forward two copies of the amended T3 Slip to the recipient beneficiary. If the original T3 Slip was filed electronically, the amendment can also be made electronically. Forward the revised data to CRA in electronic format by diskette or CD-ROM. Amendments submitted in electronic format should be sent to:

CHAPTER 15 — FILING REQUIREMENTS

MAGNETIC MEDIA PROCESSING UNIT
Ottawa Technology Centre
Canada Revenue Agency
Ottawa ON K1A 1A2

5.2 Cancelled Slips

If the trust issued a slip by mistake and it should be cancelled, send CRA another slip with the same data as on the original. Print the word "CANCELLED" at the top of the slip, and enter "1" in Box 16. Send two copies of the slip to the beneficiary.

5.3 Duplicate Slips

If the trust is required to issue a slip to replace one that a taxpayer has lost or destroyed, print the word "DUPLICATE" at the top of the slip. Send two copies to the beneficiary. *Do not send CRA a copy of the duplicate slip.*

If the amended or cancelled T3 slip results in a change to the total dollar value of amounts reported in Boxes 21 to 41, an amended T3 Summary should also be filed with CRA. (See heading 6, "Amending the T3 Summary.")

6. Amending the T3 Summary

If there is a requirement to amend a T3 Slip after having filed the original with CRA and if the amended T3 Slip results in a change to the total dollar value of amounts reported in Boxes 21 to 41, an amended T3 Summary must also be filed with the amended T3 Slip(s), reporting the revised totals on the summary.

If the amended T3 Slip(s) changes the amounts reported on Schedule 9, "Income Allocations and Designations to Beneficiaries," do not file an amended T3 Return. Instead, prepare a letter to CRA explaining the details of the adjustments required. Be sure to identify the name of the trust, the taxation year affected and the account number of the trust

PART V — COMPLETING THE T3 SUMMARY AND T3 SLIPS

assigned by CRA. Attach any supporting documents as required to support the request for an adjustment to the T3 Return and/or Schedule 9.

Part VI
Appendices

PART VI — APPENDICES

Appendix A sets out a list of Interpretation Bulletins and Information Circulars referred to in the footnotes to this text. Those documents have not been reproduced in the body of this text, as the CRA materials can be readily accessed by the practitioner on either the Carswell or CRA web sites. These sites can be found at:

www.taxnetpro.com
or
www.cra-arc.gc.ca

Where a publication has been archived by CRA, this is referred to in the attached appendix and it is correspondingly cited in the footnotes of the text. An archived publication may provide useful information and commentary on a relevant tax issue. However, the reader should use caution in its current application as the bulletin reflected the law in force at the time it was released and does not incorporate subsequent changes to the law.

Appendix B sets out a list of the Technical Interpretations cited in this text. Those documents are available through the Carswell web site noted above or to subscribers of other equivalent services, but are not available through CRA.

Appendix C sets out marginal tax rates for both *inter vivos* and testamentary trusts on a province-by-province and territory-by-territory basis.

Appendix A
Interpretation Bulletins and Information Circulars

Interpretation Bulletins

IT-66R6	Capital Dividends	May 31, 1991
IT-75R4	Scholarships, Fellowships, Bursaries, Prizes, Research Grants and Financial Assistance	June 18, 2003
IT-99R5	Legal and Accounting Fees [Consolidated]	December 14, 2000
IT-120R6	Principal Residence	July 17, 2003
IT-130	Capital Property Owned on December 31, 1971 – Actual Cost of Property Owned by a Testamentary Trust	November 20, 1973
IT-133	Stock Exchange Transactions — Date of Disposition of Shares	November 30, 1973
IT-151R5	Scientific Research and Experimental Development Expenditures [Consolidated]	July 23, 2003
IT-159R3	Capital Debts Established to be Bad Debts	May 1, 1989
IT-179R	Change of Fiscal Period	May 28, 1993
IT-201R2	Foreign Tax Credit – Trust and Beneficiaries	February 12, 1996
IT-209R	*Inter Vivos* Gifts of Capital Property to Individuals Directly or Through Trusts	May 18, 1983
IT-210R2	Income of Deceased Persons – Periodic Payments and Investment Tax Credit	November 22, 1996
IT-217R	Depreciable Property Owned on December 31, 1971 [Archived]	August 16, 1996
IT-218R	Profit, Capital Gains and Losses from the Sale of Real Estate, Including Farmland and Inherited Land and Conversion of Real Estate from Capital Property to Inventory and *Vice Versa*	September 16, 1986

PART VI — APPENDICES

IT-221R3	Determination of an Individual's Residence Status [Consolidated]	October 4, 2002
IT-232R3	Losses – Their Deductibility in the Loss Year or in Other Years	July 4, 1997
IT-236R4	Reserves – Disposition of Capital Property [Archived]	July 30, 1999
IT-238R2	Fees Paid to Investment Counsel	October 6, 1983
IT-260	Transfer of Property to a Minor[Cancelled]	November 12, 1979
IT-270R2	Foreign Tax Credit	February 11, 1991
IT-282R	Estate or Trust Distributions — Clearance Certificates [Cancelled]	August 3, 1981
IT-286R2	Trusts – Amount Payable	April 8, 1988
IT-305R4	Testamentary Spouse Trusts	October 30, 1996
IT-322R	Farm Losses	October 25, 1978
IT-332R	Personal-Use Property (Archived)	November 28, 1984
IT-337R4	Retiring Allowances	October 21, 2003
IT-342R	Trusts – Income Payable to Beneficiaries	March 21, 1990
IT-349R3	Intergenerational Transfers of Farm Property on Death	November 7, 1996
IT-366R	Principal Residence — Transfer to Spouse, Spouse Trust or Certain Other Individuals [Cancelled]	May 4, 1984
IT-369R	Attribution of Trust Income to Settlor	March 12, 1990
IT-370	Trusts — Capital Property Owned on December 31, 1971 [Archived]	April 25, 1977
IT-372R	Trusts — Flow-Through of Taxable Dividends and Interest to a Beneficiary [Cancelled]	October 25, 1985
IT-374	Meaning of "Settlor" [Archived]	May 16, 1977
IT-381R3	Trusts – Capital Gains and Losses and the Flow-Through of Taxable Capital Gains to Beneficiaries	February 14, 1997
IT-385R2	Disposition of an Income Interest in a Trust	May 17, 1991
IT-394R2	Preferred Beneficiary Election	June 21, 1999
IT-396R	Interest Income	May 29, 1984
IT-406R2	Tax Payable by an *Inter Vivos* Trust	May 11, 1990
IT-407R4	Dispositions of Cultural Property to Designated Canadian Institutions [Consolidated]	October 12, 2001
IT-410R	Debt Obligations – Accrued Interest on Transfer [Archived]	September 4, 1984

APPENDIX A — ITs and IC's

IT-419R2	Meaning of Arm's Length	June 8, 2004
IT-433R	Farming or Fishing – Use of Cash Method	June 4, 1993
IT-447	Residence of a Trust or Estate	May 30, 1980
IT-449R	Meaning of "Vested Indefeasibly" [Archived]	September 25, 1987
IT-456R	Capital Property – Some Adjustments to Cost Base	July 9, 1990
IT-459	Adventure or Concern in the Nature of Trade	September 8, 1980
IT-460	Dispositions – Absence of Consideration	October 6, 1980
IT-465R	Non-Resident Beneficiaries of Trusts	September 19, 1985
IT-484R2	Business Investment Losses	November 28, 1996
IT-500R	Registered Retirement Savings Plans – Death of an Annuitant	December 18, 1996
IT-502SR	Employee Benefit Plans and Employee Trusts	May 31, 1991
IT-506	Foreign Income Taxes as a Deduction from Income	January 5, 1987
IT-508R	Death Benefits	February 12, 1996
IT-510	Transfers and Loans of Property Made after May 22, 1985 to a Related Minor	December 30, 1987
IT-511R	Interspousal and Certain Other Transfers and Loans of Property	February 21, 1994
IT-517R	Pension Tax Credit	July 5, 1996
IT-524	Trusts – Flow-Through of Taxable Dividends to a Beneficiary – After 1987	March 16, 1990
IT-533	Interest Deductibility and Related Issues	October 31, 2003

Information Circulars

IC 78-5R3	Communal Organizations	September 11, 1998
IC 82-2R2	Social Insurance Number Legislation that Relates to the Preparation of Information Slips	November 20, 1992
IC 82-6R2	Clearance Certificate	May 19, 1999
IC 92-1	Guidelines for Accepting Late, Amended or Revoked Elections	March 18, 1992
IC 92-2	Guidelines for the Cancellation and Waiver of Interest and Penalties	March 18, 1992
IC 92-3	Guidelines for Refunds Beyond the Normal Three Year Period	March 18, 1992
IC 97-2R4	Customized Forms	December 19, 2003

Appendix B
Technical Interpretations

912081	Promissory Notes and Reserves	August 21, 1991
9233787	Election Under 104(13.1) and (13.2)	January 1, 1992
9203105	Spousal Trust	February 14, 1992
9228680	Treatment of Interest Accrued on Transferred Debt	November 25, 1992
9318775	No or Low Interest Loan	December 20, 1993
9238787	Minister's Discretion — 104(2)	January 25, 1993
9238555	Trust	February 4, 1993
9230425	Spousal Trust	February 15, 1993
9307775	Election Under 104(13.1) – Trusts	March 22, 1993
9238075	Benefit from Trust	March 31, 1993
9238487	Trust Money in Dispute	April 8, 1993
9236345	Spousal Trust and 104(13.1) Designation	April 8, 1993
9306245	Multiple Trusts Created by a Single Person	May 20, 1993
9304865	Multiple Trusts Settled by a Single Person	May 20, 1993
9311945	Benefits from a Trust	September 16, 1993
9314345	Preferred Beneficiary Election	September 17, 1993
9319185	Compensation Received by Testamentary Trust	November 29, 1993
9336735	Testamentary Trust – IT-381R2	February 23, 1994
9411115	Attribution	April 28, 1994
9407905	Reversion of Trust Property	June 6, 1994
9402515	Application of Subsection 15(1) in a Specific Situation	July 26, 1994

PART VI — APPENDICES

9406256	First and Last Taxation Year of Testamentary Trust	September 7, 1994
9501395	Spousal Trust – Subsection 104(13.1)	May 2, 1995
9514457	Special Purpose Trust and Taxable Benefit from a Trust	June 30, 1995
9514615	Benefits to Life Tenant	July 7, 1995
9528037	Benefit from a Trust – Loans	February 26, 1996
9526815	Executor's Year Passing Beneficial Ownership Estate	May 24, 1996
9613875	Definition of a Testamentary Trust	September 11, 1996
9625975	Testamentary Spousal Trust	October 7, 1996
9632335	Personal-Use Property	October 17, 1996
9606825	Death Benefit and 104(13.1)	November 14, 1996
9624905	Attribution on Trust Property Gifted from Beneficiary, Indirect	December 4, 1996
9605575	Testamentary Trust – Insurance Proceeds	December 17, 1996
9529647	Promissory Note – Discretionary Trust Amount Payable	February 26, 1997
9606227	Amount Payable to a Beneficiary of a Discretionary Trust	March 6, 1997
9702825	Subsection 104(18) – Capital Encroachment	June 23, 1997
9714835	Aggregation of Testamentary Trusts	June 30, 1997
9707317	Amounts Payable to Minor Beneficiaries and Taxable Benefits from a Trust	August 26, 1997
9708655	Pre-1972 Spousal Trust – Deemed Disposition – 104(13.2)	September 3, 1997
9717475	In-Trust Accounts	September 22, 1997
9618885	Third Party Payments and Rent Free Use of Trust Property	September 22, 1997
9707305	Rent Free Use of Trust Property	September 22, 1997
9721325	Attribution Rules and Transfer to a Trust	October 27, 1997
9726707	Dispute Re Preferred Beneficiary Election	October 31, 1997
9717815	Settlor/Trustee and Majority Decisions	November 19, 1997
9727793	21-Year Deemed Disposition Rule	January 1, 1998
9812245	Social Insurance Number	June 22, 1998
9811115	Attribution and Genuine Loan	July 6, 1998
9818696	Inter Vivos Vs. Testamentary Trusts	August 7, 1998

APPENDIX B — TECHNICAL INTERPRETATIONS

9815227	Attribution to Settlor	August 7, 1998
9801035	Successive Trusts and Definition of Trust	September 22, 1998
9802615	21-Year Deemed Disposition Rule	December 9, 1998
9901435	Status of Successive Trusts	February 16, 1999
9809755	In-Trust Accounts	February 23, 1999
9807495	Trusts for Minors	March 12, 1999
9830997	Attribution – Minors	April 8, 1999
9829145	How Are In-Trust Accounts Taxed?	April 14, 1999
9903747	Minimum Tax and Health and Welfare Trust	June 14, 1999
9926255	Spousal Trust Entitled to Receive All In	January 6, 2000
1999-0013475	Distribution from Trust to Avoid 104(4)	February 29, 2000
1999-0012305	Payment by Discretionary Trust Benefit Minor	June 5, 2000
2000-0012635	Split Income and Rentals	June 20, 2000
2000-0012557	75(2) On Transfer of Shares to Trust	July 17, 2000
2000-0000385	104(13.1) Designations	September 29, 2000
2000-0024775	Affiliated Rules and Trusts	February 23, 2001
2000-0059755	Trust Receives Property from an Alter Ego Trust	March 23, 2001
2000-0005135	Trust — property from alter ego trust	March 23, 2001
2001-0067745	In-Trust Accounts for Minors	March 27, 2001
2000-0051115	Capital Gains Reserve	April 19, 2001
2000-0052505	Trust Becoming Resident in Canada	October 23, 2001
2001-0079285	Status of Successive Trusts	November 2, 2001
2000-0038195	Indefeasible Vesting of Interest in Trust	November 7, 2001
2002-0127663	Taxation of Indian Trust	January 1, 2002
2001-0067955	Application of 75(2) and 107(4.1) to a Trust	January 3, 2002
2001-0116045	Trusts/First Nations/T3 Returns	January 16, 2002
2001-0099055	Joint Spousal Trust	January 23, 2002
2002-0116535	Subsection 75(2) Arising as Consequences of a Will	February 19, 2002
2001-0112945	Distribution from a Trust	March 19, 2002
2002-0127085	No Double Taxation of Income Attributed	April 2, 2002
2002-0126775	Spousal Trust	May 3, 2002

PART VI — APPENDICES

2002-0118255	Application of 75(2)	June 10, 2002
2001-0110425	75(2) When Settlor is Sole Trustee	June 20, 2002
1999-0013055	75(2)(B) Where Settlor is Sole Trustee	June 20, 2002
2002-0139205	75(2) Arising as Consequences of a Will	July 22, 2002
2002-0162865	Unification of Trusts	November 19, 2002
2002-0152353	First Nations Settlement – Trust	January 1, 2003
2002-0143685	RRSP/RRIF and Testamentary Trusts	January 29, 2003
2002-0157725	104(18)	February 3, 2003
2002-012676A	Attribution of Net Profit Interest Royalty Income	February 7, 2003
2003-0181705	Tax on Split Income	March 3, 2003
2003-0011587	Pension Tax Credit RRIF Payments	April 16, 2003
2002-0154435	Payment of Trust Expenses by Beneficiary	April 17, 2003
2002-0162855	Powers of Appointment	April 25, 2003
2002-0172475	Administration of Estates	May 30, 2003
2003-0014515	Spouse's Discretion to Accumulate Income in Trust	June 2, 2003
2002-014675A	Computation Interest on Bonds — Estate	June 3, 2003
2002-016643A	General Comments on 70(7)	June 3, 2003
2003-0012075	Safe Income and 104(13.1) Designation	June 3, 2003
2003-0019555	Personal-use Property	July 3, 2003
2002-017676A	In Trust Accounts	July 21, 2003
2003-0008285	Spousal Trust – Entitlement – Payable	September 23, 2003
2003-0039985	Tax on Split Income – Kiddie Tax	December 3, 2003
2003-0044495	Split Income	December 17, 2003
2003-0047727	Right of Use – Deemed Trust	December 17, 2003
2003-0050671E5	Attribution of Property Transferred to a Trust	April 5, 2004

Appendix C
Marginal Tax Rates

Testamentary Trusts

Province / Territory	Interest	Dividends	Marginal Tax Rate Actual Capital Gains	Business Income
Alberta				
$ 0 - $35,000	26.00%	7.83%	13.00%	26.00%
$ 35,001 - $ 70,000	32.00%	15.33%	16.00%	32.00%
$ 70,001 - $ 113,804	36.00%	20.33%	18.00%	36.00%
Over $ 113,804	39.00%	24.08%	19.50%	39.00%
British Columbia				
$ 0 - $ 32,476	22.05%	4.52%	11.03%	22.05%
$ 32,477 - $ 35,000	25.15%	8.40%	12.58%	25.15%
$ 35,001 - $ 64,954	31.15%	15.90%	15.58%	31.15%
$ 64,955 - $ 70,000	33.70%	19.08%	16.85%	33.70%
$ 70,001 - $ 74,575	37.70%	24.08%	18.85%	37.70%
$ 74,576 - $ 90,555	39.70%	26.58%	19.85%	39.70%
$ 90,556 - $113,804	40.70%	27.83%	20.35%	40.70%
Over $ 113,804	43.70%	31.58%	21.85%	43.70%
Saskatchewan				
$ 0 - $35,000	27.00%	7.08%	13.50%	27.00%
$ 35,001 - $ 36,155	33.00%	14.58%	16.50%	33.00%
$ 36,156 - $ 70,000	35.00%	17.08%	17.50%	35.00%
$ 70,001 - $ 103,300	39.00%	22.08%	19.50%	39.00%
$ 103,301 - $113,804	41.00%	24.58%	20.50%	41.00%
Over $113,804	44.00%	28.33%	22.00%	44.00%
Manitoba				
$ 0 - $ 30,544	26.90%	10.70%	13.45%	26.90%
$ 30,545 - $ 35,000	30.00%	14.58%	15.00%	30.00%
$ 35,001 - $ 65,000	36.00%	22.08%	18.00%	36.00%
$ 65,001 - $ 70,000	39.40%	26.33%	19.70%	39.40%
$ 70,001 - $ 113,804	43.40%	31.33%	21.70%	43.40%
Over $ 113,804	46.40%	35.08%	23.20%	46.40%
Yukon Territory				
$ 0 - $35,000	23.04%	4.81%	11.52%	23.04%
$ 35,001 - $ 70,000	31.68%	15.61%	15.84%	31.68%
$ 70,001 - $ 76,224	37.44%	22.81%	18.72%	37.44%
$ 76,225 - $113,804	38.01%	23.16%	19.01%	38.01%
Over $ 113,804	42.40%	28.64%	21.20%	42.40%

PART VI — APPENDICES

Province / Territory	Marginal Tax Rate			
	Interest	Dividends	Actual Capital Gains	Business Income
North West Territories				
$ 0 - $ 33,245	23.20%	4.83%	11.60%	23.20%
$ 33,246 - $ 35,000	25.90%	8.20%	12.95%	25.90%
$ 35,001 - $ 66,492	31.90%	15.70%	15.95%	31.90%
$ 66,493 - $ 70,000	34.20%	18.58%	17.10%	34.20%
$ 70,001 - $ 108,101	38.20%	23.58%	19.10%	38.20%
$ 108,102 - $ 113,804	40.05%	25.89%	20.03%	40.05%
Over $ 113,804	43.05%	29.64%	21.53%	43.05%
Nunavut				
$ 0 - $35,000	20.00%	3.33%	10.00%	20.00%
$ 35,001 - $ 70,000	29.00%	14.58%	14.50%	29.00%
$ 70,001 - $ 113,804	35.00%	22.08%	17.50%	35.00%
Over $ 113,804	40.50%	28.96%	20.25%	40.50%
Ontario				
$ 0 - $ 33,375	22.05%	4.47%	11.03%	22.05%
$ 33,376 - $ 35,000	25.15%	8.35%	12.58%	25.15%
$ 35,001 - $ 58,768	31.15%	15.85%	15.58%	31.15%
$ 58,769 - $ 66,752	32.98%	16.85%	16.49%	32.98%
$ 66,753 - $ 69,238	35.39%	19.88%	17.70%	35.39%
$ 69,239 - $ 70,000	39.41%	22.58%	19.71%	39.41%
$ 70,001 - $ 113,804	43.41%	27.58%	21.71%	43.41%
Over $ 113,804	46.41%	31.33%	23.21%	46.41%
Newfoundland and Labrador				
$ 0 - $ 29,590	26.57%	10.29%	13.29%	26.57%
$ 29,591 - $ 35,000	32.16%	17.28%	16.08%	32.16%
$ 35,001 - $ 58,597	38.16%	24.78%	19.08%	38.16%
$ 58,598 - $ 59,180	39.61%	26.03%	19.81%	39.61%
$ 59,181 - $ 70,000	41.64%	28.56%	20.82%	41.64%
$ 70,001 - $ 113,804	45.64%	33.56%	22.82%	45.64%
Over $ 113,804	48.64%	37.31%	24.32%	48.64%
Nova Scotia				
$ 0 - $ 29,590	24.79%	4.70%	12.40%	24.79%
$ 29,591 - $ 35,000	30.95%	12.40%	15.48%	30.95%
$ 35,001 - $ 59,180	36.95%	19.90%	18.48%	36.95%
$ 59,181 - $ 70,000	38.67%	22.05%	19.34%	38.67%
$ 70,001 - $ 80,661	42.67%	27.05%	21.34%	42.67%
$ 80,662 - $ 93,000	44.34%	28.17%	22.17%	44.34%
$ 93,001 - $ 113,804	45.25%	29.31%	22.63%	45.25%
Over $ 113,804	48.25%	33.06%	24.13%	48.25%
New Brunswick				
$ 0 - $ 32,183	25.68%	10.81%	12.84%	25.68%
$ 32,184 - $ 35,000	30.82%	17.23%	15.41%	30.82%
$ 35,001 - $ 64,368	36.82%	24.73%	18.41%	36.82%
$ 64,369 - $ 70,000	38.52%	26.86%	19.26%	38.52%
$ 70,001 - $ 104,648	42.52%	31.86%	21.26%	42.52%
$ 104,649 - $ 113,804	43.84%	33.51%	21.92%	43.84%
Over $ 113,804	46.84%	37.26%	23.42%	46.84%
Prince Edward Island				
$ 0 - $ 30,754	25.80%	5.96%	12.90%	25.80%
$ 30,755 - $ 35,000	29.80%	10.96%	14.90%	29.80%
$ 35,001 - $ 51,859	35.80%	18.46%	17.90%	35.80%
$ 51,860 - $ 61,509	37.18%	19.22%	18.59%	37.18%
$ 61,510 - $ 70,000	40.37%	23.20%	20.19%	40.37%
$ 70,001 - $ 113,804	44.37%	28.20%	22.19%	44.37%
Over $ 113,804	47.37%	31.95%	23.69%	47.37%

APPENDIX C — MARGINAL TAX RATES

Inter vivos Trusts

Province / Territory	Marginal Tax Rate			Business Income
	Interest	Dividends	Actual Capital Gains	
Alberta	39.00%	24.08%	19.50%	39.00%
British Columbia	43.70%	31.58%	21.85%	43.70%
Saskatchewan	44.00%	28.33%	22.00%	44.00%
Manitoba	46.40%	35.08%	23.20%	46.40%
Yukon Territory	42.40%	28.64%	21.20%	42.40%
North West Territories	43.05%	29.64%	21.53%	43.05%
Nunavut	40.50%	28.96%	20.25%	40.50%
Ontario	46.41%	31.33%	23.21%	46.41%
Newfoundland and Labrador	48.64%	37.31%	24.32%	48.64%
Nova Scotia	48.25%	33.06%	24.13%	48.25%
New Brunswick	46.84%	37.26%	23.42%	46.84%
Prince Edward Island	47.37%	31.95%	23.69%	47.37%

Federal and provincial income tax rates reported in these tables are based on the 2004 tax rates listed on the CRA website at the date of publication.

Index

A

Accumulations
  perpetuities and accumulations *19-21*

Age forty trusts – *see* Minors

Agency
  distinguished from trust *15*

Administration
  estate *14, 30-40*
  executor year *149, 166*
  T3 filing requirements *149-156, 159-161*

Alter ego trusts
  confidentiality *79*
  creditor-proofing *80*
  dependants' relief legislation *29-30, 53, 80*
  incapacity planning *80*
  jurisdiction shopping *81*
  opting out *54, 83*
  principal residence exemption *44, 85-87*
  probate avoidance *77-78*
  requirements *75-76*
  successor trusts not testamentary *32, 84*
  taxation of *81-85*

Allowable Business Investment Loss
  bad debts *244*
  defined *214-216*

Attribution
  contributor or settlor *44, 50-52, 61-65, 81, 85, 125, 132*
  inter vivos trusts *41-45, 52*
  minors *61-62, 65*
  spouse or common law partner *50-52*

B

Bailment
  defined *14*
  distinguished from trust *15*

Bare trust
  defined *15, 244*

Beneficiaries
  avoiding probate *77, 79*
  benefits received *96, 103-106, 217-218*
  contingent vs. vested *7*
  creditor-proofing *80*
  income payable *99-101, 179, 276-280*
  "kiddie tax" *70-72, 201*
  minors *60, 65, 72-74*
  non-discretionary income *101-103*
  non-resident *123, 138*
  party to trust, as *5, 102, 121*
  preferred beneficiary election *112-115, 118, 120, 121-123*
  taxation of distributions and allocations *135-139, 261, 269, 276-280*

Index

C

Capital gains
$500,000 capital gains deduction
54, 83, 225-226, 246, 249, 261-262, 267-269, 306
attribution *43, 51, 63-65, 85, 125, 132*
deemed gains at death *37, 150, 179, 195-196*
deemed realization *139, 140-144, 145, 181-182, 178, 206, 207*
flow-through to beneficiary of trust *66, 95, 96, 99, 100, 112-115, 123, 218-219, 278*
"qualified farm property" *83, 247-249, 261-262, 306*
qualifying small business corporation shares *245-246*
reserves *193-195, 257-258, 259-261*

Capital interests
cost to taxpayer *49-50*
disclaimer of interest *57, 110, 174*

Capital losses
164(6) election *195, 259*
attribution *50-51, 61-62, 64-65, 85, 132*
utilization of capital losses *195, 222-224*
year of death *37, 121, 195, 259*

Capital property
deemed realization *83, 139-140, 144, 145, 146, 181-182, 206-208*
depreciable *81-82, 137, 182, 207, 251-252*
proceeds of disposition *48, 138, 174, 193, 252*
spouse and spousal trust, rollover *37, 53-54, 57-58*
tax treatment on death *47-48, 267*
utilization of losses *195, 222-224, 259*

Certainties of a trust
intention *10, 13*

"in trust" accounts *73*
objects *11*
subject matter *11*

Clearance certificates *156-157, 171*

Committeeship
distinguished from trust *16*

Contributions
common-law partner trusts *74, 75, 77, 84, 120, 135-137* – see also Alter ego trusts
non-resident trusts *172, 183-185*
settlor *7, 47-49*
testamentary trusts *23-26, 84, 184*

Creation of trusts
by express words or conduct *13*
by law *12*
by will *25*
tax deferral *37, 57-58, 207*

D

Death of taxpayer
capital losses *52, 195, 221-222*
capital losses; 164(6) election *195, 259*
capital property *37, 53-54, 58*
reserves *193-195, 197, 218, 257-258*
rollovers *53-54, 57-58*

Deemed disposition
21 year rule *20, 83, 140, 143, 181-183, 206-208*
inter vivos trusts *41, 43, 139*
planning for disposition of trust assets *135-137, 207*
trust property *135-136*

Deemed disposition at death
estate *30-31*
principal residence *85-87, 255*
reserves for year of death *194*
spousal rollover *37, 54*
testamentary trusts *38-40*

332

Index

Deductions
  allowable business investment losses *214-216*
  carrying charges and interest expenses *211-212, 274*
  other carrying charges and expenses *213*
  trustee fees *213-214*

Dependants' relief legislation
  avoiding *80*
  trusts arising *29, 53*

Designations
  designated beneficiary *230-231*
  income designations *218*
  RRSP designation *210*
  subsection 104 (13.1) and 104 (13.2) *31, 40, 96, 107, 108-112, 120, 197, 276-277*

Discretion
  defined *74, 114-115, 169, 202, 251, 256*
  income distributions *99, 101, 108, 150, 275*

Distributions
  deemed realizations *136, 139, 140, 146, 206, 208, 240, 267*
  disposition of income interest in trust *49, 117, 121, 135-137, 174-175*
  inter vivos trust *32, 43-48, 52, 69, 109, 115-116, 142, 169, 180, 276-280*
  spousal trusts *37, 53, 54, 206-207, 267*
  testamentary trusts *23-26, 32-33, 37-40, 84, 276-280*

Dividends
  flow-through to beneficiary *95-97, 99, 100, 101-102, 123, 278*
  "kiddie tax" *70*
  taxable *70, 123, 199, 219-220, 272*

E

Emigration
  attribution *130*
  deemed realization *144-145*
  residence *167*

Elections
  bequests of capital property *30, 259*
  capital gains exemption *83, 121, 135, 278*
  preferred beneficiary election *52, 96, 112-123*
  principal residence election *86, 104, 255*
  qualified farm property *83, 247-249, 261-262, 306*

Estate
  administration *14, 30, 165, 213-214*
  beneficiary *5-8, 14, 49-50, 65-70, 72-74, 96-97, 99-103, 106-108, 112-120, 135, 139, 174, 179, 181, 209, 217-219, 230, 267, 304*
  clearance certificate *155-157, 171*
  distinguished from trust *14, 21, 30*
  distribution of property *137-139, 181-183, 247-249*
  executor's year – *see* Executors
  fiscal period *33, 143-144, 170*
  principal residence *85-87, 103-105, 255*
  probate planning *77-78*
  residence *91-93, 167*
  taxation of *23, 30, 99-111*
  windup *31*

Executors
  administrative tasks, overview *92*
  executor's year *14, 30-31, 101-102, 170*
  filing returns *31, 122, 150-155, 160-161, 171, 236-237, 299, 311-312*
  liability *155, 236-237*
  reassessments *36*

333

Index

F

Failure of Trust
  other relationships *14-16*

Farm property
  inter vivos transfer *41, 63, 83*
  "qualified farm property" *225, 247, 248, 249, 261, 306, 307*
  rollover at death *247*
  testamentary transfer *249*

Federal foreign tax credit
  foreign income or profit tax *284*

Foreign investment income
  foreign source income *199, 272*

G

Gifts
  attribution *63, 126, 127*
  defined *16*
  distinguished from trust *10, 16, 73*
  income-splitting *33, 38, 57, 58, 109, 113, 143*
  inter vivos trusts *41, 43, 53, 95*
  tax consequences *240, 258, 287, 288*
  will gifts *26*

I

Implied trusts
  three certainties *9-12, 13*

Income
  allocations and designations *276*
  beneficiaries *6, 15, 39, 114, 145, 179*
  benefits as form of income *103*
  business income *202*
  designated *40*
  dividend *199, 219, 220, 272, 275, 278, 289, 305*
  estate, computation *30, 150, 156*
  farming income *203, 307*
  fishing income *203, 307*
  foreign investment income *199, 272*
  general rules for inclusion and deduction *95-98*
  outlays, as form of *106*
  payable to beneficiary *65, 66, 95, 96, 99, 100, 110, 115, 179, 197, 209, 210, 277, 279*
  property income *60, 63, 71, 85, 131, 201, 204, 205, 212, 214*
  rental income *71, 202-205, 307*

Income-splitting
  attribution *50, 61, 64, 65, 85, 132*
  installment taxes *23, 34, 231*
  insurance trusts *26*
  minors *60, 62, 70*
  spousal transfers *50, 51, 53, 54, 57, 58*
  testamentary trusts *33, 38, 57, 109, 113*

Insurance trusts
  purposes *26*
  requirements as testamentary *27*

"In-trust" accounts
  whether qualify as trusts *41, 72-74*

Inter vivos trusts
  attribution *44, 50, 63, 65-66*
  deemed realization *43, 139, 178*
  defined *46, 169*
  distribution of capital *139*
  minimum tax *94, 289*
  overview *41, 46, 169*
  preferred beneficiary election *112, 114*
  taxation *47, 49, 52, 170*

J

Joint spousal trust – *see also* Alter ego trusts
  deemed realization *140, 207-208*
  distribution of capital *139*
  income allocations and designations *218-219, 279*
  planning *77-81*

Index

Joint spousal trust — *continued*
    preferred beneficiary election *119-120*
    principal residence *255*
    summary *74-77*

Jurisdiction shopping
    alter ego trusts *81*
    anti-avoidance issues *93*
    residency of trust *91-93*

K

"Kiddie Tax" – *see* Tax on split income

L

Laws
    provincial variation *16*
    trust law distinguished from tax law *14*

Land inventory
    deemed realization *207*
    restriction on income designation *218, 279*
    rollover *57*

Life interest
    beneficiary *49, 136*
    disposition of interest *174-175*
    distributions *136, 143*

M

Merger
    blended testamentary trusts *26*
    deemed realization *146*

Minimum tax
    basic exemption *269*
    inter vivos trusts *52*
    notice of objection *161*
    overview *94-95*
    testamentary trusts *140*
    when applicable *227, 261, 284, 289*
    when not applicable *94*

Minors
    age forty trusts *65-70*
    attribution of income *61, 65*
    child, trusts *26, 39, 65, 112-113, 117*
    in-trust accounts *72-74*
    "kiddie tax" *70-72, 201*
    pent up income *65*
    summary *60*

N

Non-resident beneficiaries
    Part XIII tax *123*
    withholding taxes *280, 283*

Non-resident trusts
    deemed resident *171-172*
    filing *159*
    resident contributor *183-185*

P

Perpetuities
    perpetuities and accumulations *19-21*
    Saunders v. Vautier 17-18

Personal representative
    administration *14, 30, 34, 37, 60, 80, 149, 150, 160, 161*
    clearance certificate *156, 157*
    estate *14*
    liability *155*
    power of attorney *15, 80*
    testamentary trust *25*

Power of appointment
    distinguished from trust *15*

Power of attorney
    distinguished from trust *15*
    incapacity planning *80*

Preferred beneficiary election
    calculations *118-121*
    forms of income *123*
    mechanics *121-122*
    qualifying beneficiary *116-118*
    summary *112-115*

Index

Principal residence
   benefit conferred by trust *103-105*
   deemed disposition *255*
   principal residence exemption *85-87, 255-256*
   rollover to spouse or spousal trust *53-54*

Probate
   alter ego and joint spousal or common-law partner trusts *74-75*
   insurance trusts *26*
   planning and probate avoidance *77-79*
   RRSP trusts *28-29*

Provincial considerations
   perpetuities and accumulations *19-21*
   Saunders v. Vautier 17-18

R

Registered Retirement Savings Plan
   income eligible for designation *278, 309*
   RRSP trusts *28*
   tax treatment on death *210*

Reserves
   capital property *257-258, 259-261*
   proceeds not due *193-195*
   spouse or spousal trust *194*
   year of death *195*

Rollovers
   alter ego and joint spousal or common-law partner trusts *74-75, 77, 81-83, 146*
   distribution to beneficiary *181-183*
   interest in family farm partnership *248*
   principal residence *85-87*
   qualified farm property *41, 83, 247-249*
   reserves, spouse or spousal trust *194*

   shares of family farm corporations *247-248*
   spouse or spousal trust *53-54, 57-58*
   testamentary trust *37*
   transfer from non-grandfathered *inter vivos* trust *180-181*

S

Settlor
   attribution of income *44, 50, 63, 85, 125, 132*
   defined *7*
   resident contributor *183-185*
   tax consequences *47-49*

Small business corporation shares
   $500,000 capital gains deduction *83, 225-226, 245-246, 261-262, 306*
   qualified small business corporation shares *245-246*

Spousal trusts
   capital gains deduction *54, 178-179, 225-226, 246, 249, 261-262, 267-269, 306*
   deemed realization *135-137, 139, 140, 146, 206-207, 267*
   minimum tax *94*
   principal residence *53-54, 255*
   qualifying spousal trust *53-58*
   rollovers *53-54, 57-58*
   tainted spousal trust *58-60, 182, 197, 247*
   testamentary *37, 53-58*
   untainting a spousal trust *59*

T

Tax on split income
   "kiddie tax" *70-72, 201*

Testamentary trusts – *see also* Estate
   attributing income to minors *66*
   attributing losses to T-1 return *37*
   blended *26*
   definition *23-24*

Index

Testamentary trusts — *continued*
    designated income *31, 40, 96, 109-111, 276-280*
    fiscal period *33-34, 143-144, 170-171, 202*
    loss of status *34-35*
    minimum tax *40, 94-95*
    multiple trusts *38-40, 95, 166, 173*
    qualifying and non-qualifying *25*
    reassessment *36, 157, 160, 259*
    special features *33*

Trusts
    amended slips *312*
    amendment *17, 18, 141, 145, 175*
    attribution *44, 50-52, 61-65, 65-70, 125-133*
    constructive *10, 12*
    charitable gifts *240, 287*
    charitable purposes *6*
    creation of *12-13*
    creditor proofing *80*
    discretionary and non-discretionary *99-103, 126*
    distinguished from other relationships *14*
    division of ownership *5, 8-9*
    express or implied *12, 13*
    income-splitting *33, 57, 109, 112-115*
    insurance trusts *26-28*
    inter vivos trusts for minors *60-62, 72-74*
    multiple testamentary *38-40, 95, 166, 173*
    parties to *5*
    preferred beneficiary election *112-116, 118-123*
    purpose trusts *3, 5-6, 12*
    residency *91-93, 167*
    resulting trusts *10, 12*
    revocable and irrevocable *40, 100*
    spousal trusts *37, 53-58*
    tainted spousal trusts *58-60, 182, 197, 247*

    taxation of alter ego and joint spousal or common-law partner trusts *74-77, 81-83*
    testamentary – *see* Testamentary trusts
    three certainties *9-12, 61, 73, 143, 169*
    twenty-one year deemed disposition *140-144*
    variation – *see* Variations

Trustees
    bare *15, 244-245*
    capacity *7, 141, 150*
    care and duties *8, 14, 92, 213*
    delegation of duties *93, 167*
    party to trust, as *7*
    residency *91-93, 167*
    trustee fees *213-214*

V

Variations
    provincial *16, 141-142*
    Saunders v. Vautier 17-18
    trust amended or varied *175*

Vest Indefeasibly
    deemed realization *140*
    definition *56*
    spousal rollover *168, 194*

W

Wills
    capacity to make *13, 23*
    planning *38-40*
    property passing outside *78*
    spouse *37*
    testamentary – *see* Testamentary trusts

Withholding taxes
    foreign business income tax paid *308*
    Part XII.2 tax *280-284*
    Part XIII tax *280-284*